# AIDS and the Human Survival

Dr. V Ramamurthy

AUTHORSPRESS
*under the auspices of*
INDIA HEALTH FOUNDATION

First Published 2000
by Authorspress

E-35/103, Jawahar Park (Shree Ganesh Complex),
Laxmi Nagar, Delhi-110 092



Typeset in NewCenturySchlbk by Chitra Computers

*AIDS and Human Survival*
ISBN 81-7273-017-9

Printed in India at Tarun Offset, Delhi.

# Preface

Humans live in relative harmony with a range of viruses, bacteria, parasites and fungi that do not cause disease in healthy people with intact immune defences. But these organisms can take advantage of someone with a weakened immune system, such as an individual infected with HIV. The course of HIV infection can be divided into several stages, only the last of which is defined as AIDS. In the earliest stage, an HIV infected person may be asymptomatic except for swollen lympth nodes in the neck, armpits and groin which do not make the person feel ill but may prompt a visit to the doctor.

By late 1993, close to 850,000 cases of AIDS had been reported to WHO from over 180 countries and territories. For several reasons, however, this is thought to represent only a small proportion of the true world total. Many countries were slow to admit they had an AIDS problem and to set up systematic surveillance and reporting. Moreover, where expertise and blood testing facilities are lacking, it may be difficult to differentiate AIDS from other common diseases. And in remote parts of the developing world, many people fall ill and die without ever coming into contact with modern health services. Taking all these factors into account, WHO estimates that by early 1994 more than 3 million cases of AIDS had actually occurred, including over 500,000 in infants born to HIV-infected women. HIV/AIDS does not affect populations uniformly, either at the global level or within any one country, and the epidemic is in reality the sum of many local epidemics. Each has its own distinctive characteristics shaped by local, social, economic, cultural and similar factors.

The shifting patterns of the epidemic, the logistic and other requirements of resting, and the need for anonymity and confidentiality make HIV/AIDS surveillance a very complex task. In many countries surveillance activities are yet to be implemented or are only now being built up with the help of WHO.

Apart from unprotected sex and drug injection, contaminated blood transfusions are thought to contribute to the epidemic in parts of south and south-east Asia. In India, the trading of blood for transfusion and the preparation of blood products is big business and subject to very little control. The experiences of India, Myanmar and Thailand could easily be repeated in other countries of the region—particularly Bangladesh, Indonesia, Nepal and Sri Lanka, where illicit drug injection, high STD rates, male patronage of female and male prostitutes, and/or low rates of condom usage in both casual and long-term relationships are common. Countries such as Cambodia, the Lao People's Democratic Republic and Vietnam, which are emerging from the isolating influence of communism, are also especially vulnerable to HIV infection as their people go through profound social and economic changes. It is therefore vital that education, condom promotion and community action programmes are put in place throughout the region.

By the year 2000, according to the World Health Organisation, a total of 40 million men, women and children worldwide will be infected with HIV, the virus which causes AIDS. More than 90% of those infected will be in developing countries. Above all, societies cannot afford to deny the existence of the problem, which can affect each and every person. Timely, effective and compassionate action is the only response that provides hope for the human survival.

*Author*

# Contents

# 1

# Understanding HIV/AIDs

The uncertainties of human immunodeficiency virus (HIV) infection and its relentless progression to acquired immunodeficiency syndrome place enormous burden on those affected. HIV infection drains intrapersonnel, interpersonnel and material resources and cannot be thought of as a single, stressful life event but rather as an unremitting force with uncertain course. Counsellors and therapists are not expected to be experts in the medical aspects of AIDS, it is critical that professionals who provides services to HIV-infected persons have a basic understanding of the syndrome and its manifestations.

With HIV/AIDS, the emotional trauma is compounded by a societal reaction that judges the HIV-infected person very harshly, unlike current public reactions to those with heart disease or cancer. Often that severe reaction is internalized, creating a loathing of self. Consider these issues:

— Because the human immunodeficiency virus is spread through exchange of bodily fluids—during sex, in artificial insemination, when sharing contaminated syringes during injection drug use, in transfusions and infusions of blood and blood products, and from mother to baby *in utero* and during breast-feeding—HIV and AIDS is a taboo topic for many.

— Because HIV is most often spread during sex and drug use, large portions of world society judgmentally regard persons with HIV/AIDS as moral degenerates who are to blame for their illness. The judgment is evident in the allowance made for infected children and for persons who were infected by contaminated blood products, who are viewed as "innocent" victims.

— Irrational fears of contamination have deprived many of adequate medical and other care, and even from basic human contact.

Many people still believe that their communities, their family members, and they themselves are immune to HIV. But now, and especially for the next century, no individual and no community can afford to dismiss HIV as a condition that happens to others. HIV threatens all our communities, in ways overt and in ways subtle, hidden, and complex. Mental health practitioners, especially, cannot be so dismissive or unaware.

If a mental health practitioner believes HIV infection doesn't occur in his or her community and therefore fails to learn how to address it appropriately with clients, he or she does clients a grave disservice. In fact, many would argue that discussion of HIV issues should be a part of every mental health practice. The practitioner must be able to respond empathically and skillfully to:

— Whether a person is infected with HIV or is a family member or neighbour of someone with HIV/AIDS

— When a person says a fear of HIV is preventing a desired relationship

— When a person is sexually active and doesn't fear HIV sufficiently to have safer sexual attitudes

The HIV-related tasks for mental health practitioners, then, are many and complicated. They involve constant self-scrutiny of our feelings and reactions. They also involve constant learning. Understanding HIV entails much more than assembling a headful of facts, be they medical or psychological, to be pronounced to oneself or to a person. Skillful practice requires, foremost, a conceptualisation of HIV in which many interlocking and complicated pieces of knowledge may come together and be unified. This conceptualisation enables the practitioner to make a comprehensive assessment of the HIV-affected person. The assessment findings and the model then guide the practitioner in planning care that is far-reaching. Finally, the model informs interdisciplinary practice, which will be a hallmark of the next decade of care.

### BIOPSYCHOSOCIAL/SPIRITUAL MODEL

The biopsychosocial/spiritual model acknowledges that all persons have many aspects and that these aspects all interact. These broad, interlocking aspects have the following general definitions:

— *Biological or biomedical*—pertaining to flesh, blood and bone, organisms, and entities as viruses.

— *Psychological*—having to do with the inner life of the individual, including emotions, self-judgments, motivations for relatedness with others, and internal reasons for behaviours.

— *Social*—the person's participation or lack of participation in family, community and society (including the therapist), and the effects of family, community, and society on the person. One's culture resides in this realm, although one's reactions to the culture may be psychological.

— *Spiritual*—not necessarily an attachment to organized beliefs or religious institutions, although that certainly may be present. Spiritual aspects often include an internal belief or sense that acknowledges an "other," a reality beyond normal experience, which may be a presence or meaning that surpasses current reality.

Western society views each of these aspects separately. When "health care" is mentioned, for example, most people think "medical care," an indication of our overemphasis on biomedical responses, to the exclusion or neglect of care of other aspects of ourselves.

In the biopsychosocial/spiritual model, the different realms may be separated out for purposes of distinguishing major components and for planning our assessment and interventions.

Consider application of the model to the situation of a person who, after testing, is told that she is HIV-positive.

Since the recognition of AIDS and HIV, and in many institutions still, the person who receives a test result that indicates HIV infection is immediately drawn into a whitewater torrent of months of laboratory tests, visits with medical providers, prescriptions for prophylactic (preventative) medicines, and discussions about the newest medical interventions. While the body may generally be well cared for, other aspects require attention, such as:

— The person's psychological reaction. Many patients, still unfamiliar with HIV, react with the belief they have been given a death sentence. (An unknowledgeable mental health provider may include by joining in the client's hopelessness.) Even those who cognitively "know" that HIV/AIDS is chronic are likely to have a strong psychological response that may include despair, fear, dread, guilt, shame, or even relief that comes with knowledge.

— The reactions of those who love that person, who make love with the person, go to church with the person, or are estranged from the person.

— The spiritual reaction of the person, who may or may not have a system of beliefs or feelings about God, "higher power," or meanings of life.

Clearly, the knowledge that one is infected has significant psychological, social, and spiritual consequences. Similarly, much that is psychological, social, and spiritual has led to behaviour that carries with it the risk of introducing HIV into the body.

Psychological consequences may include depression and a feeling of being cheated. Social consequences may include loss of salary and of the ability to support his family, which may also affect his emotional well-being. Being sick, the man may seek a closeness to his God, or he may curse God for his situation. And what of the effects of the illness on his family, and its response? The interplay of all these aspects is what the HIV-infected person presents to the mental health practitioner, and what must be understood as such.

The biopsychosocial/spiritual model is useful because it allows us to think through what we know intuitively. Every aspect of HIV affects and is affected by others. It allows a sophisticated response to a client who learns that he or she is HIV-positive. The practitioner who views a client as a dynamic interaction of many different aspects assumes a professional stance that responds to each component. This response is a more comprehensive assessment that takes into account the various aspects and a treatment plan that derives from that comprehensive assessment.

Arguments for viewing the person as a biopsychosocial system are decades old. The addition of the spiritual element as an important part of the model is newer, and somewhat controversial.

In 1977 Engel used the term "biopsychosocial" and listed arguments for its adoption in medicine and psychiatry. A year later Engel alluded to an integrated model of care. He noted that the posture that science and humanism are in opposition "promotes rivalry, if not antagonism, between and among health professionals. But the care of the sick calls for collaboration and smooth interaction between professionals, with complementary roles to fulfill and tasks to perform". This study details a biopsychosocial model based on general systems theory, taking into account culture, subculture, community, family, and intrapsychic factors, among other factors. In the field of HIV, several persons make reference to the model, albeit from a medical vantage point.

The multiple-aspects model is not just theoretical and a nice way to think about humankind. It is the basis of new ways of regarding health care, as well as of studies of mind-body connections. Studies that acknowledge mind-body connections have emanated from scientific areas such as psycho-neuroimmunology, behavioural medicine, and psychosocial oncology. More and more scientific data describe the mind-body connection. A statistical analysis of the results of many studies in psychosocial oncology, for example, psychosocial interventions have positive effects on emotional adjustment, functional adjustment, and treatment and disease-related symptoms in adult cancer patients.

## TOOLS FOR CLINICAL PRACTICE

The HIV-affected person's situation—both before and after

infection is complex, and the entire landscape needs to be seen and understood. To respond in a sophisticated manner, the mental health practitioner needs to survey the entire landscape by way of a complete assessment.

**Comprehensive assessment**

***Biomedical issues***

***1) Medical information***

- — Current T-helper cell counts and other markers of immune function such as viral load assays.
- — Medical history, both HIV and non-HIV. An HIV-positive person may have other significant conditions, e.g., hypertension, diabetes, history of headaches.
- — Medications being taken and those prescribed or recommended but declined.
- — Include drugs obtained on the street, herbal remedies by nonmedical practitioners, and other complementary remedies.
- — Other treatments, including chiropractic care, acupuncture spiritually based healing practices.
- — Self-care practices, including nutrition and exercise.
- — Names of all caregivers, medical and nonmedical, include dentist, ophthalmologist, occupational therapist, physical therapist, visiting nurse, nutritionist etc. Understand their roles and the person's choices.
- — Understanding of HIV-related conditions and his or h own condition.

***2) Neurological condition***

Because HIV, like certain medications, has a neurotoxic effect that affects the person's quality of life, please consider:

- — Person's baseline cognitive functioning.
- — Symptoms of central nervous system involvement, such as cognitive slowing, memory loss.
- — Person's use of compensatory strategies, such as note taking or a reminder system.

— Peripheral nervous system involvement, indicated by pain, numbness or other symptoms in arms, hands, legs, or feet.

***Psychological issues***

***1) Mental state***

— How has client's pre-HIV psychological functioning changed with knowledge of infection and progression of illness?

— Person's emotional response to HIV issues.

— Acute psychological symptoms that the client attributes to HIV status or to other stressors, *e.g.*, anxiety, unhappiness, depression, despair.

— Longstanding psychological presentation. Neglect of personality disorders severely undermines any mental health intervention and can lead practitioners to feelings of inadequacy. The personality disorders of persons must be taken into account.

— History of, and attitudes regarding, current or past experiences with mental health professionals, who may include substance abuse program counsellors; past or current participation in twelve-step programs, such as Narcotics Anonymous, Positives Anonymous.

— Use of psychiatric medications and psychoactive substances, either prescribed or obtained from street dealers. Do not overlook abuse of prescriptions and the possibilities of substance abuse in persons who do not meet your stereotype of drug abusers.

***2) Sexual functioning***

— Assess history and current sexual functioning.

— Does the client practice safer sex?

— Type of sex preferred—anal, oral, receptive?

— What has changed since diagnosis or appearance of symptoms?

— Unwanted sexual occurrences?

— If gay, lesbian, or bisexual, the person's comfort with his or her sexual preference.

***Social issues***

- For sophisticated and deeper understanding of the HIV-affected individual, strive to understand his or her culture. The person's cultural affiliations may be multiple. How does the person identify himself or herself culturally? Ask the person to explain his or her cultural identifications.
- Consider the individuals socioeconomic place in society; his or her vulnerability to racism, classism, heterosexism, and sexism; and the educational and economic opportunities denied or afforded this individual.
- Do not overlook one very important social aspect—the person's relationship with you, who becomes part of his or her social network. Note the person's ability to have a relationship with you, to accept your empathy, and to open up to you. The person's style of interaction with you is likely to mirror his or her style with similar figures outside the therapeutic relationship.
- Who are the caregivers? Does the client have two families—one of blood relatives and another of affiliation, such as friends and a partner? A genogram, or a visual display of the family, is always helpful.
- What has been the response of "family"? Consider long-time family patterns of care and current support. Are any family members likely to flee during a crisis?
- Are others in the support system HIV-positive?
- Whom does the person's designate to make treatment decisions if 'incapacitation occurs? Are the proper documents signed and filed with physicians and others? Whom should you contact in an emergency?
- Are children involved? What is their biopsychosocial status?
- What does the person want you to do if he or she misses an appointment and has no telephone or doesn't answer?

***Spiritual issues***

— History of religious observance and current attitudes.

— Person's definition, explanation, and practice of spirituality.

— Are these beliefs comforting or a source of discomfort? Do the beliefs facilitate patient's dealing with his or her HIV status or hinder it?

— With whom does the person discuss spirituality?

— What are the person's spiritual concerns?

This is by no means a comprehensive list of information that should be obtained. The information gathered should be expanded to encompass the client's specific circumstances. On the basis of the information obtained through this process and your knowledge of HIV/AIDS, enter into a realistic therapeutic contract that anticipates, as well as reacts to, biopsychosocial and spiritual issues.

— The mental health practitioner who uses the biopsychosocial/spiritual model acknowledges and responds to a person's many aspects.

Many years of experience providing mental health services to HIV-affected persons have convinced providers that rigid frames of practice do not adequately serve clients. The inadequacy has several causes, including these:

— Much current practice is based on Western European models, that is, white majority-culture models, of providing psychotherapy. These models are foreign to and perhaps inappropriate for minority-culture person and fail to meet their needs.

— Current psychotherapeutic models fail to account for the diverse and complex needs of medically involved patients.

While much is said about culturally sensitive or culturally competent practice, in fact it is so complicated that mental health practitioners largely ignore its implementation. Practitioners must realize that acceptance of, or sensitivity to, a person's culture is insufficient; they need to be well versed in the culture, to understand it, and to accept its role in the person's life. The therapist must create a therapeutic relationship and make interventions that are culturally consonant for the person. Obviously, cultural competence requires a great deal of study and experience.

— The model provides a metamodel under which many disciplines can interact.

The teamwork arises from what many of us call integrated care comes: when people talk with each other and regard each other with respect. But, often, teamwork is hindered by a lack of a common way of thinking.

Physicians, nurses, psychologists, and social workers generally emerge from training with different worldviews, including etiological presumptions, treatment strategies, and decision-making styles. The biopsychosocial/spiritual model does not require practitioners to change their worldviews. Rather, it facilitates a consensual treatment plan based on a common understanding that a person has biomedical, psychological, social, and spiritual aspects.

On the basis of that common acceptance of the model, practitioners of diverse views can sit together, view the patient in many different ways, and blend their different views into a biopsychosocial/spiritual treatment plan.

— The biopsychosocial/spiritual model assists us in incorporating knowledge from other disciplines.

The blending of knowledge within a system has to occur within each practitioner. What occurs when the person tells his social worker that his T-helper cell count has dropped below 200? Will the worker understand the implications and respond appropriately? Similarly, if the patient tells his physician that he takes pleasure in nothing, will the practitioner recognize a symptom of depression? Too often, we become prisoners of our training. But with the many aspects of HIV, this limitation is now insufficient for practice. To respond fully to the HIV-affected person, providers have to learn some of other disciplines' knowledge.

The psychologist will never have the training of a physician, a social worker, or a member of the clergy. But he or she must be able to understand the HIV-affected person's concerns, no matter the aspect from which they come.

Having a sense of other providers' knowledge allows the psychologist to work better with colleagues and extends his or her professional reach.

***Barriers***

Barriers to the implementation of a biopsychosocial/spiritual model include the following:

— Being entrapped in one own's discipline and unwilling to extend one's breadth of knowledge.

— Adaptation of a simplistic, cartoonish view of what is meant by biopsychosocial/spiritual factors.

— Current reimbursement systems for health care, both medical and mental health. These now pressure providers to be more productive, that is, to see more patient, and therefore allow less time for interdisciplinary meetings and discussions.

— Scepticism among patients. People who seek assistance in medical facilities generally believe that assistance comes in the form of medication. This belief requires mental health professionals in multidisciplinary programs to persuade patients of the worth of psychosocial, nonmedical services.

The biopsychosocial/spiritual model has been presented as a guide not only to understanding the condition but to assisting health care providers in structuring assessment and guiding intervention. The metamodel also informs multidisciplinary practice and encourages providers of HIV-related services to extend their knowledge beyond their disciplines.

Psychiatry plays a significant role in the treatment of the immense and complex mental health needs related to HIV/AIDS.

As HIV disease develops into a chronic illness, psychiatry has the opportunity to span the gulf between biological and psychosocial/spiritual approaches. Because the virus is prevalent in groups with multiple problems, such as homelessness, chronic mental illness, and substance use, diagnosis and treatment planning become increasingly complicated. One must identify symptoms as psychiatric or neurological; although accuracy in identifying symptoms improves with time and training, diagnoses are still missed and the patient is blamed for misbehaviour.

At the beginning of the HIV/AIDS epidemic, patients typically died quickly from acute infections, such as pneumocystis carinii pneumonia (PCP). The role of psychiatrists and other mental health providers was limited, if it existed at all. As more individuals became affected, experts in the field distinguished two groups of people with HIV/AIDS and mental illness: those with pre-existing chronic and/or recurrent psychiatric illness who subsequently become HIV infected and HIV-infected persons who later develop neuropsychiatric or psychosocial problems related to their infection.

Studies addressing the number of acutely hospitalized psychiatric inpatients infected with HIV-I found that between five per cent and seven per cent of individuals studied were HIV-seropositive. Among longer-stay patients at a state hospital, HIV seroprevalence has been reported as 4 percent. Injection drug use is a well-documented risk factor for HIV infection.

Recent information shows that alcoholics and non-injection drug users also are at higher risk: Seroprevalence rates in these populations range from 4.5 per cent to 11.4 percent. One cohort of 300 alcoholic patients showed 10.3 per cent of patients were HIV-infected, 77.4 per cent of whom were undetected during inpatient alcohol treatment.

Several investigators have identified higher-risk behaviours among persons with mental illness, including engaging in casual sex, trading sex for money or a place to stay, combining sex with substance use, having unprotected heterosexual intercourse with known HIV-positive partners, having unprotected anal intercourse with men, and sharing needles or drug paraphernalia.

The understanding of AIDS risk behaviours appears to be compromised among psychiatric inpatients. But few programs developed to date address the special needs that chronic mentally ill patients have regarding AIDS education.

In addition to prevention/education challenges, persons with mental illness who subsequently become HIV-infected also present providers with unique challenges around treatment compliance and diagnosis. What is the most effective method for keeping a homeless individual with schizophrenia and tuberculosis engaged for the several weeks to months of medications required both to ensure proper treatment of the lung infection and to minimize the risk of exposure to the general population? Are the current psychiatric symptoms seen in an immunocompromised patient an exacerbation of bipolar disorder or indicative of a central nervous system infection?

The World Health Organization Neuropsychiatric AIDS Study, which attempted to study a population representative of the current epidemic, reported a higher prevalence of current mental disorders among symptomatic HIV-1 infected persons than among HIV-1 seronegative controls. AIDS dementia, characterized by cognitive impairment, motor dysfunction, and changes in mood/personality, typically occurs in significantly immunocompromised AIDS patients. Earlier reports suggested a prevalence at a single point in time from 8 per cent to 16 percent, with prevalence over the life of the individual approaching 40 to 50 percent. More recent studies suggest that this illness occurs in 10 to 20 per cent of AIDS patients.

Delirium, defined as an acute confusional state with a physiological cause, is characterized by disturbances of consciousness and attention, changes in cognition or perceptual disturbances, and acute onset with a fluctuating course.

Many providers mistake delirium for dementia. Many take it for granted as a natural part of dying. Misconceptions result in underrecognition and inappropriate treatment of this condition. In one study of hospitalized AIDS patients, delirium accounted for 57 per cent of the identifiable organic mental disorders seen in the study group. The study also includes reports of other neurological diseases presenting with psychiatric symptoms: toxoplasmosis and psychosis; cryptococcal meningitis and mania; dementia and depression.

Adequate population-based descriptive studies that outline the frequency and the severity of psychiatric illness in HIV/AIDS patients, and the subsequent effect of such an illness on function and general health, remain missing from the literature. In addition to neuropsychiatric illness, mental health providers working with HIV/AIDS patients commonly address spiritual or existential crises across the spectrum of HIV disease. Farmer and Kleinman describe AIDS as human suffering despite the rational-technical language of disease. Kuhn advocates viewing spirituality as a legitimate and purposeful area of medical investigation.

Psychiatrists working in the area of HIV/AIDS certainly possess a unique role in overseeing psychopharmacological interventions. Unfortunately, much of the literature in this area consists of anecdotal information and case reports. Only recently have controlled medication trials in HIV/ AIDS patients for common psychiatric illnesses such as depression been published.

## THE ROLES OF PSYCHIATRY

The unique role of psychiatry in the treatment of HIV/AIDS patients encompasses and balances each aspect of the biopsychosocial/spiritual model; the psychiatrist is at once physician, consultant/liaison, educator, therapist, and visionary.

### Psychiatrist as physician

A person sat in the office chair breathing heavily after his walk to the clinic. Diagnosed with alcohol dependence and bipolar disorder, he saw his psychiatrist more often than his medical provider. In fact, his recent problems around accepting his HIV status had led him to avoid seeing the internal medicine doctor. A bout of alcohol use two weeks ago resulted in a fall that fractured his upper arm; the pain made it difficult to move; his sleep was decreased. Depressed, tired, out of breath, and in pain, he waited for the psychiatrist.

Upon entering the room, the psychiatrist noticed that the person looked different: He was short of breath; his colour was pale; he had lost weight. Rather than focus only on the psychiatric medications, the doctor asked several questions about the persons' current symptoms. It rapidly became clear that he needed a physical examination followed by a chest x-ray to address his respiratory disease. The need for consultation with a primary-care provider was explained to him, and he agreed to an examination. The diagnosis was pneumonia.

In this clinical example, the psychiatrist was in the best position to appreciate the interaction between medical and psychiatric illness. Alcohol abuse led to a fracture of the person's arm, which led to serious pain and decreased mobility, which facilitated the development of pneumonia, which ultimately resulted in depression and problems with sleep.

If the psychiatric provider had merely addressed the person's depression, sleep disturbance, alcohol abuse, and psychiatric medications, a serious infection would have gone untreated. As physicians, psychiatrists utilize a set of methods gleaned from basic science to understand the workings of the human body.

These methods emphasize diagnosis, which determines appropriate treatment. Identification and treatment of comorbid conditions can lead to increased level of function, decreased disability, and improved quality of life. Psychiatric facilitation of primary care for HIV patients may affect survival, given the association between survival and lack of medical care, higher T-helper, also known as $CD_4$, cell count at the initial visit, and pneumocystis carinii pneumonia prophylaxis and antiretroviral therapy.

**Psychiatrist as consultant/liaison**

Consult/liaison psychiatry is a speciality area within the area of psychiatry. This function provides a remarkable opportunity to influence patient care without being directly responsible for the patient. This unique perspective often results in a more neutral evaluation than is given by primary-care providers, nursing staff, and social workers who have ongoing interactions with the patient and who may be emotionally involved.

One assumption in having psychiatrists service as consultants is that direct-care providers recognize the need for psychiatric consultation. This is a documented problem throughout medicine and is not unique to HIV/AIDS. Psychiatric liaison services tend to work toward better recognition of psychiatric illness in primary-care settings, as well as assist in the discussion of various legal and ethical issues confronted in the care of complicated patients.

Liaisons take a more proactive role: affiliating with specific providers or clinics, providing continual reinforcement regarding the importance of psychiatric intervention, and bridging gaps between more medically oriented providers and psychosocial or spiritual heaters. The psychiatric consultant/liaison relies heavily on the relationships forged with direct-care providers. Without the information obtained from discussion with these providers or from review of their chart notes, the psychiatric consultant cannot complete his/her assessment. Without support from the staff caring directly for the patient, the best-formed treatment plan will surely fail.

**Psychiatrist as educator**

One key outcome of having psychiatrists serve as educators is the reduction of stigma associated with mental illness. HIV/AIDS is a disease already characterized by shame, discrimination, and misunderstanding. When psychiatric illness is added to this tenuous situation, even the most empathic caregiver can succumb to stereotypes and frustration.

Psychiatrists, because of their unique biological perspective, can assist HIV/AIDS providers to recognize better psychiatric illness and understand better psychiatric pharmacological subtleties. Psychiatrists can educate other physicians, physician assistants, and nurse practitioners in prevention of iatrogenic disease due to medication toxicity. Psychiatrists, because of their appreciation for the psychosocial/spiritual characteristics of the patient, can listen carefully to providers' and family members' concerns, presenting their information in a manner that the recipient can relate directly to the patient or loved one. Optimal care for HIV/AIDS patients requires an educational component for patients, providers, and family members.

**Psychiatrist as therapist**

Psychiatry is not synonymous with psychotherapy. In fact, in recent years some psychiatrists have distanced themselves from the practice of psychotherapy and embraced the definition of psychiatry as strictly a medical discipline. Nevertheless, 50 per cent of residents in psychiatric training are in therapy and believe that therapy is essential to becoming a psychiatrist. The "art" of medicine resides in the understanding and expertise that addresses that which is human, such as relationships, conscious and unconscious thought, and the complexity of cc volitional" behaviour. Psychiatry, and medicine in general, would suffer tremendously if no medical discipline devoted its time and resources to the better understanding and practice of this art.

Concerns regarding cost of care and limited funding may preclude psychiatrists from only performing psychotherapy in the future. Psychiatric psychotherapy may one day be restricted to complicated patients with severe personality disorders or who require both medications and psychotherapy.

Because of their ability to integrate medical and psychosocial/spiritual perspectives, psychiatrists treating HIV/AIDS patients may be in a unique position to differentiate neurologic sequelae of the virus, psychiatric illness needing medications, psychological distress, and existential dilemmas. Research into the relationship between psychosocial factors and improved immunologic status and physical functioning needs to be a priority area for HIV psychiatric psychotherapy.

**Psychiatrist as visionary**

The word psychiatry stems from the Greek for mind and soul; psychiatrists are healers of the mind and the soul. Advances in the late 20th century established a union among the mind, the soul, and the brain that should not end in divorce. Psychiatrists must work diligently to strengthen this union if HIV/AIDS patients are to be served properly. The changing demographics of the HIV/AIDS population suggest an increasing need for psychiatric services in the 21st century.

As patients continue to live longer with the disease, there will be a greater opportunity for development of psychiatric illness, both as a result of HIV neurological disorders and as a reaction to living with a chronic illness. It is hoped that efforts to strengthen the collaborative partnerships among primary-care providers, non-physician providers of mental health services, and psychiatrists will lead to increased recognition of psychiatric morbidity in HIV/AIDS patients, for diagnosis always precedes proper treatment. The epidemic's movement into populations with multiple problems increases the complexity of addressing psychiatric illness in HIV/AIDS patients.

Psychiatrists wishing to work with HIV/AIDS patients must prepare to leave the private practice and medical clinic settings in which they currently work. Creative treatment approaches, including housing programs for people with mental illness, substance use, and HIV disease, will need on-site psychiatric services in order to maintain these challenging patients in the community and to decrease the need for psychiatric or medical hospitalization.

Mobile treatment units that meet patients where they live may be one option for the care of homeless. University- and community-based agencies must be encouraged. Pooling academic and front-line resources will result in better understanding of the HIV population needing care, treatment ideas that work effectively, and archaic perspectives that must be abandoned. Psychiatrists must fully engage in the effort to abolish the stigma associated with HIV/AIDS and mental illness.

Working with other physicians, non-physician providers of mental health care, patients, and families, psychiatrists can provide a unique perspective on the biopsychosocial/spiritual aspects of HIV disease and impact the highly political process that determines health policy. Until the economic stigma surrounding HIV disease and mental illness is decreased, HIV/AIDS patients needing psychiatric care will suffer. The practice of psychiatry in the setting of HIV/AIDS must be determined by local circumstances and not merely by ideology. The increasing complexity of mental illness in HIV-infected patients demands the best that all providers can offer.

General psychiatric practice of the future, as well as HIV-specific psychiatric practice, demands better definition of diagnostic subtypes in order to achieve improved treatment outcomes. Is the depression seen in an AIDS patient due to a "major depressive episode" or to depression associated with AIDS dementia? Do the two illnesses respond equally well to current modes of depression therapy, or does a different etiology require a different intervention? Improvement in diagnosis will also achieve more uniform application of diagnostic labels, resulting in better communication among care providers. Improvement in identification and communication will then allow a clearer definition of treatment outcomes, providing the opportunity for a clearer demonstration of benefit from psychiatric services.

Future advances in the understanding of individual drug metabolism will facilitate more individualized dose-response targets for each patient. In other words, patients may one day benefit from truly individualized medication treatment plans, rather than population-based medication dosage recommendations. This is especially important in HIV/AIDS patients, who tend to be prescribed ten and twenty medications simultaneously, to be particularly susceptible to adverse medication effects, and to exhibit altered patterns of drug metabolism.

## TOOLS FOR CLINICAL PRACTICE: UTILIZING A PSYCHIATRIST

Psychiatrists can serve many roles in the provision of care to HIV/AIDS patients, even when those patients receive the bulk of their care from other providers.

### Psychopharmacology

Many patients seek mental health care from a non-physician provider because medication is not their treatment of choice. Patients deserve to have clear explanations of the risks and benefits of medication for a given psychiatric illness in making this choice. It is important for non-physician providers of mental health care to HIV/AIDS patients to form a relationship with a psychiatrist purposes of medication consultation and referral, by taking these steps:

1) If possible, find a consultant with HIV/AIDS experience and interest. Medication management in HIV/AIDS patients is complex. Differentiating medication side effects from underlying illness or other possible causes requires special understanding of the biopsychosocial/spiritual aspects of HIV/AIDS.
2) Develop a relationship with the consultant before it is needed. It is always easier to call and ask a question of someone you know than it is to call someone "out of the blue." Be clear about your agenda in establishing a relationship with a consultant, and determine what the consultant sees as limitations to that relationship.
3) Remain neutral in your discussion with the patient about the "best" treatment options. As in any other area of the therapeutic relationship, neutrality is vital. Allow exploration of issues such as whether to use medications or which particular medication is most appropriate. Help the individual to clarify his or her own biases without introducing your own.
4) If a referral for a medication evaluation is made, obtain releases of information, and provide the consultant with as much information about the individual's illness and potential need for medication as possible. Important information to include in your referral includes:
   - Demographics, such as age, ethnicity, and relationship status.
   - HIV disease status, including category (A,B,C), T-helper ($CD_4$) count/$CD_4$ per cetn/viral load (if known). If you do not know or feel comfortable about gathering this information, give the psychiatrist the name and the phone number of the patient's physician.
   - Past psychiatric diagnoses, including substance use.

- — Current psychiatric diagnoses, including substance use.
- — Current symptoms that suggest a need for medication (*i.e.*, why you are making a referral).
- — Past medication trials, if any, including the patient's experience with the medicine.
- — Concerns the patient has expressed about seeing a psychiatrist or using medication.

In making a referral for a medication evaluation, it is important to be clear with the client and the consultant about the working relationships between each of you and how information will be shared after the consultation occurs.

**Diagnostic dilemmas**

In addition to helping to resolve psychopharmacology questions, psychiatrists can assist with diagnostic conundrums. HIV/AIDS patients may have several things going on simultaneously: mental illness, substance use, HIV-related illness, and other physical illness. Obtaining a second opinion on a patient's condition can help clarify your treatment approach as well as reassure the patient, who may be concerned that symptoms represent the first stages of some frightening illness, such as dementia.

A unique aspect of HIV/AIDS is the psychiatric presentation of many serious, and in some cases life-threatening, neurological diseases. In cases where a patient presents with psychiatric symptoms in the setting of severe immunocompromise (T-helper or $CD_4$ count less than 200; $CD_4$% less than 14), a psychiatric referral is indicated to ensure that a medical explanation for the symptoms cannot be found.

In cases where the person is mildly to moderately immunocompromised ($CD_4$ count between 200 and 500), a phone consultation is warranted to determine if farther evaluation is necessary. It is important to remember that any change in mental status, even a relatively subtle one that develops over a period of weeks, may reflect an underlying physical problem. It is best to err on the side of referral. The nonphysician provider may be the first to encounter this change in the person and therefore has the responsibility of informing the patient's other providers if the patient cannot do this her or himself.

With HIV disease, the borders between the biological, psychological, social, and spiritual disappear. Individual practitioners, regardless of their disciplines, need to acknowledge this and practice accordingly. Institutions and agencies can no longer retain divisive care systems when dealing with a condition that demands new, integrated models of care.

# 2

# HIV: The Most Disarming Virus

Viruses are infectious agents like bacteria, but they are far smaller and unlike bacteria, not self-sufficient. They are parasites that need a host. They can often exist on their own, in a kind of suspended animation, but to reproduce they must use and subvert the mechanisms of a host cell. Some viruses can thrive in only one type of cell within one type of plant or animal. Others are not so fussy. The HIV prefers certain T-helper cells and macrophages of the human immune system. (*Macrophage* means "big eater" in Greek because these defender cells neutralize invaders by engulfing and digesting them.)

In the early 1980s, a strange new epidemic emerged among North American homosexual men. It was first seen in the large gay communities of New York and California among young men who were very sexually active. These men became mysteriously ill with infections and tumors that, according to previous experience, were rarely serious and rarely combined in the same individual. Certainly they had never been seen in epidemic proportions in such a narrowly defined risk group.

One of the infectious agents was *Pneumocystis carinii,* a usually harmless microorganism that thrives around us and even inside of us. Like many other organisms in our environment, *P. carinii* routinely colonizes most of us, at an early age, with no ill effects under ordinary circumstances. It could harm only severely malnourished or ill people or children, not vigorous young men.

The same was generally true for Kaposi's sarcoma (KS), the tumour most often seen in the new epidemic. KS had previously been seen in aging men in the United States and Europe, but it was uncommon and rarely aggressive. It was more frequent and serious in Africa, but still no great threat. It was soon discovered that some impairment of the immune system that normally protects us from invaders had allowed the bizarre and fatal combination of infections and tumours. The condition was marked by a rapid decline of certain blood cells, or T-helper cells, whose cell wall includes a crucial molecule known as $CD_4$.

These $CD_4$-positive cells are major players in our immune system. $CD_4^+$ cells are essential to fight all types of invaders. In this epidemic, their impairment was apparently not inborn but somehow acquired, so the disorder came to be called AIDS: acquired immunodeficiency syndrome. The Center for Disease Control (CDC) found that those who developed AIDS had invariably had sex with someone who concurrently had AIDS or later developed the disease. Apparently it was transmitted sexually, most likely by means of seminal fluid.

Then AIDS began to occur among hemophiliacs, but not by sexual transmission. Hemophilia is a congenital disease, seen only in men, in which the blood does not clot normally. It is effectively treated with transfusions of blood that contains clotting factors, but apparently blood could also transmit AIDS. This transmission route was later confirmed when AIDS appeared among intravenous drug users who had shared needles with infected gay men.

The transmission of AIDS in semen and blood, its epidemic spread, and its sudden occurrence in otherwise healthy men suggested an infectious agent, probably a virus. In 1982 or 1983, only two years into the epidemic, a likely suspect was found at the Institute Pasteur of Paris by Franqoise Barre-Sinoussi, Jean-Claude Chermann, Luc Montagnier, and colleagues.

The new virus was discovered in an enlarged lymph node taken from a young homosexual man. He had not yet developed AIDS, but AIDS patients were found to have the same virus in their blood. In 1984, American researchers Mika Popovic, Bob Gallo, and colleagues showed that most AIDS patients had this virus, while a control group of healthy subjects did not. (With today's finer techniques, they would have found the virus in all their AIDS patients.) Meanwhile, the virus infected three lab workers who later developed AIDS.

As far as most scientists were concerned, this tragedy supplied the last piece of the puzzle. According to a reasoning process based on Koch's postulates, an agent is linked to a disease in four steps. First, the agent is observed in every case of the disease. Second, it is isolated from people with the disease, then grown in pure culture. Third, the culture causes the disease when inoculated into susceptible subjects (in this case, the unfortunate lab workers). Fourth, the agent is observed and recovered from the experimentally infected subjects.

But these researchers identified the new virus, and the Gallo team grew the virus to high levels of infectivity, 'enabling rapid production of kits to diagnose the infection. The virus was soon known as HIV: human immunodeficiency virus. Perhaps no other virus in history has become so widely known in so short a time.

$CD_4$ does not exist solely to give passage to HIV. It did not evolve to serve as the HIV receptor. In fact, its main job is sentry duty: it recognizes intruders and arouses various fighter cells against them. In an ironic twist, HIV uses this guardian molecule to enter and ultimately destroy the cells that carry it on their surface. For survival, HIV defends by attacking: it cripples the immune system that would destroy or control it. Its effects are slow to show because, up to a point, the cells it destroys can be replenished. But eventually its steady killing reduces the quantity and quality of $CD_4^+$ cells, causing immunodeficiency. By the time people have full-blown AIDS, they cannot cope with invading organisms that normal people accommodate or fight off every day.

The organisms that threaten AIDS patients are not only invaders from our external environment but insiders like *P. carinii.* These members of our internal ecosystem—our natural flora—are usually kept in their place by many factors, including a healthy immune system. But given the opportunity to overgrow or grow in the wrong place, they can cause "opportunistic" infection.

Several studies of the natural course of AIDS have shown that certain opportunistic infections always become fatal once HIV is acquired and persists in the blood and other organs of the body. Where did this treacherous and apparently new virus come from? As the Bible says, "There is no new thing under the sun." HIV may be truly new, but it is more likely an old virus that has gained a new level of virulence, enabling it to cause human immunodeficiency. Or perhaps it has always been virulent but has only now entered the human species.

When AIDS was first seen in North America and then in Europe and Africa, epidemiologists were baffled. Most epidemics can be traced to one focal point, but this one seemed to be spreading independently on three continents. North American and European AIDS were soon regarded as one epidemic, brought to Europe from America by gay men. Meanwhile, a different type of AIDS surfaced among a few central Africans living in Belgium and France. This disease was transmitted heterosexually, appeared mainly in women, and had come directly from Africa.

Today AIDS is generally accepted to be more than one epidemic caused by a whole family of HIV types, subtypes, and strains. The main epidemic in North America and Europe is caused by HIV type 1 (HIV-1). Now spreading fast to South America, this Western HIV is apparently becoming ever more lethal or virulent as it is passaged through the human population. That is, it gains strength each time it enters a new person, reproduces in the $CD_4^+$ cells, then bursts out to circulate and infect another person.

This process of cycling to virulence seems to be an HIV family trait. All members of the family, including HIV-1, were probably much less deadly when they first encountered humans. They had to reach a threshold of cycles and new infections before they could cause AIDS and premature death. If so, then HIV may have been with us for millennia.

It can suddenly cause AIDS because of some change in us or in its own makeup. So far, research indicates that all members of the HIV family can cause AIDS (some faster than others)-but a very few people can block the disease.

The study began with a sample of more than one thousand gay men, who were examined every three months. These subjects belonged to the subgroup known to be at highest risk for AIDS: young gay men who seek rough and anonymous .sex with multiple partners. Some of the sample were HIV-infected before the study began, but they focused on those who became infected as the study proceeded. These men, who so far number about fifty, had been followed for an average of ten to twelve years.

As usual with HIV-1, each case started with acute infection. Though brief and sometimes hardly noticeable, that flu-like illness was accompanied by the generation of permanent and specific HIV antibodies. Our immune system normally greets any invader by producing specific antibodies. They remain forever on call, should the invader reappear. If it does, they are geared to recognize and tag it as an enemy to be destroyed. HIV antibodies are evidence of seropositivity.

Their appearance signifies seroconversion: the first point at which serum was found to contain the virus. The acute stage was followed by a period free of symptoms or disease, which usually lasted several years. But of those infected early in the study, more than 75 per cent had developed AIDS, and twenty-three have died. Three individuals developed the disease within only eighteen months of initial infection. At the opposite end of the spectrum, the two lucky ones shown no sign of immunodeficiency.

Incidentally, their work offers further proof that HIV is the agent of AIDS. Of the twenty-three men who died, each acquired HIV infection before development of any immune disturbance. And not a single case of AIDS-or any sign of immunodeficiency-has developed among the many hundreds of men who had remained HIV-negative over the years. However, a few researchers still doubt HIV is the agent of AIDS. One of their arguments is that Kaposi's sarcoma has occurred, though rarely, in young gay men with no sign of immunodeficiency. Recent evidence indicates that a newly discovered virus, sexually transmissible but unrelated to HIV, may be involved in KS. And while KS can occur without HIV, it clearly runs a much more aggressive course in HIV-positive people.

Based on the linear progression of AIDS development, it is found that about 95 per cent of homosexual men infected with HIV-1 will eventually develop AIDS. Their symptom-free period will vary according to a bell-shaped curve. Very few individuals will develop AIDS in the first year after infection or in the "last" year, projected to be fifteen to twenty years after infection. Most people will progress to AIDS after an average asymptomatic period of about ten years.

Their two nonprogressors remain well not because of virus variation but because of host variation. In other words, these men did not get an unusually weak virus but are, for some reason, unusually well defended hosts. All of us are genetically programmed to offer a more or less effective immune response to HIV and other invaders. The response to any invader involves many factors, all of which can vary. With HIV, an important variation is seen in the cells that carry the $CD_4$ molecule.

From person to person, these cells are more or less hospitable to HIV access, entry, and multiplication. Their two AIDS-free subjects have maintained extremely low levels of circulating virus since their initial infection. In contrast, subjects who have developed AIDS quickly have had extremely high levels during the entire period. Naturally, we are looking hard for the precise factor that seems to protect the nonprogressors.

More clues to virus and host variation can be found by comparing HIV and AIDS in the three, major risk groups: homosexual men, IV drug users, and hemophiliacs. All three groups are susceptible to HIV-1, but they differ in their AIDS frequency rates and their length of symptom-free periods. AIDS occurs at a somewhat higher rate among gay men than among IV drug users and hemophiliacs, even though the sexual transmission of HIV is far less efficient than its transmission by injection. For IV drug users and hemophiliacs, certain host factors are known to lower AIDS frequency and lengthen the symptom-free period. All other things being equal, the younger a hemophiliac the better his defense against AIDS.

As for drug users, the frequent sharing of syringes means frequent exposure to HIV. However, once infected, they derive a small benefit from this dangerous practice. The constant injection of foreign blood seems to dull or confuse the immune response, leading to cell *anergy* (the opposite of *energy),* which slightly curbs reproduction of the $CD_4^+$ cells. This, in turn, slightly curbs multiplication of HIV, since the virus depends on host reproductive mechanisms.

Much evidence indicates that host factors, more than virus factors, are responsible when HIV is thwarted; conversely, host factors are less responsible when the virus thrives. All HIVs seem to be viable and virulent, and some have found ways to increase their damage. So HIV needs no help from a weak defense, but apparently it can be slowed by a strong defense. One may say that increases in the rate of disease progression are more virus-dependent, while decreases are more host-dependent.

Whether sex is homosexual or heterosexual, the probability of acquiring HIV-1 is related less to promiscuity than to the type of contact and the sex of the partner. Especially among men who have sex with men, the number of partners is far less important than the kind of sex they practice. The most dangerous sex is anogenital: anal penetration by the penis. The more often an uninfected man is anally penetrated by a man infected with HIV-1, the greater his chance of acquiring HIV and AIDS, whether his partners are few or many.

The safest sex is that between two women, even if they engage in anal stimulation. In fact, two women engaged in such contact (i.e., nonpenile but involving some kind of penetration) are at less risk than two men engaged in the same type of contact, possibly because force is less often a factor.

HIV virulence, or damage, is directly related to its rate of circulation. This is because the virus load needed for efficient

HIV transmission depends on virus reproduction within host cells that are crucial to host well-being. As already noted, the faster and more often HIV changes hosts, the more deadly it becomes. Our own studies have shown that the virus is more aggressive in times of rapid spread and less aggressive when spread is relatively slow. Spread depends on two factors: the opportunity to transmit HIV and the infectivity of the virus.

Opportunity depends on the frequency of the transmission event, whether it is unprotected sex, blood transfusion, or IV drug use. Infectivity depends on the level or amount of virus in the transmitting fluid as well as the susceptibility of the host cells to that particular virus. Looking at sexual transmission (by far the most common of the three routes), we have seen that virtually all newly infected individuals have high virus loads during the first few months. As measured by the HIV RNA in their blood, they have about equal amounts of circulating virions, making them equally HIV-infectious.

But soon a distinction develops between progressors and nonprogressors (*i.e.*, those rapidly progressing to AIDS and those progressing slowly or not at all). The progressors are highly infectious due to persistent high virus loads in all their body fluids. They transmit a highly aggressive virus that reproduces fast and sustains high levels in its next host. However, progressors are highly infectious for a relatively short time due to rapid disease progression. As their $CD_4^+$ cells fall, their sexual activity tends to decline because they feel increasingly ill and develop unattractive symptoms: the dark red Kaposi lesions, the continual cough of *P. carinii* pneumonia, or devastating diarrhea. In contrast, the nonprogressors are less infectious for a relatively long time because the virus load declines in their fluids.

As their immune systems keep AIDS at bay, they feel healthy enough to continue sexual activity, but 'they transmit a weaker virus. It reproduces relatively slowly and cannot sustain high levels in the next host. Of course, as the epidemic continues, the progressors with their aggressive HIV contribute less and less to the viral mix. They drop out of sexual activity and ultimately die. Therefore, we see that a new AIDS epidemic is dominated by the more infectious virus of progressors, but a late-stage epidemic is dominated by the weaker virus of nonprogressors.

At times of high spread, the stronger virus shrinks the average symptom-free period because it needs less time to break down the immune system. At times of low spread, the weaker virus leads to a longer average symptom-free period. We have compelling evidence that breakdown occurs faster when HIV is acquired (by any route) from an AIDS patient whose symptom-free period was relatively short. These observations are based on various studies. Although many gay men have stable long-term relationships, this highly active subgroup combines youthful potency with militant expression of emancipated homosexuality.

Such promiscuity, practiced routinely throughout a good-sized community, may be unprecedented in history. It may be approximated by heterosexual men who continually visit many different prostitutes, but such men are rare, as far as we can tell. For one thing, prostitutes cost money. In contrast, gay encounters in bathrooms and bathhouses are largely free of charge. It is a tragic accident that HIV- 1 was introduced to a population where such activity—so perfectly suited to its passage!—had become the hallmark of liberation. This first HIV epidemic got off to a very good start.

Fortunately, preventive measures can reduce HIV infections and actually reverse the spiral of aggressive infection. Fewer people get HIV and AIDS. They stay healthier longer because the virus is weaker and gives them a longer symptom-free period. However, HIV remains. To keep HIV in check, everyone who is sexually active-gay or straight-must avoid the high-risk behaviour that gives HIV the advantage. In North America and Europe, AIDS is epidemic but seems to be holding, and HIV-1 incidence has dropped. In South America and Asia, the disease is fast reaching epidemic proportions. It could easily become endemic because of factors such as poor education, communication, and medical care, which have already made it near endemic in much of Africa.

Evidence suggests that the HIV family could kill faster. It could shorten the symptom-free period that follows the initial acute infection. If so, instead of developing AIDS over several years, people might develop the disease in a matter of months. We would then see many millions more cases of AIDS than are projected on the basis of today's average disease-free period.

Outside Europe and North America, AIDS spreads mainly by heterosexual relations, perinatal infection, and contaminated blood and hospital supplies. Control strategies must aim to safeguard the blood supplies and hospital equipment. But if HIV thrives on rapidity of consecutive transmission, these strategies will not be enough. Somehow people in Africa, Asia, and South America must be educated to lower their number of sexual partners and, even more important, their high-risk sex acts. Gay men in Amsterdam and other areas have shown this can be done. Even in North America and Europe, HIV incidence is dropping.

The decreased incidence may lead to decreased virulence and even to a weakened or attenuated virus. But virulence could just as well be boosted by ominous changes in the Western epidemic. At first HIV-1 was spread mainly by homosexual relations, then by needle sharing among drug users. Now it is infecting more women and children, most of whom have no direct connection with drugs or homosexuals.

Nature and science will hopefully ultimately show us the way, but two promising avenues have so far been disappointing. The first involves searching the HIV family for types that are relatively harmless, either because of inherently low infectivity or loss of infectivity (attenuation). Such relatively weak viruses could give insight into more harmful types. They might ever protect us against them, as cowpox was used by Jenner to protect against smallpox. At this point, we have discovered and studied two possibilities that will later be discussed in depth. The first is HIV type 2 (HIV-2), which emerged in the West African interior. This virus causes AIDS, but very slowly and with lower frequency than HIV-1. HIV-2 is mainly confined to West Africa, where HIV- 1 subtypes are appearing with increasing frequency.

More time and study are needed to tell how well HIV-2 infection protects people against HIV-1. Although most West African AIDS victims harbor only one of the two viruses, a rare few harbor both. This could mean HIV-2 offers incomplete or temporary protection.

However, with a double infection we cannot yet tell whether the two viruses entered simultaneously or, if sequentially, which came first. We can still hope that HIV-2 has some protective potential, and new data point tentatively in that direction. Meanwhile, HIV- 1 is overtaking the slower HIV-2 in West Africa, but HIV-2 is not likely to disappear. It has a proven monkey reservoir or home base: the sooty mangabey. This monkey comfortably hosts an SIV that becomes HIV-2 when transmitted to the human body.

The other new type to be studied is HIV type 0 (HIV-0). It was discovered in 1990 by Belgian researchers Guido van der Groen and Peter Piot. Some have called it "0" for "outgroup", but "zero" is now preferred. Originally found only in Cameroon and Gabon, HIV-0 was isolated from several AIDS patients by different researchers, leaving no doubt that it can cause the disease in humans. Its virulence is unknown, but its spread is extremely limited. The virus has just recently been seen in Europe, mainly France, in a handful of immigrants from Cameroon and Gabon. In Africa, it is only rarely seen outside its accustomed area. Even there, HIV-0 occurs in much less than 10 per cent of AIDS victims. The rest are infected with the more common HIV-1 subtypes.

As with HIV-2, the closest relative to HIV-0 is not another human AIDS virus but a monkey virus. Found in chimpanzee, it is called *chimpanzee immunodeficiency virus* (CIV) or, more often, SIV cpz. Like other SIVs, it does not harm its natural host. While HIV-2 and HIV-0 have great research value, they are not too promising as barriers against HIV-1. Though they spread and act slowly, they still cause AIDS.

The second avenue is to find a virus outside the HIV family: something similar but harmless to its natural host. We have already found CIV, other SIVs and even analogs beyond the primate family. These viruses offer tantalizing clues to the HIV family. But so far, none offers us protection from HIV. Although closely related to the killer, these viruses are remarkable and they never cause the slightest harm to their natural hosts. SIVs can even move among various types of African monkeys without harm.

In fact, they seem to inhabit a different virus world than our HIV. Without knowing the terrible AIDS story, we would never believe that these innocent monkey viruses could kill. Yet they kill humans, and some of them kill Asian monkeys. What makes these simian viruses perfectly harmless to some primates and deadly to others? How can they be so well adapted to multiply in human immune cells? Since we find no harmless HIVs, it appears that SIV just naturally develops into an AIDS-causing pathogen after roaming from human to human for a number of viral generations.

# 3

# Roots of HIV

HIV-1B is extremely rare in Africa, but a few strains have been found in certain countries of the sub-Saharan rain forest: Gabon, Cameroon, Ivory Coast, Uganda, and Rwanda. Proto-1B must have reached Europe from one of these areas, but probably not Uganda or Rwanda. Before 1940, the lack of commercial air transportation made these interior countries virtually inaccessible. The virus more likely came by ship from a coastal area. It could have come from Ivory Coast, then a French colony, but since 1939 the epidemic began in Germany, a German colony is more logical. This points to Cameroon, which then included the northern parts of Gabon.

Proto-1B must have descended from the African ancestor of all HIV-1 subtypes. Even if not always fatal, a serious disease would have been noticed in a colony like Cameroon, a colony with a good infrastructure dating back to the nineteenth century. Historical records would tell us if a deadly illness was endemic among colonists or local plantation workers. It would have made the country less prosperous and attractive to European superpowers, but England, France, and Germany never stopped fighting for this treasure. No reports hint that Cameroon was a dangerous place to colonize. So we can assume that, in colonial times, most HIV strains circulating in the territory must have been harmless and unnoticeable. They were largely unable to cause disease and, as will be argued, had not yet grown into subtypes. The strain that became proto-1B had deadly potential but perhaps never caused *P. carinii* pneumonia (PCP) or other opportunistic infections and tumours until it got to Europe. This odd variant that mutated into a disease-causing virus no doubt left Cameroon by sheer chance.

Proto-1B would have been closely related to the common HIV-1 ancestor, so that ancestor must have lived nearby. Whereas proto-1B ultimately went to Europe, other descendant strains travelled eastward in Africa. Like proto-1B, they would evolve from harmless to AIDS-causing viruses, mainly HIV-1A.. And if HIV subtypes form only during an epidemic in which disease is linked to passage among human hosts, then this same area gave rise to all the HIV-1 subtypes that favour heterosexual transmission.

Only HIV-1B, which favours homosexual transmission, developed its full potential elsewhere—in Europe. This historical scenario, with its two paths, may explain the divergence of 1B from the others: its preferential spread through anal intercourse versus their spread through vaginal intercourse. Since the common ancestor in Cameroon was harmless, a few HIV-1 strains could unknowingly be transported eastward, where they would quietly evolve by heterosexual passage. Likewise, strains that remained in Cameroon and Gabon evolved, unnoticed, into what became proto-1B. Then, during epidemics in Europe and the United States, they formed HIV-1B, the only HIV-1 subtype formed through serial passage by anal intercourse.

The common ancestor of HIV-1 must have passed from its source animal to humans in some outlying part of Cameroon, in the deep rain forest where people would be hunting and eating this animal. Once cross-species transmission had occurred, a human epidemic was perhaps inevitable. Given enough time, the natural movements of African peoples might eventually have given HIV-1 the opportunity to become a large-scale human killer. But as it happened, the evolution of dangerous HIV-1 subtypes was vastly assisted by German colonialism.

European colonialism caused turmoil in Africa, especially the mixing and movement of peoples. Europeans not uncommonly had sexual relations with their subject people. In Cameroon, for example, many German officials reportedly had local black mistresses. These relationships sometimes erupted in scandal and bloodshed. We can assume that circulating HIV strains, though relatively harmless, were sometimes passed from Africans to Germans by sexual transmission.

In this same period there were major military movements against subject people who rebelled against cruelty and injustice. Such movements of the army and particularly the navy gave HIV ample opportunity to spread from one territory to another. It is easily envisioned that, around the turn of the century, a German sailor or adventurer-or an African servant-became infected in Cameroon and took the virus, by ship, to German East Africa, on the other side of the continent. When World War I broke out in 1914, the conflict was initially confined to Europe. Soon, however, the fighting spread to Africa, where French and British joint forces invaded German colonies.

Most important, the Europeans used Africans in their colonial armies. The majority of soldiers on both sides of the African conflict were Africans. The colonial powers also recruited Africans to fight their battles in Europe. At the end of World War I, German colonies were distributed among the victors. In 1919 the Belgians claimed Rwanda and Burundi; the British took the rest of East Africa. The French took 80 per cent of Cameroon and Britain took 20 percent. By this time, HIV- 1 was already seeded around Lake Victoria, where it would grow slowly into HIV-1A and the other African HIV-1 subtypes. But what about HIV- 1B?

The first cases of opportunistic PCP and cytomegalovirus (CMV) infections and tumours did not occur in Germany until 1939. If German colonists coming home after World War I brought proto- 1B, we would expect such cases to occur in the 1920s. How do we account for the lag time? Apparently those returning expatriates were not infected, or else they carried harmless strains of HIV. The potentially lethal proto-1B must have been imported later among about three hundred Germans who came home in 1939 when war was declared between England and Germany.

## RISE OF AFRICAN AIDS

Pinpointing AIDS-like disease is not easy, especially in

Africa. This is true today and was even more true in the past. After all, AIDS is not one disease but a collection of clinical manifestations that occur only because HIV has damaged the immune system. All known HIVs can cause this damage, but they rarely cause the diseases that follow.

HIV has been established as the cause of certain dementias, and evidence is increasing that it causes certain diarrheas. But most AIDS-related diarrhea is caused by other agents, as are AIDS-related pneumonia and tumours. These other agents, such as *R carinii* or herpesviruses, commonly infect people early in life but cause no harm if the immune system is healthy. To spot AIDS we must look for unexpected or odd cases of pneumonia, diarrhea, or tumours. This is an easy task in Europe, where such problems were extremely rare before HIV emerged in the 1970s and 1980s. It is not easy in Africa, where such problems have long been common, Many Africans without HIV have Kaposi's sarcoma (KS), diarrhea, or wasting (i.e., severe weight loss) because their immune systems are compromised by malnutrition or multiple infections that have nothing to do with AIDS. Still, some sense can be made of the records, especially if we look at KS.

Kaposi's sarcoma is the most common tumour seen in Euro-American AIDS patients. It is a major risk not so much for HIV-positive hemophiliacs but for HIV-positive gay men. Of men infected by homosexual, or anal, transmission of HIV, one out of two gets KS, at least in Europe.

This agent has quite recently been identified as a herpesvirus. It can be detected in the KS lesions of virtually all patients, whether or not they are HIV-positive. The virus belongs to a group of herpes viruses known to multiply in white blood cells.

Beyond AIDS patients, KS is quite rare in the United States and Europe. It appears almost exclusively in two very distinct populations. By far the largest of these consists of gay men who are HIV-negative. The appearance of KS in HIV-negative gay men again points to the risk of orofecal contact through homosexual as in relations. But KS also occurs, if rarely, in a population with no HIV or history of homosexuality: elderly men of Mediterranean, Middle Eastern, or Eastern European descent. So far, nobody can explain how these men acquired the KS agent or why they are susceptible.

Though rare in the Western world, KS has long been endemic in Africa. Its ubiquity makes it a tricky indicator of HIV or AIDS, but changes in KS frequency or severity may give us clues. Interestingly, Cameroon is the first African country from which it was reported. In 1914 a German doctor named Hallenberg described KS-like lesions in a Cameroonian man.

Since then, many cases of severe and mild KS have been reported from many countries, particularly eastern and western Zaire, Rwanda and Burundi, western Uganda, and Tanzania. Kaposi's sarcoma was clearly endemic in these areas before AIDS appeared in the 1970s. Was an ancestral HIV allowing the KS agent to bloom, or did HIV have nothing to do with these early KS cases? There is no way to be sure, since it was 1983 or 1984 before HIV was identified and we had good tests to assess immune function. Studies of the early 1970s suggest that, at that time, the most severe KS was sometimes, but not always, associated with immunological abnormalities.

The earliest report is from Uganda in 1970. A 1973 report, using more refined technology, suggested that the most aggressive forms of KS were always linked with immunological abnormalities. However, as noted, in Africa such abnormalities can stem from many causes besides AIDS. Once good testing was available, a study was conducted at the seven-hundred-bed Fomulac Hospital in Katana, Zaire, in 1984. The hospital's outpatient population included hundreds of thousands of residents on the eastern side of Lake Kivu, of whom 10 to 15 per cent were already infected with HIV. The study found HIV in none of fourteen inpatients with KS but in two of twelve controls, that is, people without KS who were admitted for trauma or elective surgery. One must assume that if most Zairian cases of KS were not associated with HIV in 1984, earlier cases were probably not associated either.

Even more revealing studies were done in Uganda during the 1980s. They found that while the KS agent was clearly present before the 1970s, it had not yet joined with HIV to create an epidemic of aggressive KS. Ugandans diagnosed with KS between 1971 and 1975 showed no HIV antibodies when their frozen samples were later analysed. The same was true for healthy controls bled during the study period. Taken together, these findings strongly indicate that, in Uganda and Zaire in the 1970s, HIV had not yet enhanced the aggressivity and transmissibility of the KS agent. They suggest that, as late as 1975, HIV had not yet entered Uganda at all.

The question remains, Did HIV-1 increase virulence by forming subtypes, or did it become virulent and then form subtypes during epidemic spread? By the mid-1970s, HIV-1 subtypes were apparently established, spreading west through central Africa and causing predominantly a wasting disease with high mortality. Unlike HIV-1B, the African HIV does not seem to have gone through an intermediate state of aggressivity. However, such a stage may have occurred but gone unnoticed in Africa because of the generally poor health and record keeping there.

These points suggest that HIV-1 had to form subtypes to achieve the kind of disease frequency we see with AIDS. Each subtype consists of many strains that share certain defining characteristics, including optimal spread and an asymptomatic period. For example, all strains of HIV-1 subtype B spread optimally by anal intercourse and cause disease after a symptom-free period of about ten years.

If the ancestral HIV-1 from Cameroon lay nearly dormant for decades, some change in the environment or population must have caused it to blossom into aggressive diarrhea-causing subtypes. This change most likely occurred where Uganda and Tanzania meet, west of Lake Victoria. In that area a new disease emerged in the early 1980s. Locally called "slim disease" because of its wasting effects, it was characterised by the diarrhea, weight loss, and fever.

So for half a century, African HIV-1 was transmitted only fast enough to sustain a low level of endemicity—not fast enough to increase its virulence. Then, in the late 1960s and early 1970s, it encountered new opportunities in rural areas of Uganda and northwestern Tanzania. Transmitted more rapidly by the mainly heterosexual activity of traders and particularly soldiers, the virus formed the well-documented HIV-1A and other subtypes adept at heterosexual transmission.

Morbidity and mortality increased in the process. The subtypes then spread their lethal wasting syndrome beyond Uganda and Tanzania, launching the outbreak of AIDS in Africa in last half of the 1970s. One might ask why so many HIV-1 subtypes formed in a relatively small area, all causing the same disease. The answer is that the virus was apparently nonpathogenic or very weak when imported from Cameroon to German East Africa. Unlike the "proto-1B" that went to Europe in 1939, the African precursor had no evolutionary direction when it met its opportunity for increased transmission. Its nature was to infect a host, then rapidly to form a swarm of genetically linked, yet distinct, virus clones.

Following sexual transmission, one of these clones is selected by its ability to survive in the new host. However, in some cases, the selected variant can infect the host but causes little or no disease. Initially, before the African HIV- 1 grew into subtypes, there was as much or more variation among strains as now exists among subtypes. Out of an enormous swarm of HIV-1 variants, all those ill adapted to heterosexual spread gradually disappeared. This left only the most well-adapted progeny, including the A, C, and D subtypes.

Another reason for the formation of multiple HIV-1 subtypes may be the health condition of African hosts. As we know, HIV-1 replicates best when its host cells are activated. Activation occurs when the immune system is alerted by invasion of foreign organisms or substances, or the resulting infection. Invasion by parasites (as in malaria), bacteria (as in typhus), and viruses (as in hepatitis) is only too common in Africa. All of these invaders activate white blood cells or T cells, including the $CD_4^+$ cells that attract HIV. The more these cells are activated when HIV appears, the more likely HIV is to establish a widespread infection with multiple strains.

The higher state of T cell activation in African hosts may well be the main reason why multiple HIV-1 subtypes are so rapidly formed in Africa. Yet after their formation, they remain recognizable subtypes despite strain variation that increases in the course of an epidemic. As integrity is preserved in HIV- 1B after ten to fifteen years of the Amsterdam epidemic, so it is preserved in HIV-1A after almost twenty years of spread in Africa. This phenomenon can only be explained by virulence equilibrium. HIV-1 subtypes are directly linked to the course of infection in humans, that is, an asymptomatic period just long enough to transmit the virus to others by some sexual route.

From the time HIV-1 was seeded in the former German East Africa, about 1900, to the emergence of "slim disease" in what are now Uganda and Tanzania, the virus probably created far more variants than it has since 1975. Many of those early variants died out from lack of transmission. Some failed because of too little infectivity. Others failed because of too much: they grew so fast to such high titers, or levels, that the host sickened and died before he or she could transmit the virus to a new host. The current HIV-1 subtypes were created by decades of constant elimination of too-weak or too-strong variants from the pool. This process continues, so we can predict that subtypes may disappear from a given locale if they are too aggressive to allow the host time for sexual activity. Indeed, we have preliminary evidence that this is happening right now in Uganda, an area dominated by HIV-1 subtypes A and D, whose shares of infections were initially about equal. But it seems that subtype D is more aggressive than the other known subtypes. It replicates to enormously high levels at the moment of acute infection and maintains this high virus load, causing AIDS to occur in a few years instead of a decade. We now see this subtype becoming less and less prevalent. Its history seems to support the idea that a virus can be too aggressive—too successful at killing its host—to survive in a population.

## DISTRIBUTION BY TRUCK ROUTES

Of course, HIV is not carried by roads or trucks. It is carried by people: the truckers who drive the routes in relay, and the prostitutes or village women they meet along the way. Starting at Mombasa and Dar es Salaam on the eastern coast, two main cast-west routes link Nairobi in Kenya, Kampala in Uganda, Kigali in Rwanda, Kinshasa in Zaire, and cities farther west. North-south routes run to Addis Ababa in Ethiopia and down to Lilongwe in Malawi and Lusaka in Zambia.

Once HIV-1 subtypes were established just west of Lake Victoria, these agents and their wasting variant of AIDS began to fan out. Mainly subtypes A and C spread along the north-south axis and the east-west axis. HIV-1A favoured the latter, becoming the predominant subtype from Kenya in the east to Cameroon and Ivory Coast in the west. HIV-1C has travelled the other axis, flourishing from Ethiopia in the Horn of Africa to Zambia, Malawi, and South Africa. The two axes of HIV-1 distribution tend to follow the rain forest. More to the point, they follow the roads through the rain forest, which head out from Lake Victoria in all directions. These are used mainly by trucks since cars are scarce.

If the virus has travelled these routes, we should find two kinds of evidence. First, the truckers who live and work nearest to Lake Victoria should be infected at the highest rate, compared with truckers who live and work in outlying areas. Second, the prevalence of infection along the routes should be highest in individuals and villages closest to the truck routes, compared with those farther from the routes. Both types of evidence have been documented. More than half of Rwandan truck drivers are HIV-1 positive, compared with about a third of Ugandan drivers and about a fifth of those in Kenya or Ethiopia. Similarly, in the early 1990s, most prostitutes of the interior were infected, compared with half of those in Ethiopia. And the farther a village population lived from a truck route, the lower its percentage of HIV-1 infections. So we now have the final piece of the puzzle. According to the scenario proposed in this chapter, HIV- 1 arose in Cameroon and was carried to German East Africa about 1900, and to Germany in 1939. HIV- 1B adapted to spread by anal intercourse, causing the Western AIDS epidemic.

In Africa, HIV-1 viruses adapted to spread by vaginal intercourse, launching AIDS epidemics on that continent. They caused the African wasting form of AIDS by forming subtypes, mainly 1A and 1C. Sometimes called "slim disease," African AIDS arose in northern Tanzania west of Lake Victoria in the early 1970s. It spread to neighbouring Uganda, Rwanda, and Zaire in the late 1970s. From there, along rain forest truck routes, HIV-1A spread east and west, while HIV-1C spread north and south.

# 4

# AIDS: Clinical Course and Manifestations

The HIV infection is silent for most of its duration, only becoming overtly symptomatic at its later stages. The natural history of HIV infection is highly variable and changes over the course of the epidemic. There is now considerable evidence that people infected with HIV will develop AIDS and will die of an AIDS-related illness. The length of time from infection to an AIDS-related condition varies from as short as 1 year to 15 years or longer. Studies have shown that 5 per cent to 10 per cent of HIV-infected people progress to AIDS within 4 years, and nearly 50 per cent develop AIDS by 10 years after initial infection.

No single factor or combination of factors accounts for variability in HIV progression. Differences in rates of decline occur among individuals who contract HIV through different modes of transmission. For example, the San Francisco City Cohort Study, comprising primarily gay men, found that 54 per cent of HIV-positive men progress to AIDS within 11 years of being infected, whereas 49 per cent of people infected through blood transfusions develop AIDS within 7 years. Other studies have not found survival differences across transmission groups.

Most studies have, however, found that the average duration from time of HIV infection to AIDS, in the absence of treatment, is between 7 and 10 years. The time between contracting HIV and developing AIDS is for the most part characterised by an absence of serious illness. Several descriptive systems are available for staging HIV disease. In an early classification scheme, the CDC had a four-stage progressive model that included an acute infection syndrome, a long period of asymptomatic infection, the development of persistent generalized lymphadenopathy (enlarged lymph nodes), and later disease manifestations.

A second staging system developed by CDC included an expanded list of diseases associated with AIDS and an early symptomatic phase of disease referred to AIDS-related complex. In the 1987 CDC system, stages I and II consist of asymptomatic periods, stage III is characterised by chronic lymphadenopathy, and the substages of stage IV represent later phases. More recent staging systems rely on tracking the number of T-helper lymphocyte cells over the course of infection.

*Table 1:*
*Centers for disease control (1987) staging system for human immunodeficiency virus infection*

| *Stage* | *Description* |
|---|---|
| I | Actuate HIV infections; asymptomatic or possible acute viral reaction latent infection |
| II | Latent infection |
| III | Chronic lymphadenopathy |
| IV-A | Constitutional symptoms: weight loss, fever, chronic diarrhea |
| IV-B | HIV-induced neuropathology: dementia, myelopathy, peripheral neuropathy |
| IV-C | Opportunistic infections |
| IV-D | HIV-associated tumours |
| IV-E | Other conditions |

The course of HIV infection varies across subpopulations. For example, perinatally HIV-infected infants and children have shorter survival times compared with adolescents and adults. Although there are few significant differences between HIV-positive and -negative newborns at birth HIV-positive infants become ill early, with a median onset of symptoms between 8 and 10 months of age and the majority of children becoming ill within one year. HIV-positive infants have higher rates of certain complications, such as neurological diseases, which occur in 30 per cent to 60 per cent of infected infants.

Failure to thrive is also common, as are delays in developmental milestones and the actual loss of milestones once achieved. HIV-positive infants are particularly susceptible to disease because HIV inhibits the development of the immature immune system, accelerating the course of HIV infection. The criteria for diagnosing AIDS in infants and children consist of the same AIDS-defining conditions that diagnose AIDS in adults, along with other specific and recurrent infections. Unlike infants and young children, the clinical progression of AIDS for adolescents is more like that for adults. The following sections review HIV disease processes from the point of infection to later phases of illness.

### Primary HIV Infection

The body mounts an immune reaction that unfortunately, is ineffective in stopping HIV infection, following the introduction of HIV into the bloodstream. In response to HIV, the body may react with a brief period of acute infection symptoms. The usual time that lapses between exposure and acute illness is about two to four weeks, with the duration of symptoms lasting only one to two weeks. Acute retroviral illness, when it does occur, is the earliest clinically recognizable event in the natural history of HIV infection. Response to retroviral infection is similar to vague symptoms of mononucleosis.

However, retroviral infection actually consists of a distinct and recognizable clinical syndrome. Most typically, acute HIV symptom illness, or primary HIV infection, presents with persistent fever, lethargy, malaise, muscle weakness, headache, pain in or around the eyes, sensitivity to bright light, sore throat, and skin rashes. In most cases, primary HIV infection symptoms resolve themselves and usually do not recur. Not all people infected with HIV, however, develop symptoms of primary infection. Studies have found that between 40 per cent and 90 per cent of individuals experience an acute response to HIV infection. Symptoms occur among people infected through each major route of HIV transmission, and, at present, there is no conclusive evidence that any particular group is more likely to develop symptomatic acute illness. In addition to the aforementioned early symptoms, HIV-positive persons may develop persistent generalized lymphadenopathy, defined by enlarged lymph nodes that are detectable by touch and remain enlarged for a minimum of three months.

Swollen lymph nodes in the armpits, neck, or groin are common in HIV infection, as well as in other viral infections. In the case of HIV infection, swollen lymph nodes are the result of disseminated HIV throughout the lymphatic system. Most studies show that persistent lymphadenopathy does not have prognostic value for disease progression towards AIDS. Following acute symptoms of HIV infection, although not dependent on the occurrence of such symptoms, antibodies are produced against HIV.

Establishing HIV antibodies, or seroconversion to HIV, most likely results after a threshold of HIV replication has occurred and depends on the immune competency of the host to mount the antibody response. On average, HIV antibodies are detectable through serological testing slightly more than 2 months after viral transmission, and 95 per cent of HIV-infected individuals develop antibodies within 6 months of becoming infected.

However, the incubation period for HIV may last longer than 6 months, and in rare cases incubation may last 2 to 3 years. Variability in establishing HIV antibodies can come from numerous factors, including the virulence of viral strains, the dose of virus transmitted, the frequency of exposure, and an individual's immune response. Once antibodies have developed, they are detectable through HIV testing.

## HIV TESTING

Some diagnostic tests for HIV infection involve detecting HIV genetic material directly in blood cells or actually culturing the virus. However, the most widely used tests identify antibodies to the virus rather than the presence of HIV itself.

Antibodies produced by the immune system provide immunologic "footprints" to viral infection. Antibody tests are safer for laboratories to perform than actual viral-detection procedures because antibody tests do not require direct contact with HIV. Antibody tests also tend to be less expensive than, viral cultures and genetic testing. The standard procedures for HIV antibody testing involve providing written informed consent, pretest counselling for 30 to 90 minutes (including an explanation of the test), discussions of limited confidentiality when tests are not anonymous, personalized risk assessments, and exploration of individual concerns.

The test procedure itself involves drawing blood and sending samples for laboratory analysis. Post test result notification and counselling usually occur about two weeks after the initial visit. Blood collected for testing is first subjected to an *enzyme-linked immunosorbent assay* (ELISA) that tests for antibodies to HIV. ELISA tests are done first because they are highly sensitive to HIV antibodies. If an ELISA test is negative, it is highly improbable that the person is HIV infected. Positive ELISA tests must be repeated because the procedure is not specific to HIV antibodies. For this reason, ELISA tests are used to screen blood samples for HIV antibodies. After a blood specimen receives a repeated positive ELISA, the test is confirmed using a western blot procedure. Like ELISA, western blot detects HIV antibodies, but western blot is highly specific because it determines the exact antigens toward which antibodies are directed.

A positive western blot result means detection of two out of three precise antigen groups from components of HIV. This level of specificity reduces the chances of false positive results to an extremely low probability. Thus, both a positive repeated ELISA screening test and a positive western blot confirmatory test are required for diagnosis of HIV infection.

HIV antibody testing is now among the most accurate diagnostic tools in medicine. In tests that indicate a false negative result (*i.e.*, that the person is not found infected when he or she really is infected), the most common cause is that the blood sample was collected during the incubation window period before the presence of HIV antibodies. A person cannot, therefore, know that they are HIV infected during the first month or two of infection, although HIV can be transmitted to others during this time. The potential for false negative tests requires that all persons who receive this result be tested again approximately 3 months later. People who test HIV-positive and have no identifiable risk history should also be retested, although false positive test results only occur because of laboratory errors.

In addition to receiving either a positive or a negative result, a third possible outcome is an, indeterminate result: neither conclusively positive nor negative. Indeterminate HIV test results usually occur when the ELISA test is positive and only one of the two required specific antigens is detected by western blot.

Ambiguous results occur with respect to both HIV-1 and HIV-2 antibody tests, and are most commonly found among individuals infected with HIV who are in the process of developing antibodies, and require that the test be repeated 2 to 6 months later. HIV testing is the only reliable means of determining HIV infection. Even after symptoms, many HIV-related illnesses can be caused by non-HIV immune-suppressing conditions. Thus, individuals with symptoms should be tested for HIV antibodies rather than assuming that they are HIV infected on the basis of illness alone.

## ASYMPTOMATIC HIV INFECTION

During most of HIV infection, patients appear, feel, and are otherwise healthy. As much as 50 per cent to 80 per cent of the time that a person has HIV, they are symptom free. The virus is actively depleting T-helper lymphocytes during clinically asymptomatic phases, and HIV is also transmittible to others during this time. It was once thought that HIV replicated less during asymptomatic periods, primarily because of low concentrations of virus in the bloodstream. Although termed a latency period, asymptomatic HIV infection does not constitute a time of microbiological inactivity. Recent studies have shown that HIV is productive in lymph nodes when patients are symptom free. Following years of destruction, the immune system slowly degenerates, increasing vulnerability to illness. The primary target of HIV, T-helper lymphocytes, is one of three types of thymus-originating cells (T-cells) of the immune system. These cells function to distinguish self from nonself and rid the body of foreign agents. Cytotoxic T-cells identify and destroy infectious agents, suppressor T-cells reduce immune responses, and T-helper cells induce responses from several branches of the immune system.

T-helper lymphocytes are the only of the three that express the $CD_4$ surface receptor, and HIV therefore binds with and infects these cells. T-helper lymphocytes have several functions, including the induction of non-T-helper cell activity. Cell-mediated immunity results from the production of cytokines that guide a number of immunologic responses. For example, T-helper lymphocytes mediate through cytokines the activity of natural killer cells, which in turn destroy viral-infected and certain cancerous cells. Impaired natural killer-cell activity is an outcome of T-helper cell dysfunction. Cytokines also direct the proliferation and maturation of several other immune cells.

Decreased numbers of T-helper lymphocytes were among the first immunologic abnormalities described in patients with AIDS. The single best predictor of developing AIDS in HIV-positive gay men is the rate of T-helper cell decline and blood concentration of T-helpers relative to other immune cells.

Because the number of T-helper cells is inversely related to symptoms, low T-helper cell counts indicate impending illness. During asymptomatic periods, T-helper cell counts are usually between 500 and 200 cells/$mm^3$, although nearly half of individuals with counts below 200 cells/$mm^3$ are also asymptomatic at any given time. T-helper cell counts are a marker for HIV disease progression, but they are limited by extreme fluctuations because of a number of factors, including variability in laboratory procedures and changes in cell concentrations over diurnal cycles.

Changes in cell counts are also difficult to interpret because there are no normative data for HIV-infected patients and noninfected risk groups. Despite their limitations, T-helper lymphocyte counts set guidelines for prognostic decisions, for initiating medications that suppress HIV production, and for determining when to initiate prophylaxis against opportunistic illnesses. Thus, the risk for AIDS-related conditions increases over the course of HIV infection, and the most reliable marker for disease progression is the number of functional T-helper lymphocytes present in the immune system.

Vulnerability to disease increases as the immune system loses T-helper cells and T-helper-cell-mediated immunity. Although immune-system suppression does not necessarily mean symptomatic illness, having an HIV-related illness does suggest severe immune suppression.

Only 2 per cent of cases progress to AIDS within 2 years of becoming infected, whereas as many as 10 per cent progress to AIDS within 4 years. The mean length of time between infection and developing AIDS is 8 to 10 years among homosexually active men, and it is considerably shorter for adults who contracted HIV through blood transfusions. Evidence suggests, however, that the interval between infection and illness is lengthening as a result of advances in medical treatments.

## FACTORS ASSOCIATED WITH HIV PROGRESSION TO AIDS

The variable clinical manifestations of HIV infection have led to several hypotheses concerning factors that facilitate or inhibit the virus. There are several potential influences on the duration and course of most infectious diseases. Among sociodemographic characteristics, age is consistently associated with HIV progression, with older people having more rapid rates of immune suppression.

Moss and Bacchetti found that people infected with HIV at ages over 40 years were more likely to become ill sooner than individuals infected at younger ages. Men who were infected after age 30 also have poorer survival than their younger-age counterparts. Similarly, once diagnosed with AIDS, older adults die sooner than younger adults. For example, Clement and Hollander reported that being diagnosed with AIDS at age 35 and older is associated with a substantially poorer prognosis. Decreased survival time observed with advancing age is not, however, entirely understood. The accelerated rate of disease may involve a general decrease in ability to contend with opportunistic infections. Ethnic minorities demonstrate a more rapid decline in T-helper lymphocytes than do Whites, and there are ethnic differences in the relative frequency of AIDS-related illnesses. Sex differences in prognosis have also been suggested; men live longer after an AIDS diagnosis than do women, aside from differences in lag time to diagnosis and inattention of the AIDS definition to variations among women.

Disease progression also varies by primary route of HIV transmission. Individuals who become infected through injection drug use survive longer compared with those infected through other modes of HIV transmission, whereas contracting HIV by blood transfusion results in the most rapid death following an AIDS diagnosis. The route of contracting HIV is also related to relative frequencies of AIDS-related illnesses. Men who contract HIV sexually from other men are more likely to develop Kaposi's sarcoma, and injection drug users are more likely to develop *Pneumocystis carinii* pneumonia, recurrent bacterial pneumonia, and pulmonary tuberculosis.

Differences in transmission routes may also account for most of the differences in opportunistic illnesses between men and women. However, the associations between disease and HIV transmission routes are not well understood. Exercise and nutrition may slow HIV disease, although there is thus far little empirical support for direct relationships. There is also little evidence that alcohol and other psychoactive substance use to play a significant role in HIV infection. The most widely accepted cofactors for HIV infection, although not universally accepted, have been infections with other pathogens.

In particular, the interaction between HIV and other viruses (*i.e.*, herpes viruses) has been considered important. Sexually transmitted pathogens and infectious agents spread through nonsterile preparations of drug-injecting equipment trigger immune responses that can stimulate HIV and activate HIVs replication cycle. Co-infection with other immune-suppressing viruses can also facilitate the progression of HIV. Even worse, multiple infections are synergistic and make prognosis dependant on a chain of unpredictable biomedical events. Repeated exposures to HIV complicate the picture further by multiple strains of the virus with varied properties.

Variation in viral strains occurs because of the drift in molecular composition demonstrated in HIV isolates within and between infected persons. Although these and other factors appear related to HIV progression, no true cofactors for HIV disease have been conclusively established. Potential cofactors of HIV infection tend to co-occur and have inextricable effects. For example, studies that have found shorter survival times for women and ethnic minorities could be explained because women and people of color are often infected through injection drug use.

In addition, exposure to infectious agents that may facilitate HIV disease occurs in different patterns among ethnic groups, sexes, and sexual-orientation subgroups. Therefore, associations between potential cofactors and disease progression are open to multiple interpretations, including bidirectional causes and unidentified third variables.

### Later-stage HIV Infection

Following long periods of asymptomatic infection, any number of general and nonspecific early symptoms may develop. Symptoms of HIV infection include chronic low-grade fever, persistent fatigue, diarrhea lasting at least 2 weeks, rashes or other skin conditions, unintentional weight loss of at least 10 pounds, night sweats, and mild infections of the mouth or throat.

The later stages of HIV infection are characterised by severe depletion of T-helper lymphocytes and the onset of specific illnesses. Most clinical manifestations of HIV infection are evident relatively late in the course of disease, occurring only after significant immunologic impairment.

Illnesses that occur late in HIV infection reflect the defective-cell-mediated immunity caused by diminished numbers of T-helper lymphocytes. Similar immune dysfunction is common among cancer patients receiving chemotherapy, patients with certain lymphomas and other malignancies, and organ transplant recipients. T-helper lymphocyte counts below 200 cells/mm$^3$ mark what otherwise would be unexplained significant weight loss, chronic diarrhea, new or persistent outbreaks of genital herpes, skin rashes, and infections of the mouth, esophagus, and vagina. Over 35 per cent of all HIV-related hospitalisations, 29 per cent of hospital costs, and over 35 per cent of HIV-positive hospital inpatient deaths occur among people who become systemically ill but have not yet been diagnosed with AIDS.

Cohorts followed before the widespread availability of antiretroviral medications showed that most people survive between 11 and 12 months after receiving an AIDS diagnosis, less than 11 per cent survive 3 years, and yet others are known to have a slow-progressing disease, surviving 15 years and beyond. T-helper cell counts below 200 cells/mm$^3$ substantially increase risk for developing AIDS-related conditions, with 80 per cent of people developing an AIDS-related illness within 3 years of T- helper cell counts dropping below 200/mm$^3$. The probability of serious illnesses increases as T-helper lymphocytes decline, with survival times for people with T-helper cell counts below 50 cells/mm$^3$ being generally less than 1 or 2 years. Several factors appear to predict length of life following AIDS-related symptoms. Studies have shown that the initial condition leading to an AIDS diagnosis strongly predicts the period of survival.

Most consistently, individuals first diagnosed with Kaposi's sarcoma are more likely to survive longer than are people diagnosed with *Pneumocystis carinii* pneumonia, who in turn survive longer than those initially diagnosed with other AIDS-associated illnesses. Rothenberg, Woelfel, et al. found that 72 per cent of patients initially diagnosed with Kaposi's sarcoma survived one year and 30 per cent survived 5 years, a substantially greater survival time than is associated with other AIDS-related illnesses. Friedman et al. concluded that the role of initial AIDS diagnosis in survival may be attributed to the organ systems involved, the degree of immune suppression that characterises its onset, and the effectiveness of available treatments.

Survival time is also associated with characteristics of individuals, among which the sex of the infected person is the most controversial. Friedman et al. found that women who received an AIDS diagnosis survived for a significantly shorter time than men. However, subsequent research has failed to show that nongynecologic manifestations of HIV infection differ between men and women, and there are no known sex differences in AIDS prognosis or in the rate of disease progression from HIV infection to AIDS.

A history of using injection drugs also contributes to an earlier death for women with AIDS. Sex differences in survival also appear related to women historically having less access to adequate health care, including clinical trials for experimental treatments. Ethnicity also predicts AIDS survival. African Americans survive a shorter time with AIDS than do their White counterparts. Ethnic differences in survival may be the result of several factors, including differences in immune functioning, prevalence of cofactors for disease progression, and differences in routes of contracting HIV.

Interpreting survival studies requires close attention to their methodological limitations. For example, early studies conducted in New York City demonstrated survival times substantially longer than those reported in San Francisco cohorts. It was at first thought that the difference reflected relative numbers of gay men versus injection drug users in the respective cohorts. Differences in survival, however, have been accounted for by data management strategies.

The New York City studies, unlike those conducted in San Francisco, assumed that people who moved or could not be reached for follow-up were still alive, an assumption that would necessarily increase estimated survival. Finally, there are problems in trying to compare different survival studies, not only because AIDS has been defined differently over the course of the epidemic, but also because treatment has changed over time.

Later stages of HIV infection are the result of a progressive depletion of the immune system. Loss of T-helper lymphocytes directly and indirectly impairs immune functioning over long clinically asymptomatic periods. Although studies show that some demographic and risk-related characteristics may be related to survival following an AIDS diagnosis, only initial AIDS-defining illnesses have reliably predicted prognosis. Most differences in survival are related to sociocultural factors, particularly access to medical care. Nearer the end of the disease process, people with HIV infection face an array of serious health threats as their immune system declines.

Clinical manifestations of HIV-related conditions fall within one of two general classes. Although most conditions result from a depleted immune system, others are a direct result of HIV infection itself, including HIV infection of the lymph nodes, brain, kidneys, abdominal cavity, and lungs. Most AIDS-defining conditions, however, result from a deteriorating immune system, including the growth of malignant tumours and development of opportunistic infections that would otherwise be kept in check.

Bartlett identified the 10 most common clinical presentations of HIV infection: persistent lymphadenopathy; pulmonary symptoms suggestive of pneumonia; cytopenia (diminution of blood cells); fungal infections; constitutional symptoms including persistent fever and diarrhea; weight loss; bacterial infections; tuberculosis; persistent symptoms of sexually transmitted diseases; and nervous system disorders. The first formal diagnostic criteria were established in 1982 as a result of early clinical experiences with men who contracted HIV infection through homosexual activity. The diagnosis was updated in 1985 and again in 1987 to include additional indicator diseases that characterised the diversity of HIV-infected persons. The 1987 case definition for adults and adolescents consisted of 23 clinical diseases. The case definition for children differed from adults by including recurrent bacterial infections and pulmonary problems among indicator diseases and by not considering children under 15 months old with HIV antibodies to be HIV infected because of passive perinatal transfer of maternal antibodies.

The CDC AIDS case definition was once again expanded in 1993. The revised case definition also addresses several criticisms of previous diagnostic criteria, such as failure to include manifestations of HIV common among women. The CDC case definition retains the 23 conditions included in the previous diagnosis and adds three new diseases: pulmonary tuberculosis, recurrent pneumonia, and invasive cervical cancer. Pulmonary tuberculosis (TB) was added because HIV-induced immune suppression increases the likelihood of activating latent TB.

Recurrent pneumonia was added to the case definition because of the prevalence of bacterial pneumonia, with as much as a fivefold increase among HIV-infected injection drug users compared with their non-HIV-infected counterparts. Finally, invasive cervical cancer was added to the revised case definition because as many as 22 per cent of HIV-infected women present signs of early cervical disease. The major change in the 1993 AIDS case definition was the inclusion of immunologic diagnostic criteria. Unlike previous AIDS diagnoses, the definition specifies that individuals who are asymptomatic but receive an accurate, although not necessarily most recent, T-helper lymphocyte cell count below 200 cells/mm$^3$ in conjunction with HIV infection meet the criteria for diagnosis with AIDS.

Immune dysfunction is included in the new case definition because immunologic markers are associated with disease progression and used as clinical prognostic indicators. Another reason for including an immunologic marker independent of specific illnesses is that T-helper cell counts carry similar meaning among subgroups of infected persons who may vary in illness presented, some of which may not yet be listed in the case definition.

Finally, people with suppressed immune systems who did not yet have a case-defining illness became eligible for disability benefits. A substantial increase in the number of diagnosed AIDS cases occurred as a result of the expanded 1993 definition. The increase was due to the sudden inclusion of individuals with T-helper counts below 200 cells/mm$^3$ among persons living with AIDS.

Each AIDS-defining condition entails its own disease processes and implications for prognosis. The majority of AIDS cases have been initially diagnosed with *Pneumocystis carinii* pneumonia. Numerous other AIDS-defining conditions are rare and do not typically occur as initial diagnoses. The signs, symptoms, and complications of each condition pose substantially different challenges for people living with AIDS. Immune suppression can mean multiple, simultaneous illnesses.

The manifestations of HIV infection represent a wide spectrum of diseases and a multitude of problems for infected persons. Mental health professionals, of course, are not in a position or role to diagnose or treat these ailments. However, professionals who provide services to clients with HIV infection should be aware of the symptoms, course, and potential outcomes of each illness.

### Conditions caused directly by HIV

#### *HIV-related wasting syndrome*

HIV wasting syndrome is an AIDS-defining condition. Although several disease processes affect the gastrointestinal system and cause chronic, persistent, disabling loss of weight and body mass, HIV itself can directly cause these symptoms. Diagnosis is determined by involuntary loss of at least 10 per cent of body weight along with either chronic diarrhea or chronic weakness and fever over the course of 30 days, in the absence of other illnesses that could otherwise explain these symptoms. In association with severe weight loss are symptoms of fatigue, lethargy, and physical weakness.

#### *HIV-related neurological disease*

Mild to moderate cognitive, affective, and motor dysfunctions can occur in HIV infection, with individuals at later stages of AIDS more often experiencing such symptoms. Subtle signs of dysfunction, however, can appear earlier in the course of HIV infection. Early signs of HIV-related neurological disease include difficulty maintaining concentration, memory problems, and motor disturbances, including slowing of arm, leg, and eye movements.

HIV-related neurological disease is usually diagnosed when symptoms become moderate to severe and disrupt occupational, basic self-care, intellectual, social, or motor functioning. HIV-related neurological disease is caused by the toxic effects of HIV infection of the brain. Clinical symptoms are almost always caused by diffuse brain damage.

**Conditions caused by viral infections**

***Cytomegalovirus (CMV)***

Cytomegalovirus is a herpes virus and is a very common cause of disease in HIV infection, with a majority of people with AIDS developing some form of active CMV infection. Cytomegalovirus can cause pneumonia, vaginal infection, hepatitis, encephalitis, and colitis. However, the most common manifestations are CMV retinitis, CMV esophagitis, and CMV colitis. Among the most distressing manifestations of CMV infection is retinitis, which threatens the vision of a significant number of people with AIDS. Irreversible loss of visual acuity and blindness often result from untreated CMV retinitis.

Almost all patients who develop CMV retinitis have T-helper lymphocyte counts below 50 cells/mm$^3$, making it a later manifestation of HIV infection. In addition to symptomatic illness, CMV also has immune-suppressing effects of its own, potentially complicating the course of HIV infection. Although CMV infection is difficult to treat, advances in antiviral medications have been effective in managing this condition.

***Herpes simplex virus infection***

Studies have found that as many as 95 per cent of gay men with AIDS were previously infected with herpes simplex virus. Symptoms of herpes simplex infection include small, painful, erupting blisters. When outbreaks of herpes lesions are persistent for at least one month, they constitute an AIDS-defining condition. Herpes simplex virus causes ulcerations of the oral, genital, and anal mucous lining. In non-immune-suppressed persons, herpes blisters heal within 3 to 4 weeks of their onset.

People with compromised immune systems, however, may have chronic prolonged lesions lasting months if untreated or unresponsive to treatment. Herpes simplex lesions may occur in the esophagus, causing pain and possibly interfering with swallowing. Pneumonitis, pulmonary infection, and encephalitis are also possible manifestations. Finally, like cytomegalovirus, herpes simplex virus is a potential cofactor in the progression of HIV infection.

### *Epstein-Barr virus and hairy leukoplakia*

Epstein-Barr virus is associated with infectious mononucleosis. Among people with HIV infection, Epstein-Barr virus infection also involves hairy leukoplakia, an AIDS-defining condition the symptoms of which include white lesions on the tongue and other areas of the oral cavity.

### *Progressive Multifocal Leukoencephalopathy (PML)*

Caused by a human papovavirus, progressive multifocal leukoencephalopathy occurs in approximately 2 per cent to 4 per cent of AIDS cases. The papovavirus infects the oligodendrocytes of the brain, cells responsible for producing the myelin sheath that coats and insulates neurons. The neurologic symptoms of PML are usually rapid, progressive, and fatal, with the majority of afflicted persons dying within months of symptomatic disease.

## Conditions caused by fungal infections

### *Candidiasis*

Candida is a fungus that normally exists in the mouth and esophagus. With immune suppression, however, candida often progresses to an active disease. Oral infection with candidiasis is commonly called thrush, usually forming removable white plaques on the surface of the tongue and oral cavity. Plaques may be small or widespread and can alternatively appear as small red areas rather than white patches. Although for an AIDS diagnosis, candidiasis must involve the esophagus, bronchi, trachea, or lungs, infection may also occur in other organ systems, including the gastrointestinal system and the female genital tract.

### *Coccidioidomycosis*

An infection that occurs after fungus particles are inhaled into the lungs, coccidioidomycosis is among the least frequent AIDS-defining conditions.

There are two general forms of coccidioidomycosis, primary and chronic. The primary form is an acute self-limiting condition involving only the respiratory system. In contrast, the chronic form of the disease may involve several organ systems. People with severely impaired immune systems are most likely to develop pulmonary disease followed by widespread dissemination. For coccidioidomycosis to allow an AIDS diagnosis, the disease must become disseminated to nonpulmonary organs.

***Cryptococcoses***

Advanced HIV infection increases susceptibility to cryptococcal infections, affecting as many as 6 per cent to 9 per cent of people with AIDS. Cryptococcal infection tends to occur with severe immune suppression. Although the disease may occur in any organ system and often affects the respiratory system, the most common form of infection is cryptococcal meningitis presenting with headache, stiff neck, nausea, vomiting, malaise, and possible seizures. Other common symptoms include hypersensitivity to light and marked changes in mental status.

***Histoplasmosis***

Histoplasmosis first occurs through inhaling fungus particles, with infection potentially disseminating to other organ systems. Clinical manifestations of infection include fever, skin rashes, anemia, lymphadenopathy, and involvement of vital organs. Histoplasmosis occurs at varying rates across regions of North America, with the central and south-central United States and Ontario and Quebec Canadian provinces having the most concentrated number of cases. As many as 27 per cent of AIDS patients in these areas develop histoplasmosis, as compared with other regions, where infection is virtually nonexistent.

***Pneumocystis carinii pneumonia (PCP)***

Prior to the wide-scale use of prophylaxis, active *Pneumocystis carinii* (PCP) occurred in as many as 80 per cent of advanced HIV disease cases. First classified as a protozoan, most authorities now agree that *Pneumocystis carinii is* a fungus, although this is not conclusive and the taxonomy remains debated. *Pneumocystis carinii* is only clinically expressed under severe immune suppression, particularly when T-helper lymphocyte cell counts fall below 200 cells/ $mm^3$.

However, children infected with HIV develop PCP at earlier stages of infection. Thus, because almost everyone is exposed to *Pneumocystis carinii,* and because the fungus is suppressed by cellular immunity mediated by T-helper lymphocytes, it has been the predominant manifestation of AIDS in the United States and the most frequent identifiable cause of AIDS-related death. Pneumocystis carinii pneumonia can present with early and diffuse symptoms, including mild tightness of the chest, chronic fever, fatigue, abd weight loss.

Respiratory symptoms usually include dry/nonproductive cough and progressive shortness of breath. As the pneumonia progresses, tasks with even limited demands become taxing and exhaustive.

**Conditions caused by Protozoan infections**

***Cryptosporidiosis***

Infection with cryptosporidiosis occurs after spores of the microorganism are either inhaled or ingested. Cryptosporidia causes chronic diarrhea and is responsible for all diarrhea-related illnesses in AIDS cases. Infection can involve any area of the gastrointestinal tract, but the usual site is the small intestine. The AIDS case definition requires that symptoms of chronic diarrhea caused by cryptosporidia persist for a minimum of one month. Cryptosporidiosis also causes gallbladder disease in AIDS cases.

Treatment for this infection is extremely limited, and symptoms, therefore, are chronic, debilitating, and often lethal. Outbreaks in cities where drinking water and swimming pools have been contaminated by cryptosporidiosis have resulted in several deaths among people with suppressed immune systems. People with HIV infection are therefore advised to routinely boil their drinking water or use bottled water.

***Isosporiasis***

Like cryptosporidiosis, this infection strikes the gastrointestinal tract, causing diarrhea, abdominal cramping, and weight loss. However, unlike other protozoan infections, effective treatments are available for Isosporiasis.

***Toxoplasmosis***

The intercellular protozoan Toxoplasma gondii is the cause of toxoplasmosis, the most common infection of the human central nervous system. Exposure to *toxoplasma gondii* occurs principally through contact with cat feces. Immune suppression allows for toxoplasmosis infection because of defective cellular immunity. Between 20 per cent and 47 per cent of people with AIDS who carry *Toxoplasma gondii* eventually develop toxoplasmosis encephalitis.

Manifestations are often insidious and usually include a mixture of focal and generalized neurological symptoms, including disturbances in thought processes, lethargy, confusion, memory and language deficits, and motor disturbances. Although Toxoplasma gondii can infect vital organ systems outside of the central nervous system, a disseminated course of infection is atypical even among HIV-infected persons.

**Conditions caused by Malignancies**

***Invasive cervical cancer***

Cervical abnormalities, or cervical dysplasia, are a common precursor to cervical cancer. Several studies have shown that HIV-infected women frequently develop cervical dysplasia, with prevalence rates as high as ten times greater than those found in non-HIV-infected women. The occurrence of cervical dysplasia in women with HIV infection is related to increased immune suppression. Studies of women who receive organ transplants, however, suggest that progression to cervical cancer may require prolonged periods of immune suppression.

Therefore, relatively few cases of invasive cervical cancer have been reported among HIV-infected women. Because invasive cervical cancer usually occurs late in HIV infection, and because it has been reported in some HIV-infected women, it was added to the 1993 AIDS case definition following controversy about previous exclusion of conditions related to AIDS in women. Inclusion of invasive cervical cancer as an AIDS-defining condition was also meant to emphasize "the importance of integrating gynecologic care into medical services for HIV infected women. Early detection of cervical cancer is possible with pap smears, which should be a regular part of health care for HIV-positive women.

***HIV-related lymphomas***

Non-Hodgkin's-disease lymphomas were among the earliest recognized manifestations of HIV infection. Unlike other lymphomas, those related to HIV infection tend to progress rapidly and have extremely poor prognoses. Although most non-HIV-infected lymphomas involve disease contained to the lymph nodes, HIV lymphomas are distinguished by their widespread involvement of vital organs.

Approximately 26 per cent of HIV-related lymphomas involve the gastrointestinal system, 25 per cent bone marrow, 12 per cent liver, 9 per cent kidneys, and 9 per cent lungs. Most common, however, is central nervous system involvement, occurring in 25 per cent to 32 per cent of HIV-related cases of lymphoma and only rarely in non-HIV lymphomas. Symptoms of central nervous system lymphoma include seizures, localized neurologic dysfunction, and headache. HIV-related lymphoma usually occurs late in infection, after other AIDS-related conditions have occurred and when T-helper lymphocyte counts drop below 50 cells/$mm^3$.

***Kaposi's sarcoma***

Although rare before the HIV epidemic, Kaposi's sarcoma has been the most common malignancy among people with AIDS, with the majority of cases occurring among men who sexually contracted HIV from other men. Homosexually infected men are 20,000 to 40,000 times more likely to develop Kaposi's sarcoma than same-age HIV-negative men. Relatively few cases of Kaposi's sarcoma have occurred among injection drug users, and only 2 per cent of cases have an initial diagnosis of Kaposi's sarcoma.

Kaposi's sarcoma typically develops as a mass on the skin, mucous membranes, or internal organs. The disease is usually first noted by skin lesions that appear as dark red-to-violet-colored areas on light-skinned persons, and black or brown lesions on dark-skinned persons. Lesions commonly first occur near the head and neck, as well as on the inside of the mouth. It is also common for Kaposi's sarcoma to afflict internal organs, with 20 per cent to 50 per cent of cases involving the lungs. Thus, the lethality of Kaposi's sarcoma is entirely dependant on the site of disease. In most cases, however, Kaposi's sarcoma has an aggressive and unpredictable course.

The exact etiological agent of Kaposi's sarcoma remains unknown, although, as discussed earlier, there is evidence that a pathogen causing the disease, possibly a virus, is transmitted through contact with human feces. When Kaposi's sarcoma develops in the absence of other HIV-related diseases, it usually occurs early in immune suppression. People who have Kaposi's sarcoma are likely to later develop opportunistic infections and other malignancies.

In addition to being an AIDS-defining condition and a life-threatening malignancy, Kaposi's sarcoma carries additional psychological burden because of its skin lesions. Symptoms of Kaposi's sarcoma are disfiguring, and their appearance will frequently mark a person as being seriously ill and can lead to identifying a person as having AIDS. The result of Kaposi's sarcoma's symptoms, therefore, can interfere with rights to privacy and add a stigmatizing dimension to an already stigmatized disease.

### Conditions caused by bacterial infections

#### *Mycobacterium diseases*

Mycobacterial infections include mycobacterium TB, mycobacterium avium complex, and other disseminated mycobacteria. It is estimated that between 4 per cent and 40 per cent of people with AIDS in the United States have active TB and that up to 40 per cent of individuals with active TB are HIV infected. The scenario is even worse in developing counties, with the number of cases of TB in sub-Saharan Africa doubling in recent years.

In some South African countries, nearly one third of HIV infections present clinically with TB as their first manifestation. Mycobacterial TB is contracted person-to-person through respiratory routes of transmission, posing a highly alarming chance for spread. Active mycobacterial TB occurs relatively early in HIV infection, usually with T-helper lymphocyte cell counts between 500 and 200 cells/mm$^3$. Tuberculosis can become disseminated to a number of organ systems, with less than half of all TB cases in AIDS being confined to the respiratory system. The course of TB in pecple with AIDS is typically aggressive, particularly when it remains untreated.

Symptoms may include fever, night sweats, fatigue, malaise, and weight loss. When TB; is pulmonary, symptoms will usually include persistent cough, production of sputum, and chest pain. Pulmonary disease occurs in 70 per cent to 90 per cent of HIV-infected individuals with TB. However, antituberculosis drugs are highly effective when used properly. Unfortunately, as the TB epidemic has escalated, several multiple-drug-resistant strains of mycobacterium TB have emerged. Thus, HIV infection and TB; reciprocally complicate each other's disease processes: Persons with HIV are at greater risk of developing TB, standard medical interventions for TB are less effective in HIV-infected persons, and TB may be more infectious in persons with HIV infection.

In addition to mycobacterium TB, mycobacterium avium complex (MAC) is common in HIV infection. Although discussed as a single disease, MAC consists of two closely related organisms, mycobacterium avium and mycobacterium intracellular, with mycobacterium avium being the more frequently occurring. These mycobacterium are contracted through contaminated soil, food, water, and air-borne water droplets.

Cases of MAC have increased each year of the HIV epidemic. Disseminated MAC infection usually occurs late in HIV infection, typically with T-helper lymphocyte counts below 100 cells/mm$^3$. Clinically, MAC presents as diffuse symptoms of infection that include fever, weight loss, malaise, severe anemia, anorexia, and a number of possible gastrointestinal symptoms, including chronic diarrhea, abdominal pain, and malabsorption. Disseminated MAC infection is often lethal among people with AIDS. Because MAC occurs late in HIV infection, other opportunistic illnesses commonly precede MAC. Unfortunately, there are few effective treatments available for MAC infections, although there have been many advances in preventive and therapeutic medications.

***Recurrent bacterial pneumonia***

Pneumonia caused by any one of nine different bacteria are frequently seen in people with HIV infection. Bacterial pneumonia was observed early in the HIV epidemic, and pulmonary infections have contributed substantially to HIV-related deaths, with as many as 10 per cent of pneurnonias in AIDS patients the result of community-acquired bacterial infections. The onset of bacterial pneumonia is typically abrupt, and the duration can last several days, making it distinguishable from the insidious onset and persistent symptoms of *Pneumocystis carinn* pneumonia.

Pneumonia caused by bacteria in HIV-infected persons has a course of disease similar to that found among immune-competent individuals, including persistent fever, productive cough, dyspnea (laboured or difficult breathing), and chest pain. However, unlike people with functional immune systems, symptoms of pneumonia in HIV infection persist for long periods of time. Recurrent bacterial pneumonia is now an AIDS-defining condition.

***Non-pneumonia-causing bacterial infections***

Compromised immune systems increase susceptibility to a wide range of bacterial infections. The most common infections associated with HIV involve the gastrointestinal system, skin, meninges, and sinuses. Bacterial infections tend to occur early in immune suppression, reflecting the aggressive disease-causing capabilities of bacteria in even relatively healthy people.

Recurrent salmonella infection occurs frequently and early in HIV infection and is an AIDS-defining condition. More than 50 per cent of cases of salmonella infection cause severe diarrhea, and nearly half involve febrile illness: high fevers that may result in seizures. Salmonella infection in HIV infection is most likely to recur because of incomplete elimination of the disease during what would usually be adequate treatment. The bacteria are also likely to become resistant to treatments following recurrent use.

Sinusitis is another common bacterial infection that is persistent when it occurs among HIV-infected persons. Caused by as many as four different bacteria, symptoms of sinusitis include fever, headache, and upper respiratory distress. Symptoms are most chronic among people with T-helper lymphocyte counts below 200 cells/mm$^3$. Additional bacterial infections common to HIV infection include oral infections such as gingivitis and periodontitis, both of which can be progressive and painful. Other frequent bacterial infections are sexually transmitted diseases. Pelvic inflammatory disease resulting from gonorrheal infection becomes persistent and aggressive in HIV-infected women. Syphilis also takes an aggressive course in HIV infection and includes an increased risk of neurosyphilis. HIV infection further complicates syphilis by speeding up its course and reducing the effectiveness of antibiotic treatments. Thus, similar to other bacterial infections, co-infection of HIV and sexually transmitted bacteria poses specific problems not encountered when bacterial infections occur in people with functional immune systems.

Virtually any infection or malignancy that is normally suppressed by immune responses can become a complication of HIV infection. For example, although only three cancers are included as AIDS case-defining conditions (non-Hodgkin's lymphoma, Kaposi's sarcoma, and invasive cervical cancer), HIV infection is associated with Hodgkin's disease, melanoma, and cancers of the colon, lung, and testes. Numerous viral, protozoan, fungal, and bacterial infections that are usually managed by immune responses frequently cause serious illness.

For example, varicella-zoster virus causes chicken pox in childhood and usually remains inactive throughout adulthood. When reactivated in adulthood, varicella-zoster virus is the cause of shingles, painful skin eruptions in association with nerve endings. However, shingles are common to early and late HIV infection and usually take a severe and aggressive course.

Manifestations of HIV infection result from interactions among several defects in the protective immune system resulting from interference with and destruction of T-helper lymphocytes. Thus, as HIV infection progresses, disease-causing agents that are usually either completely suppressed or easily managed by immunity become potentially fife threatening. Serious immune suppression is also likely to result in simultaneous infections and malignancies that require multiple medical interventions. For these reasons, medical treatments that slow the loss of T-helper lymphocytes, prevent malignancies, or protect against opportunistic infections have been the principal means of combating HIV infection.

## BIOMEDICAL INTERVENTIONS

People with HIV infection live longer today than at any other time in the history of the HIV epidemic and can expect to live even longer in the future. Advances in the medical management of HIV disease are constantly emerging. Treatments for HIV infection and its associated complications generally fall into three categories: interventions directed at impeding the progress of HIV, prevention and treatment of opportunistic illnesses, and complementary treatments.

### Antiretroviral therapies

Immune system responses are intact and antiviral medications synergize with the body's immune system to effectively suppress infection, for most viral infections. However, because HIV selectively eliminates the branch of the immune system that recognizes antigens and coordinates immune responses, antiretroviral treatments act entirely on their own to suppress HIV. HIV's cycle provides points of potential attack on HIV. For example, tat, one of HIV's regulatory genes, is essential for the synthesis of proteins used for HIV production.

A drug that inhibits the activity of the tat gene disrupts the HIV replication cycle and stops production of HIV in chronically infected as well as newly infected cells. Several tat inhibitors have demonstrated some effectiveness in clinical trials and show promise as a future treatment. Drugs that inhibit reverse transcriptase, the enzyme necessary for HIV activation, interfere with the transcription phases of virus production. Reverse transcriptase inhibitors have been the most widely developed and studied antiretroviral medications. Reverse transcriptase is necessary for the replication of HIV and is not found in non-HIV-infected cells. Thus, inhibiting reverse transcriptase does not interfere with normal cell functioning.

Viral replication is interrupted by the drug when RNA is transcribed to DNA. A nucleic acid from the antiretroviral drug is incorporated into the RNA-DNA transcription process, causing a termination in the chain of nucleic acids. Reverse transcriptase inhibitors, however, only suppress HIV replication in newly infected cells. Once HIV is established in a cell, the effects of reverse transcriptase inhibitors become limited. The first approved and most widely used reverse transcriptase inhibitor is zidovudine (AZT), a drug first developed in the 1960s to treat murine retroviruses.

Numerous studies have shown that zidovudine is effective in slowing HIV progression for most people treated. Effects of zidovudine treatment include increased numbers of T-helper lymphocytes, decreased HIV activity, reduced frequency and severity of opportunistic illnesses, and improved general health status. There is also evidence that AIDS is delayed by zidovudine. Zidovudine appears to extend survival for some people with AIDS. For example, Lemp *et al.* found that patients receiving zidovudine had increased survival times across subgroups of people infected through various modes of HIV transmission.

In addition, Moore, Hidalgo, Sugland, and Chaisson showed that survival with AIDS has increased substantially since 1987, and zidovudine therapy was attributed with much of the improvement. People with AIDS treated with zidovudine demonstrate greater longevity than those who, for what ever reason, did not receive treatment. Zidovudine has its greatest effects when started within 1 year of receiving an AIDS diagnosis. Zidovudine is typically initiated when T-helper lymphocyte counts fall between 200 and 500 cells/mm³. Early use of zidovudine, before the onset of overt immune suppression or opportunistic illnesses, has been recommended but controversial.

Some patients treated before the onset of AIDS survive longer after an AIDS diagnosis when compared with people not treated early in the course of infection. Antiretroviral therapy is tolerated best when a person is generally healthy, because zidovudine is highly toxic for people with advanced immune suppression. However, results from clinical trials show that the maximum benefits of zidovudine are time limited, and there is disagreement about exactly when treatment should be initiated. It is generally recommended that antiretrovirals be started when T-helper counts drop below 200 cells/mm³.

There are a number of limitations associated with zidovudine therapy. Zidovudine may slow down the replication of HIV, but it will not prevent persistent infection. People treated with zidovudine, particularly at high doses, are vulnerable to early side effects that result from its toxicity, including headache, insomnia, nausea, vomiting, abdominal pain, diarrhea, fatigue, rashes, muscle pain, and fever. However, most side effects resolve within 8 weeks. The most threatening adverse effect of zidovudine is bone marrow suppression, causing anemia and other potentially serious conditions. Bone marrow suppression therefore leads to immediate discontinuation of zidovudine treatment. Prolonged use of zidovudine, particularly when started early in HIV infection, can result in long-term, often irreversible side-effects.

Zidovudine toxicity is directly related to dose, and adjustments often relieve adverse symptoms. Also related to toxicity are the possible teratogenic effects on pregnancy, although they have not yet been fully determined. Expectations of potential adverse effects of zidovudine are among the most common reasons for refusing treatment.

Three additional reverse-transcriptase-inhibiting drugs have been developed and tested: Dideoxycytidine (ddC), Dideoxyinosine (ddC), and 3' -Deoxythmidine-2'-ene (d4T). Each functions similarly to zidovudine by inhibiting the action of reverse transcriptase and therefore interfering with HIV replication. The antiretroviral actions of ddC are increased when taken in combination with zidovudine. Unfortunately, ddC also has toxic side effects, including peripheral neuropathy (numbness, tingling, or pain in the hands and feet), oral ulcerations, and skin rashes. Similarly, ddI presents problems with peripheral neuropathy, diarrhea, and pancreatitis.

Although d4T has not been as fully tested, it has shown promise as an antiretroviral treatment, although it too has potential adverse effects. Other antiretroviral treatments are under development and may effectively inhibit reverse transcription with lower levels of toxicity.

For example, phosphonosformate (foscarnet) is an effective antiviral drug used to treat herpes viruses, particularly cytomegalovirus, that also has antiretroviral properties. Foscarnet exerts an inhibitory effect against viral enzymes that are important in HIV replication, without interfering with normal cell enzymes. Foscarnet, however, requires intravenous administration and can have many toxic effects. Advances in antiretroviral medications have been most promising in the area of combination therapies. Concurrent use of two or more treatments, or convergent combination therapy, may increase effectiveness and prohibit HIV resistance to these medications.

For example, synergistic reverse transcriptase inhibitory effects of zidovudine and ddI have been well established. Zidovudine in combination with ddC has also shown promise in slowing HIV infection, and 3TC (lamivudine), another antiretroviral, has also shown promise when combined with zidovudine. Certain antiretroviral drugs used in combination with other treatments have also been effective. For example, zidovudine in combination with prophylactic treatments against *Pneumocystis carinii* pneumonia increase survival times for people with AIDS.

Combination therapies have potential for future developments in treating AIDS because new drugs are constantly appearing in clinical trials and because when given in the right combination, they may create an effect greater than any single drug. Treatments targeted to other points of the HIV replication cycle have, unfortunately, been less successful at slowing down HIV infection. One avenue has been to interfere with HIVs binding with $CD_4$ receptor molecules.

Receptor-based therapy is geared toward blocking HIV from attaching to the surface of and entering T-helper lymphocytes. Because HIV has such a strong affinity for $CD_4$ surface molecules, infusion of soluble $CD_4$ molecules into the bloodstream of infected persons could allow HIV to bind directly with free $CD_4$ molecules, preventing the virus from subsequently binding with T-helper lymphocyte cells. Unfortunately, HIV is substantially less sensitive to recombinant, or free, $CD_4$ than to $CD_4$ surface receptors.

Other treatments include drugs that inhibit proteins necessary for the production of regulatory genes specific to HIV and drugs that inhibit cellular enzymes important in HIV production. For example, a new group of drugs that inhibit protease, an enzyme that is essential for HIV replication, has shown efficacy in clinical trials. These drugs bind with the protease enzyme, interfering with its usual functions. It appears that protease inhibitors can effectively slow HIV progression with few toxic side effects, and may synergize with zidovudine, ddI, ddC, or d4T. Promising HIV treatments like protease inhibitors have accelerated government approval procedures for life-threatening illnesses and reach the stage of clinical trials much more rapidly than almost any other treatment in medical history. At any given time, there are hundreds of investigational drug trials for HIV infection and AIDS.

**Prophylaxis and treatments for opportunistic illnesses**

Most manifestations of HIV infection involve opportunistic infections and malignancies that are usually protected against by T-helper lymphocytemediated immunity. Prevention of opportunistic illnesses results in sustained illness-free periods for people with HIV infection. Because many opportunistic illnesses were rare before the HIV epidemic, there has been a rush to establish prophylactic and treatment guidelines.

For example, guidelines for prophylaxis against *Pneumocystis carinii* pneumonia (PCP) include actions to prevent an initial episode of pneumonia, primary prophylaxis, where individuals with T-helper lymphocyte cell counts below 200 cells/mm$^3$ routinely begin treatment with anti-PCP drugs. Dapsone, bactrim, and aerosolized pentamidine are effective in preventing primary and secondary episodes of PCP. Prophylaxis is credited with reductions of PCP ranging from 62 per cent in 1988 to 46 per cent in 1990. Prophylactic treatments against PCP have also extended the longevity of HIV-infected individuals.

Prophylaxis has also been established for toxoplasmosis encephalitis and mycobacterial infections. Antiviral drugs are widely used to control recurrent symptoms of herpes viruses and members of other virus families. Interferons have been effective in treating Kaposi's sarcoma. Additional advantages are offered by some prophylactic agents because they frequently guard against multiple opportunistic illness. For example, TMP-SMX, used as a PCP preventive, also helps protect against other diseases, including toxoplasmosis. Standards of care are also in place for preventing HIV-related malignancies.

In addition to prevention, treatments are available to manage several opportunistic illnesses. Most treatments effective in dealing with diseases in the context of a functional immune system do so in conjunction with cell-mediated immunity.

Unfortunately, as the immune system deteriorates the effectiveness of opportunistic-illness interventions requires greater doses and more time to achieve equal effectiveness. This is problematic in and of itself because many treatments have adverse side effects with prolonged use, particularly in immune-compromised individuals. Another limitation is the potential for resistance to treatments over time, as has been the case with some strains of HIV and several bacteria. It is important to note that advances in the treatment of HIV-related diseases develop rapidly.

New treatments are the product of converging areas of medicine including, but not limited to, infectious diseases, immunology, oncology, hematology, neurology, and pharmacology. For example, oncology has shown that bone marrow transplantation has promise in treating non-Hodgkin's lymphomas in AIDS patients. Similarly, clinical immunology has experimented with transplanting thymus gland tissue in AIDS patients, also suggesting limited results that warranted further testing. As treatment approaches from different disciplines emerge, they *will likely* be combined into promising new therapeutic avenues.

### Complementary Treatments

Treatments for HIV infection and related illnesses that have not yet gone through rigorous approval processes are often sought by HIV-infected people. Searching for unconventional treatments when faced with a chronic, life-threatening disease is often an outgrowth of disillusionments and frustrations with traditional medicine. Although initially considered alternatives to standard medical care, unapproved treatments are now referred to as *complementary* therapies because they are not necessarily replacements as much as they are adjuncts to mainstream treatments. Complementary therapies have become part of a social activist movement within communities heavily affected by AIDS.

People who seek out complementary treatments are likely to reestablish a sense of personal control over their health and therefore increase their attempts to deal with illnesses. Underground organizations have established routes for disseminating information and complementary therapies, including "buyers' dubs" that serve as distribution centers for otherwise unavailable treatments. Several newsletters inform people of the progress and development of traditional and complementary treatments.

The demand and accessibility of complementary therapies has increased to where many primary care physicians routinely discuss these options with their patients. For example, a study of mostly homosexually HIV-infected men receiving treatment from an AIDS clinic in San Francisco found that 40 per cent had received a prescription medication from someone other than their primary care provider and that 11 per cent received treatment from an unorthodox provider. Complementary therapies intervene at different points along the HIV replication cycle. Among those that are more commonly used are megadoses of vitamin C, which have been shown to have antiretroviral activity against human retroviruses in laboratory studies.

Also used is AL-721, a mixture of lipids believed to alter the membrane of T-helper lymphocytes and viral protective envelope proteins, in an effort to disrupt virus-to-cell binding properties. Other presumed antiretroviral agents include Compound Q (a purified root of a Chinese cucumber), hypericin (an herbal tea), and several preparations related to proteins necessary for HIV biosynthesis. In addition to antiretrovirals, several complementary therapies may act as modulators of the immune system (*e.g.*, naltrexone and disulfiram).

Most of these agents showed early promise but have not stood up to rigorous scientific testing. Other treatment modalities have been suggested, such as chiropractic methods, acupuncture, herbal remedies, multiple vitamins and mental imagery. These treatments are acceptable to traditionalists only to the extent that they do not interfere with standard medical care.

Although complementary treatments can involve holistic and naturalistic approaches, there are invasive procedures that have not yet demonstrated effectiveness but are nonetheless undertaken by many HIV-infected patients. Two examples are passive hyperimmune therapy and ozone treatments. In passive hyperimmune therapy, or passive immunotherapy, HIV-positive people who are unusually healthy are sought to donate blood plasma, which is pooled for antibodies against multiple strains of HIV and treated to clear disease-causing microbes. The treated plasma is transfused into an HIV-infected recipient, usually with advanced HIV disease or AIDS.

The idea behind the treatment is that antibodies from healthy patients may suppress HIV. The process is similar to that used in intravenous immunoglobulin treatment, which is a general approach to building immunities in immune-suppressed patients. Passive hyperimmune therapy for HIV infection differs because it attempts to concentrate antibodies against HIV. Passive immunotherapy is highly controversial for treating HIV-AIDS, and rigorous clinical testing has been limited.

Ozone therapy is another unorthodox technique for treating HIV infection that involves removing the blood of an HIV-infected person over a series of transfusions, treating it with heat and exposing it to ultraviolet light, ozone, or both. The entire process is intended to inactivate HIV. The treated blood is then replaced into the original patient. Unfortunately, there is little support for ozone therapies and some evidence against their effectiveness.

There are several potential risks associated with complementary therapies. First, many complementary approaches have serious adverse effects, such as AL-721, which can cause abdominal pain, nausea, and increased cholesterol. Second, it is likely that many of these agents result in immune stimulation or immune suppression, either of which can interact in unpredictable and dangerous ways with HIV infection and traditional medications. Finally, the use of complementary therapies may prohibit individuals from participating in standard medical care and AIDS clinical trials. People with HIV infection who are considering complementary treatments should be advised by a physician about their use.

# 5

# The HIV/AIDS Pandemic

The HIV infection, the cause of AIDS, today beyond the range of any previous global epidemic, has reached the proportions of a pandemic, having infected millions and promising to infect millions more. Understanding how HIV rapidly spread to its current status of a global health threat is just beginning. There is substantial evidence that the HIV infection has occurred in Africa for at least the past 50 years. Antibodies specific to HIV were identified in stored blood specimens collected from regions of central Africa dating back to the 1950s.

However, the HIV infection went unnoticed because it was overshadowed by numerous other fatal illnesses that afflict developing countries. AIDS also remained hidden because its clinical manifestations are expressed as other more readily recognizable infectious diseases. The exact origin of HIV and its introduction to humans is unknown, but there is much speculation and theorizing about where and how the HIV infection first developed.

One proposed explanation for HIV is that it was well established in all areas of the world but has only recently been recognized. However, this theory has not been well substantiated. A second proposition holds that HIV evolved through the mutation of an older and nonpathogenic virus. Virologists, however, have dismissed this as a plausible explanation for HIV on the basis of specific characteristics of the virus and its relationship to other viruses. A third and widely discussed possible origin of HIV is zoonosis, the recent entry of a nonhuman virus into human populations. This is a plausible explanation for the emergence of HIV because similar viruses appear to have existed in old-world apes who lived in areas that surround African regions where HIV is endemic. Still, zoonosis has not been universally accepted as the source of HIV. The most widely held view of HIV is that it represents a virus that developed in humans in Central Africa and only recently spread because of social changes, most importantly global travel and transcontinental commerce. Epidemiological data provide the strongest support for this last theory.

The first identified cases of AIDS occurred in the spring of 1981, when the Centres for Disease Control and Prevention (CDCP) reported that five young, previously healthy, homosexually active men in Los Angeles exhibited a rare type of upper respiratory infection: pneumocystis carinii pneumonia. One month later, the CDCP reported another 10 cases of this illness and 26 cases of Kaposi's sarcoma, a rare cancer of connective and vascular tissues. All of these unusual cases occurred in New York City, San Francisco, and Los Angeles among previously healthy, young homosexual men.

By the end of 1981, the number of AIDS cases had grown to 257, and to over 2,000 cases by the end of 1983, setting into motion the rapid accumulation of over 100,000 AIDS cases in the first decade of the epidemic and reaching 360,000 cases by the end of 1993. Today new case of AIDS is reported in the United States every 15 minutes, more than 5,000 people in the world become infected with HIV each day, and a person in the world dies of AIDS complications every 30 minutes.

Evidence that AIDS is caused by a new human virus emerged between late 1983 and early 1984. Considered the most rapid progression of scientific advances in response to a new disease in the history of biology and medicine, the accelerated rate of investigation into the cause of AIDS is represented in volumes of research. The 24 published papers on HIV-AIDS in 1982 is in contrast with 8,300 articles published in 1990. The proliferation of HIV-AIDS research is also shown by the emergence of several scientific and professional journals dedicated solely to publishing AIDS-related articles (e.g., *AIDS, Journal of Acquired Immune Deficiency Syndromes, AIDS Education and Prevention, International Journal of STD and AIDS, AIDS Patient Care* and *AIDS Care),* as well as the annual International Conference on AIDS. Articles concerning various aspects of HIV and AIDS regularly appear in scientific and professional journals across the world.

## THE HUMAN IMMUNODEFICIENCY VIRUS

Human immunodeficiency virus belongs to a group of viruses called retroviruses, specifically to a subgroup of cytopathic lentiviruses. Lentiviruses integrate their genetic material with a cell's genetic material through the complicated process of reverse transcription. Retroviruses are often communicable, as is the case with feline leukemia virus, which causes immune deficiency and malignancies. Whereas animal retroviruses have been known since the early part of the century and pose no threat to humans, human retroviruses have only recently been identified.

The first human retrovirus was discovered by Robert Gallo and his associates at the National Cancer Institute. Amid great controversy as to whether or not it was even possible for retroviruses to exist in humans, Gallo's lab identified the human T-cell lymphotropic virus type-I (HTLV-I) in the late 1970s. The clinical importance of HTLV-I is that it causes a type of leukemia involving T-helper lymphocyte cells, which play an integral role in the human immune system. HTLV-I does not cause AIDS, but results in a depletion of T-helper cells that are the same target of the virus that does cause AIDS. HTLV-I also causes progressive myelopathy, a disease of the spinal cord, and lymphomas in some infected persons.

Subsequently, Gallos lab discovered a second human leukemia-causing retrovirus, HTLV-II, establishing the likelihood that other undiscovered human retroviruses exist. The discovery of two leukemia-causing human retroviruses held answers to many questions raised nearly a decade later by AIDS. On the basis of epidemiologic evidence and disease symptoms, it was believed that AIDS resulted from a viral infection. Because the disease shares several characteristics with HTLV-I and HTLV-II, including the fact that it results in a loss of T-helper lymphocyte cells and that it is spread through blood, perinatal exchange, and sexual contact, AIDS appeared to be caused by a human retrovirus. Between 1983 and 1984, the virus that causes AIDS was discovered by three laboratories and given three different names: lymphadenopathy associated virus (LAV), discovered by Luc Montagnier of the Pasteur Institute of France; human T-cell lymphotropic virus type-III (HTLV-III), identified by Gallo at the National Cancer Institute; and AIDS associated retrovirus (ARV), discovered by Jay Levy of the Cancer Research Institute of the University of California at San Francisco.

All three virus isolates were essentially the same in terms of structure, apparent mechanisms of transmission, and disease manifestations. It is now believed that these early discoveries were actually variants of the same virus; they were therefore renamed in 1986, by a subcommittee on the taxonomy of viruses, the human immunodeficiency virus type-1.

A great deal of controversy has surrounded which lab first discovered the virus that causes AIDS. Patent rights to the antibody test and the royalties for the test complicated matters further. Although still unsettled for some, the consensus is now that researchers at the Pasteur Institute in France should be credited with the initial identification and isolation of what is now referred to as HIV-I.

Subsequently, a second AIDS-causing virus common in West Africa, HIV-2, was discovered in 1986. The differences between HIV-I and HIV-2 are mostly on the molecular level, with few differences in clinical symptomatology. It is thought that HIV-2 is evolutionarily related to HIV-1, because the two viruses share several molecular and pathogenic characteristics. However, HIV-2 has not spread across populations to cause disease at nearly the magnitude of HIV-1, and remains relatively contained in West Africa. As of 1992, there were only 32 cases of HIV-2 infection reported in the United Stutes, and most were among West African immigrants. Concern about potential increases in North American HIV-2 cases has lead to mandated screening for HIV-2 antibodies in addition to HIV-1 antibodies in the national blood supply. Although HIV-2 may become a greater health threat in the future, HIV-1 accounts for the vast majority of AIDS cases in the world.

There is a great deal of diversity found among laboratory isolates of HIV-I, both when samples are taken from different infected persons as well as when isolates come from a single patient. The variation within infected persons makes HIV particularly difficult for the immune system to manage because alterations in its biochemistry evade targeted immune responses. Similar but distinct HIV-1 substrains cause deterioration of the immune system because each variant of the virus kills T-helper cells. The profusion of biochemically different strains of HIV-1 poses great obstacles to developing effective treatment as well as a preventive vaccine.

There are two known groups of human retroviruses, the leukemia-causing retroviruses, HTLV-I and HTLV-II, and the viruses that cause AIDS, HIV-I and HIV-II. Both are transmitted through close intimate contacts where blood, semen, or vaginal fluids are exchanged; both share T-helper cells as a common pathogenic target; they both become dormant and integrated into the genetic material of infected cells; and they are both related to viruses found in old-world primates. These commonalities suggest that HTLVs and HIVs have a convergent evolution.

However, the clinical manifestations of HTLV and HIV are distinctly different, with the HTLVs causing leukemia, characterised by unrestrained growth and proliferation of white blood cells, and the HIVs causing profound deterioration of the immune system because of loss and dysfunction of T-helper lymphocytes. The global AIDS epidemic is the result of HIV-I infection. How HIV-I destroys central components of the immune system is the key to understanding AIDS.

## VIRAL CYCLE OF HIV

Viruses typically consist of a core of genetic material, almost always deoxyribonucleic acid (DNA), and a surrounding protein coat. However, retroviruses have at their genetic core a strand of ribonucleic acid (RNA). Following infection of a target cell, the RNA is converted into DNA through a process of reverse transcription that relies on the enzyme reverse transcriptase. The new viral DNA then either proliferates in the infected cell or integrates itself directly with the cell DNA.

The ability of retroviral RNA to transcribe itself into a DNA copy and integrate with host cell DNA is the hallmark of a retrovirus. The virus can then he dormant for long periods of time, safely hidden within host cells; the process also allows the virus to assemble, package, and replicate itself as a free virus, using the host cell's resources. Upon entry into the bloodstream of an infected person, the HIV becomes attached to the membrane of a target cell.

HIV is highly selective in its binding properties, only targeting cells that express a surface molecule designated duster determinant 4 ($CD_4$), that usually acts as a receptor site for infectious agents. T-helper lymphocytes are one type of cell that express the surface molecule $CD_4$, which has an extremely high affinity for an HIV envelope surface protein, gp120. In fact, the binding between HIV gp120 and $CD_4$ is stronger than between $CD_4$ and most non-HIV infectious agents.

After binding with the cell membrane, the virus enters the host cell by means of the same $CD_4$ surface molecule involved in viral attachment. Once in the cell, the viral core genetic material, RNA, is reverse transcribed into a DNA copy. The retroviral DNA usually then becomes integrated with the genetic material of the host cell. The integrated viral DNA, or proviral DNA, works in the cell to transcribe viral messenger-RNA, which serves to produce more retrovirus.

Viral messenger-RNA produces structural proteins for the production of HIV, RNA and envelope proteins. The new viral RNA is encapsulated as the core of newly produced proteins in the assembly of new HIV. Replicated virus particles eventually bud and release from the host cell, infecting a multitude of new host cells. Thus, the natural flow of genetic information, from DNA to RNA, is reversed in the case of retroviruses, flowing from RNA to DNA, making retroviruses extremely difficult to understand and treat.

Shortly after infection with HIV, there is a brief period of intense viral replication, where HIV multiplies and disseminates rapidly. This period is characterised by mass quantities of virus, or viremia, and is followed by a decline in virus replication. When not replicating, HIV hides within cells in a latent phase. HIV can exist in latent form in T-helper lymphocytes, as well as other infected cells, for long periods of time.

Latent HIV infection occurs while the viral genetic material (provirus) is integrated with the host cell DNA, constituting a silent infection, undetectable by the body's immune system. Viral latency should not, however, be confused with clinically asymptomatic periods. Although during viral latency there is often an absence of clinical symptoms, viral replication is occurring in host cells during asymptomatic periods. Thus, HIV can be latent during periods of symptomatic illness and can actively replicate during asymptomatic periods.

Activation of dormant HIV in T-helper lymphocytes can occur under a number of conditions. The slow and persistent progression of immunologic destruction and clinical symptomatology characteristic of HIV infection results from its complex genetic regulation as well as the interaction between HIV, its host cell, and networks of modulating infectious cofactors.

Several other infectious agents possibly facilitate HIV activation, including herpes simplex virus type-2, HTLV-I, HTLV-II, Epstein-Barr virus, and hepatitis B virus. Thus, stimulation of the immune system and activation of HIV are intricately connected. When activated, proviral DNA in host cells transcribe messenger-RNA, which in turn initiates protein synthesis and the assembling of new HIV.

### HIV AND THE IMMUNE SYSTEM

T-helper lymphocytes are destroyed when HIV irrupts, or

buds, from host cells. However, there are a number of mechanisms in addition to viral budding that destroy lymphocytes. For example, when HIV irrupts from an infected cell, the virus sheds fragments of envelope protein gp120, which adhere to the $CD_4$ surface molecules of neighbouring T-helper cells. HIV gp120 binding with the membrane of uninfected T-helper cells can cause several adverse effects. First, gp120 adheres uninfected T-helper cells together, forming a giant multinucleated clump of functionally incapacitated cells called syncytia. Syncytia have been found in the lymphatic systems and brains of HIV-infected patients.

Another effect of gp120 bound to the surface of T-helper cells is that it triggers an immune response against the cell itself. When gp120 is detected as a foreign particle by the immune system, it is destroyed along with the uninfected lymphocytes. In addition to total cell destruction, HIV can interfere with the fundamental T-helper cell functions. For example, unintegrated DNA within infected cells can have significant effects on T-helper lymphocytes. Several other means by which HIV destroys T-helper cells have been well established.

Quantitative loss of T-helper lymphocytes was the earliest and most widely cited immunologic abnormality resulting from HIV infection, and it is the depletion of T-helper cells that results in the profound immune suppression of AIDS. T-helper lymphocytes rapidly decline by a factor of one third in the first 12 to 18 months after the occurrence of HIV infection, with a subsequently slower rate of cell loss, approximately 80 T-helper cells per unit measure per year, over the course of several years. A second accelerated period of T-helper cell decline usually occurs prior to the onset of clinical conditions of AIDS.

The close association among persistent effects of HIV infection, loss of T-helper cells, and immunosuppression provides the strongest evidence that HIV is the cause of AIDS. Studies consistently show that the progression of HIV infection can be monitored through T-helper lymphocyte counts in conjunction with other markers of immune system functioning. For example, independent of declines in the numbers of other immune cells, T-helper cell counts below $200/mm^3$ are a reliable marker for development of full-blown AIDS and have, therefore, been included as a diagnostic criterion in revised case definitions of AIDS.

In addition to absolute numbers of T-helper cells, the ratio between T-helper and T-suppressor ($CD_8$) cells is a key indicator of immune system functioning. Healthy people have more T-helper lymphocytes at any given time than T-suppressor cells, with 60 per cent of peripheral lymphocytes being T-helper cells and 30 per cent T-suppressor cells. However, with HIV infection, the ratio is often inverted. Although other infections result in increases in the number of T-suppressor cells relative to T-helper cells, HIV causes the inversion because of the loss of T-helper cells as opposed to an increase in T-suppressor cells. This immune system abnormality suppresses immunity and results in a substantial increased susceptibility to infectious diseases.

Aside from direct damage to T-helper cells, immune dysfunction occurs as a result of indirect effects of HIV infection on immune functioning. As a part of the cell-mediated branch of the immune system that deals with infection-causing microorganisms, T-helper lymphocytes coordinate immune responses to viruses. T-helper cells become impaired when the HIV envelope proteins adhere to their cell membrane, disrupting the normal cell signaling and feedback systems.

Progressive T-helper cell dysfunction therefore accounts for immunological disturbances caused by HIV infection, which ultimately interfere with multiple branches of immunologic functioning. The widespread and diffused effects of HIV were at first surprising because it selectively infects a single type of immune cell, the T-helper lymphocyte. However, the effects of HIV infection are pronounced because the loss of T-helper cells and accompanying cell disturbances result in functional deficiencies across several branches of the immune system.

Although the primary target of HIV is the T-helper lymphocyte, several other immune system cells are indirectly affected by HIV infection. For example, although there is not a significant loss of T-suppressor cells and natural killer cells, these immune cells are functionally impaired because of the mediating role played by T-helper cells in coordinating immune system responses. Also of particular importance are the monocyte macrophages, which also express the $CD_4$ surface molecule to which HIV selectively binds. Monocyte macrophage cells are phagocytic: they engulf and destroy infectious agents.

Thus, HIV may enter macrophages after binding with the $CD_4$ surface molecule, or HIV may be engulfed by the cells through phagocytosis. HIV-infected macrophages are unable to attack and destroy other micro-organisms. While inside the macrophages, HIV is also protected from immunologic responses. It is widely held that macrophages harbour, transport, and disseminate HIV throughout the body, particularly to the lungs and brain.

*Table 1*
*HIV Mechanisms that Cause Immune Impairment*

| *Impairment* | *Description* |
|---|---|
| HIV budding | HIV reproduced in cells erupt and infect a multitude of new target cells |
| Syncytia | HIV envelope proteins adhere to the receptor area of one cell, which then adheres to another until a cluster of immune cells are bound together |
| gp120 binding | HIV envelope proteins bound to a cell membrane can cause impaired cell functioning |
| Autoimmune responses | Virus components bound to cell membranes can trigger an immune response that eventually attacks the infected immune cells |

Although the scientific community has mostly accepted HIV as the cause of AIDS, there have been alternative etiological theories. Alternative perspectives discount HIV as being a sufficient cause of disease and place greater weight on combinations of other infectious agents and life-style factors that may impede immune functioning, such as substance abuse and malnutrition. Theories of AIDS that de-emphasize the role of HIV are becoming increasingly popular among lay persons and activist groups but have, thus far, lacked scientific verification.

Although many unanswered questions remain, much has been learned about HIV infection. The link between HIV, on the one hand, and immunologic impairment and AIDS, on the other, is well established. As the immune system is suppressed and deteriorates, the body becomes susceptible to infectious diseases that are normally controlled by immune responsiveness. HIV affects immunity through several pathways, including the direct loss of T-helper lymphocyte cells, indirect effects on T-helper cell functions, and impairment of other immune system cells whose functions are mediated by T-helper cells.

## ROUTES OF HIV TRANSMISSION

Early epidemiological studies demonstrated that AIDS was the result of a communicable disease. Because the first U.S. AIDS cases almost exclusively involved homosexually active men, the causal agent, not yet known to be a virus, was quickly thought to be contracted through sexual practices. At that time, any possible means of contracting the disease through intimate as well as casual contact were not quickly dismissed, and there was much speculation about how a person might get AIDS. Hysteria was commonplace and understandable given that the cause of a new and devastating illness was unknown. Careful epidemiological study over the past decade, however, has provided several conclusive findings.

To date, HIV and HIV-infected cells have only been isolated in substantial quantities from human blood, vaginal secretions, semen, and breast milk, with significantly lower quantities in other body fluids such as saliva and urine. Thus, there are four primary modes of HIV transmission: person-to-person through fluid-exchanging sexual behaviours; use of HIV-contaminated injection equipment; mother to infant during pregnancy, labour and delivery, or breast feeding; and through transfusion with infected blood or blood products.

**Anal intercourse**

Anal intercourse was the first identified route of HIV transmission in North America. Among homosexually active men, anal intercourse is the primary reason for the large number of AIDS cases in this population. Receptive anal intercourse is the only homosexual practice that is definitively associated with contracting HIV. The risk of becoming infected with HIV accelerates in direct proportion to the number of receptive anal intercourse partners men report.

Prospective studies of gay men have also shown increased risks of infection when there is rectal tissue damage during anal intercourse. Chmiel et al. found that rectal trauma resulting from anal sex provides highly efficient access for HIV to enter the bloodstream. Ninety percent of men in the large Chmiel et al. sample who experienced rectal injuries or bleeding caused by anal sex acts were HIV infected.

*Table 2*
*Routes of HIV Transmission*

| *Risk behaviour* | *Transmission mechanism* |
|---|---|
| Anal intercourse | Infected semen or blood enters the anal/rectal mucosa or penis through absorption or micro-openings |
| Vaginal intercourse | Infected vaginal fluids, semen, or blood enter the vaginal or penile mucosa, or through micro-openings |
| Oral-genital contact | Infected semen or vaginal fluids enter bloodstream through micro-openings in oral cavity, or infected cells enter vagina or penis through micro-openings |
| Perinatal transmission | Transplacental transfer of virus during gestation, transfer of virus |

| | |
|---|---|
| | or maternal blood during labour/ delivery, breast feeding |
| Injection drug use | Use of needles and other injection equipment previously used by an infected person; virus or infected cells directly enter blood stream |
| Blood transfusion—receiving blood products | Principal risk in U.S. occurred prior to 1984 blood screening programs; blood or blood parts from an infected person enter bloodstream |

In another longitudinal study, Keet, van Lent, Sandfort, Coutinho, and van Griensven followed 102 men who contracted HIV infection and found that the majority attributed becoming infected to having engaged in anal intercourse. Thus, there is conclusive evidence that anal sexual intercourse affords highly efficient transmission of HIV, and the risk seems highest for receptive partners with rectal trauma. It should be noted, then that proceptive and insertive anal intercourse also carries substantial risk for HIV infection and should not be dismissed as a low-risk sexual activity.

Risk associated with anal intercourse results from the high degree of vascularisation of anal-rectal tissue and its relatively thin mucosal lining. The practice of anal intercourse is not found exclusively among homosexually active men. Gayle and D'Angelo reported that 25 per cent of female adolescents engage in anal intercourse and that anal intercourse is often practiced among adolescents as a method of avoiding pregnancy and "maintaining virginity."

Padian et al. found that anal intercourse was frequently engaged in by women infected with HIV, and this was most commonly the case when their partner was bisexual.

**Vaginal intercourse**

Penile-vaginal intercourse accounts for the greatest number of cases of HIV infection in the world. Heterosexual transmission of HIV, primarily through vaginal intercourse, has been widely documented in North America, and transmission between men and women is bi-directional.

During the course of one prospective study, approximately 10 per cent to 20 per cent of 307 women married to HIV infected men contracted the HIV infection.

Although HIV transmission from women to men occurs during vaginal intercourse, the rates of transmission are not as high as those for men to women. One study that followed 730 couples with one HIV-positive partner found that the risk of male-to-female infection is 2.3 times greater then female-to-male transmission. Exact rates of male-to-female and female-to-male HIV transmission are not known, but two reasons for higher male-to-female efficiency may be the greater mucosal surface area of the female genital tract and the large number of potentially infected cells in seminal fluids. Although there may be differential rates of infection for receptive and proceptive partners, as in anal intercourse, there are no exact probabilities for calculating risk for HIV infection from vaginal intercourse.

**Oral-genital contact**

Among sexual behaviours that involve the exchange of semen or vaginal fluids, the most controversial in terms of risk for HIV is oral-genital contact. Unlike anal and vaginal intercourse, oral-genital contact has not been definitively linked to HIV transmission. However, there are cases of HIV-infected men who report oral-genital contact and deny engaging in anal or vaginal intercourse as well as any other known risks for HIV transmission.

Rozenbaum, Gharakhanian, Cardon, Duval, and Coulaud studied five men who denied engaging in anal or vaginal intercourse and who tested positive for HIV antibodies subsequent to a negative antibody test three months earlier. Similarly, a prospective study in Amsterdam reported four men who allegedly contracted HIV solely through oral-genital sex.

Lower rates of HIV infection via oral-genital contact may be accounted for by several factors, including minimal exposure to the bloodstream through the oral cavity. Additional factors may therefore increase the risk of oral-genital transmission of HIV, such as lacerations, trauma, or open sores in the mouth, including those caused by gingivitis, herpes infections, cracked lips, and canker sores. However, it should be noted that there is no evidence that such potential ports of entry are necessary for oral HIV transmission to occur. Another factor contributing to apparent low rates of oral-genital transmission is that oral sex does not necessarily occur in isolation from other forms of sexual contact. Thus, although oral-genital contact appears to carry lower risks for HIV transmission than do anal and vaginal intercourse, it is not possible to say that oral sex with semen or vaginal fluid exchange constitutes a low-risk sexual behaviour.

**Protection against HIV transmission**

Once HIV was established as the cause of AIDS and it was determined that HIV was transmitted through sexual contact, tests were conducted evaluate the effectiveness of condoms as barriers against HIV transmission. Laboratory tests conclusively showed that latex condoms are impermeable to HIV and other retroviruses. The effectiveness of latex condoms as a primary means of preventing HIV transmission has resulted in the widespread dissemination of condoms and mass media promotion of condom use.

To further increase the use of barrier methods of protection, and to offset power differentials in condom-use decision making in heterosexual relationships the United States government approved a vaginal insertive condom-like lubricated polyurethane sheath. There is also considerable evidence that some spermicidal applications, in particular nonoxynol-9, have virucidal effects and may add to the protective value of condoms.

Laboratory studies have shown that some spermicides have virus-deactivating properties by disrupting the viral envelope. Spermicides therefore offer an additional level of protection against HIV infection when used in proper combination with latex condoms, but provide no protection when used alone.

Condom use is also infrequent among injection drug users, with 46 per cent of men who inject drugs reporting never using condoms with their steady sexual partners and 52 per cent never using them with casual partners.

Individuals with multiple sexual partners are more likely to use condoms than those who have a long-term sexual partner, even among injection drug users who are at risk of infection from sharing needles. Likewise, prostitutes are less likely to use condoms with their steady partner than with their clients. Thus, even among persons at high risk for HIV infection, condom use is infrequent.

When latex condoms are used they reduce risk but do not eliminate risk for HIV infection. Failure of condoms to protect against HIV, as well as other sexually transmitted infections and pregnancy, has been widely documented. Condom failure frequently occurs during vaginal intercourse and anal intercourse. Small, undetectable tears in latex condoms permit HIV transmission because HIV is considerably smaller than other sexually transmitted viruses, including herpes simplex virus and cytomegalovirus.

Thus, it is not only essential that condoms be used, but that they be used properly, including using a new condom for each occurrence of sexual intercourse, keeping the condom on for the entire sexual act from start to finish, leaving an adequate reservoir at the tip to collect semen, ensuring that there is no air between the condom and penis, and using adequate and proper lubrication to reduce strain on the latex. Proper lubricants which are oil-free and water based should be used.

**Perinatal transmission**

Pregnant women infected with HIV can transmit the virus to their unborn or newborn children. In developing countries, between 18 per cent and 40 per cent of infants born to HIV-I-infected women acquire HIV-I infection, although the risk for HIV-2 transmission is much lower. The first cases of AIDS in children were reported in 1982, and AIDS is now among the top 10 leading causes of death in children older than 1 year. Infection from mother to offspring occurs by HIV crossing the placenta, usually during the second and third trimesters, and through contact with infected maternal blood and vaginal fluids during labour and delivery.

Studies have shown that newly infected women and women with advanced HIV infection are more likely to transmit HIV to the foetus than are women who are pregnant during times when HIV is less active. In addition, HIV is present in breast milk, making it possible for transmission to occur during breast feeding. Risk for perinatal HIV transmission is, however, reduced by maternal use of anti-retroviral medications and other interventions. The results of AIDS Clinical Trial Group Protocol 076 demonstrated that the anti-retroviral drug zidovudine (AZT, ZDV) administered to a select group of pregnant women and their infants resulted in a two-thirds risk reduction for HIV transmission, suggesting an effective means of preventing perinatal HIV transmission.

An estimated 6,000 births to HIV-infected women occur each year in the U.S. The majority of infants born to HIV-infected mothers test HIV antibody positive because maternal antibodies, although not necessarily the virus, cross the placental barrier during gestation. Actual HIV infection occurs in 20 per cent to 40 per cent of infants born to infected mothers. Conclusive testing for HIV antibodies in newborns can therefore only occur after maternal antibodies dissipate from the infant's bloodstream and are replaced with the infant's own HIV antibodies, if the infant has been infected. However, a test for the presence of HIV itself can be done earlier.

**Injection drug use**

Transmission of HIV many occur when needles, syringes, and other injection equipment is used by an infected person and shared with other injectors. Residual blood contaminates the injection apparatus and can directly transmit HIV to a sharing partner. As many as 40 per cent of injection drug users share needles and syringes, although the rate of infection has declined since the threat of contracting HIV through contaminated needles was first publicized. Legal exchange of needles has the potential to prevent many HIV infections. Unfortunately, public health benefits of needle exchange are often overshadowed by political issues surrounding substance abuse.

Thus, HIV has been widely transmitted among injection drug users by way of injection equipment shared by a circle of friends as well as strangers. Once infected, injection drug users can transmit HIV to sexual partners, who may or may not also inject drugs.

**Blood transfusions**

Proper to the AIDS epidemic, donated blood could not be tested for HIV antibodies, which were therefore unknowingly transmitted to transfusion recipients. Receiving a single unit of HIV-infected blood carries a 90 per cent chance of HIV infection. Persons at greatest risk for HIV infection through U.S. blood transfusions are those who received blood or blood products between 1978, when the U.S. HIV epidemic began, and 1984, when the HIV-antibody test became available and blood screening programs were initiated. Prior to blood screening, haemophiliacs were highly susceptible to HIV infection because of multiple blood transfusions and treatments with blood components combined from multiple donors. As a result of exposure to contaminated blood products in the early 1980s, 50 per cent to 65 per cent of U.S. hemophiliacs are HIV infected, and AIDS is the leading cause of death in this population.

Furthermore, HIV-infected haemophiliacs unknowingly transmitted HIV to their sexual partners, and women infected with HIV through blood transfusions often infected their offspring. However, blood-donor screening programs were implemented in March 1985 in the United States, the result of which has been to dramatically reduce HIV infection through blood transfusions. Unfortunately, most developing countries have not established widespread donor screening programs, making HIV transmission through blood transfusion a continued global problem.

**HIV transmission to and from health-care professionals**

Invasive medical and dental procedures allow for bidirectional exposure to HIV. Health-care workers serving HIV-infected patients can become HIV infected when professionals have open wounds exposed to patient blood or when patient blood splashes on mucous membranes. HIV infection from contact with patient blood has occurred in several health-care professions. Among all occupationally infected health-care workers, 84 per cent were exposed through percutaneous injury, such as a cut or needlestick puncture, and 13 per cent through mucous-membrane exposure, such as through the mouth or eyes. Still, the risk for occupational HIV infection is very low.

*Table 3*

*Total number of possible health-care occupationally acquired HIV infections in the United States*

| *Occupation* | *Number of possible cases* |
|---|---|
| Nurse | 16 |
| Laboratory technician | 15 |
| Health aide | 14 |
| Emergency medical technician/paramedic | 9 |
| Nonsurgical physician | 9 |
| Other health-care occupations | 7 |
| Dental worker | 6 |
| Embalmer/morgue technician | 3 |
| Surgical physician | 2 |
| Respiratory therapist | 2 |
| Surgical technician | 1 |
| Total | 84 |

HIV transmission can also occur from health-care workers to patients. Provider-to-patient transmission can result from direct exposure to an infected provider's blood during an invasive procedure or through the use of contaminated instruments. It is important to emphasize that transmission from HIV-infected providers to patients is extremely rare. Illustrating this is a study of 19,036 persons treated by 57 HIV-infected health-care workers that did not identify a single case of HIV transmission to patients.

## Transmission Through Casual Contact

There is conclusive evidence that HIV infection occurs as a result of direct exposure to the blood, semen, or vaginal fluids of an infected person. Direct contact with the blood or other body secretions of a person with AIDS can result in HIV transmission, but cases of transmission after direct household exposure are rare. However, a great deal of speculation and fear exists concerning HIV transmission through a variety of nonspecific, casual contacts with infected persons and through mediating mechanisms of transmission. There is, however, no evidence to support such claims.

Numerous studies conducted with individuals who live with HIV-infected persons, who have daily household exposure to body fluids and who share eating utensils and bathroom facilities, have consistently shown that people who do not engage in sexual acts with infected persons do not become infected. In one investigation, Friedland et al. studied 68 children and 33 adults who shared dose personal contact with 39 AIDS patients. The study failed to find any evidence of casual transmission of HIV. Likewise, no cases of HIV transmission have been known to occur in schools or day care-settings.

Because HIV has been isolated in body fluids other than blood, semen, and vaginal fluids, it is commonly believed that contact with these other fluids carries risk for HIV infection. Although HIV can be in tears and urine, there is no evidence that contact with these fluids results in HIV infection. Even if infection from tears or urine were possible, it would require long and extensive exposure for transmission to occur.

Infection from saliva, on the other hand, has been more controversial, with studies yielding conflicting results. The consensus is that contact with the saliva of an infected person through kissing, cardiopulmonary resuscitation (CPR), or other such contacts carries no risk for infection. Thus, aside from genital sexual contact and shared injection equipment, close contact poses no known risk for HIV transmission.

Other behaviours and mediating mechanisms once believed to present at least some risk for HIV infection have not been supported by epidemiological studies. Studies in areas with both high rates of AIDS cases and dense populations of mosquitos have shown that HIV infection is unrelated to mosquito exposure and that elderly persons and children do not show high rates of HIV infection despite multiple insect bites. Other theoretically possible modes of HIV transmission, such as tattooing, which involves needle puncture, and human bites have not demonstrated risk for HIV transmission.

## PATTERNS OF THE EPIDEMIC

Tracking the HIV-AIDS epidemic relies on two sets of data. First, local health departments, the CDCP, and the World Health Organization closely monitor the number of people diagnosed with AIDS. Surveillance programs track persons infected with HIV who have progressed to AIDS. Thus, even the most accurate AIDS case monitoring only estimates the extent of the HIV epidemic as it existed about 10 years earlier.

A second set of data that tracks the epidemic is collected through HIV-antibody testing. The number of HIV-positive persons per population tested, or seroprevalence studies, yields the rate of HIV infection in specific populations. However, these studies provide only a snapshot of current infections because only certain subgroups in a given geographic area, such as homosexually active men, injection drug users, or medical patients, are included in any single study. Seroprevalence data that rely on testing volunteers underestimate the magnitude of the HIV epidemic because participants in these studies demonstrate substantially lower rates of HIV seroprevalence than do people who refuse to participate. HIV-AIDS is a pandemic affecting all continents and virtually every country of the world. Mathematical models show that the AIDS pandemic has a continuous expansion. It is estimated that 11.8 million adults and 1.1 million children in the world were infected with HIV by 1992. The most heavily affected regions include sub-Saharan Africa, Latin America, the Caribbean Islands, and North America, with the highest prevalence occurring in developing countries.

There are several explanations for the higher prevalence of AIDS in developing as compared with industrialized countries, including coepidemics of ulcerative sexually transmitted infections that facilitate HIV transmission, culturally related sexual practices such as prostitution, resistance to condom use, and sexual networks that span across high-risk groups.

Cases of AIDS in North America and the Caribbean have increased substantially each year since 1980. For example, the first case of AIDS reported in Canada occurred in 1982, and 5,246 cases of AIDS were reported as of 1991. In Canada, nearly 70 per cent of all AIDS cases have occurred among homosexually active men. In contrast, HIV infection in Puerto Rico has primarily resulted from heterosexual contact. Puerto Rico represents the second highest rate of AIDS among U.S. cities and territories, with 99 per cent of all AIDS cases from U.S. territories occurring in Puerto Rico.

The number of U.S. AIDS cases increased 10 per cent from 1990 to 1991, and over 48 per cent from 1992 to 1993. Through 1993, there were over 361,000 cases of AIDS reported in the United States. Because the number of AIDS cases includes people infected with HIV over 10 years ago, it is impossible to know exactly how many people are HIV infected at any given time. However, on the basis of the best available data, over one million adults in the United States were infected with HIV as of 1991, with an additional 40,000 to 80,000 new HIV infections occurring between 1991 and 1992.

Epidemiologic studies piece together a picture of the U.S. epidemic that shows the HIV infection occurring across diverse subgroups in varying degrees depending on geographic areas, HIV-risk behaviour histories, and the date of study. AIDS cases have been reported in every state in the United States, with the greatest number in larger metropolitan areas AIDS became the leading cause of death among men aged 35 to 44 in the United States and the second leading cause of death among young women. HIV is the leading cause of death among young men in 64 of 170 major U.S. cities, with AIDS accounting for 51 per cent of deaths of young men in Fort. Lauderdale, 33 per cent in New Haven, 29 per cent in Minneapolis, 39 per cent in Seattle, and 37 per cent in San Diego. AIDS now ranks in the top three causes of death for young men in 21 U.S. states, with most deaths concentrated in metropolitan areas.

The disproportionate number of AIDS cases in urban centers has characterised the epidemic since its beginning. For example, in New York state, AIDS is the leading cause of death among men 25 to 44 years old and among women 20 to 39 years old, and the vast majority of deaths because of AIDS in New York state have occurred in New York City. Between 1990 and 1991, the number of AIDS cases increased 19 per cent in Philadelphia, 11 per cent in Chicago, 24 per cent in Washington DC, and 22 per cent in Miami.

Among U.S. cases of AIDS 85 per cent occur in metropolitan areas with populations greater than 500,000, compared with 9 per cent of cases in cities with populations between 50,000 and 500,000 (CDC, 1994b). Thus, like previous epidemics dating back as early as the Black Plague, cities constitute the most heavily devastated geographic areas.

The spread of infection in any given area is determined by three principal factors: First, rates of infection depend on the probability that an infected person will infect another person. Second, the number of partnerships an individual has with potentially infected persons determines the chances of infection. Finally, the length of time that an infected person can potentially infect others influences rates of spread.

For HIV, individuals remain infectious for the remaining years of their life and are often unaware of being infected for the majority of that time. Links within and between sexual and drug-using networks determine the pattern and rate of the HIV epidemic. Thus, there are numerous subepidemics emerging across several subpopulations, both globally and within the United States.

## RISK CHARACTERISTICS OF HIGHLY AFFECTED SUBPOPULATIONS

Although HIV infection occurs across all geographic and demographic segments of the United States, several groups have been affected longest over the course of the epidemic. People at risk for HIV infection are defined on the basis of two necessary conditions for HIV infection. The first condition is the prevalence of HIV in a population, because this rate determines the probability that any given risk-related contact will result in HIV transmission. The greater the HIV seroprevalence in a subpopulation, the higher risk of infection. The second condition that determines infection is the frequency of behaviours that confer varying degrees of risk for HIV transmission. Thus, although it has become less relevant to discuss traditional risk groups as the HIV epidemic has expanded, certain subpopulations continue to represent the highest rates of HIV infection and AIDS.

**Homosexually and bisexually active men**

Because the first and greatest numbers of AIDS cases in the United States have occurred among homosexually active men, most attention regarding the AIDS epidemic has been given to this group. Although high HIV seroprevalence rates occur in gay communities, men who have sex with men are only at very high risk for HIV infection when they practice unprotected anal intercourse.

**Injection drug users**

High rates of infection and sharing injection equipment account for HIV risk among persons who inject illicit drugs. Although actual rates of sharing practices are not known, more frequent injectors are likely to be HIV-positive. Younger male injectors are among the most likely to borrow needles and syringes, even when dean injection equipment is available. Needle sharing, like sexual behaviours, occurs within dose, intimate, and private relationships as well as between anonymous partners.

Sharing injection equipment is often an important aspect of social bonding among users. HIV transmission occurs when needles are shared within a network of users, where an infected person contaminates injection equipment that is subsequently used by others. Injection drug users often congregate in "shooting galleries," where injection equipment is loaned or rented. Shooting galleries are common in cities with a large number of injection drug users and where HIV seroprevalence rates are highest.

Patterns of HIV transmission among injection drug users are complicated by several sociocultural factors. First, people infected with HIV may infect their non-injecting sexual partners. Second, a close association exists between injection drug use and prostitution, with 30 per cent of female injectors engaging in sexual commerce and 76 per cent of HIV-infected prostitutes using injection drugs. Third, noninjected drugs are also closely connected to sexually transmitted infections, particularly the use of cocaine. It is common for noninjected drugs, particularly crack cocaine, to be traded for sex and vice versa, further illustrating the complex link between drug use and HIV risk.

**Heterosexual men and women**

Men and women who practice vaginal or anal intercourse constitute the most prevalent HIV-risk population in the world. Heterosexual transmission of HIV accounted for the largest jump in AIDS cases from 1991 to 1992. People living in U.S. cities with greater numbers of sub-Saharan African and Caribbean immigrants, such as South Florida and New York City, may also be at higher risk for heterosexually transmitted HIV infection. Across geographic regions, heterosexuals in the United States demonstrate substantial rates of HIV-risk-related behaviours. In a random digitdial telephone survey, Catania, Coates, et al., found that 15 per cent to 31 per cent of 10,630 adults were at behavioural risk for HIV infection. The study also found that 7 per cent reported two or more sexual partners in the previous year.

Among heterosexuals, women are at particular risk for HIV infection. The number of women diagnosed with AIDS in the United States increased 15 per cent between 1990 and 1991 and rose an additional 10 per cent from 1991 to 1992, making AIDS the leading cause of death among young women in New York City and in the top four leading causes of death among women nationally. The number of women with AIDS who were heterosexually infected surpassed the number infected by injecting drugs for the first time in 1992. AIDS has thus far occurred disproportionately among women of color and women living in U.S. inner cities. Eighty-nine percent of HIV-infected newborns in New York City are born to women of color.

**Persons with non-HIV sexually transmitted diseases**

Women and men who contract sexually transmitted infections other than HIV are at risk for HIV infection because the virus is transmitted through the same pathways as other sexually transmitted diseases (STDs) and because HIV and non-HIV infections frequently co-occur. STD patients are likely to maintain high rates of sexual risk behaviours after STD treatment, increasing the chance of spreading HIV. A history of STD is a strong independent predictor of HIV infection, particularly when non-HIV infections involve genital ulcerations, as is the case for nearly 25 million people with genital herpes in the United States. Chlamydia and gonorrhea infections also facilitate HIV transmission because of microscopic ulcerations from inflamed mucous membranes. Nonulcerating diseases form a discharge that contains infected or susceptible cells.

Among sexually transmitted infections, syphilis is the single best predictor of HIV infection. Genital ulcers facilitate viral transmission because they provide an entry point for HIV infection and because they are likely to contain large amounts of HIV-infected (or infectable) immune cells. Open sores caused by a STD infection contain T-helper lymphocytes, which, when infected with HIV, carry a massive dose of virus when introduced to an uninfected person. Studies have shown that risk for HIV infection is increased between three and five times in the presence of other sexually transmitted diseases and that the risk increase is greater for women than for men.

**Adolescents**

Given that the average length of HIV latency between the point of infection and a diagnosis of AIDS spans several years, most of the 20 to 29 year-olds with AIDS, representing 19 per cent of all AIDS cases, were likely infected during their teens. Approximately 17,000 people between the ages of 13 and 19 were infected with HIV between 1981 and 1987. Among women between 20 and 24 years old diagnosed with AIDS, 48 per cent resulted from heterosexual contact, whereas 64 per cent of male cases resulted from homosexual contact.

Thirty-five percent of women and 12 per cent of men with AIDS contracted HIV infection from injection drug use. Risk among adolescents varies by gender, ethnic background, and geographic area, with males, ethnic minorities, and adolescents from inner cities being at greatest risk. Ethnicity is also a factor, with 8 per cent of African-American youth reporting previous sexually transmitted infections. The prevalence of co-occurring sexual infections and increasing rates of HIV are particularly problematic given the frequency of sexual risk behaviours found among adolescents.

Several factors indicate that HIV contracted during adolescence will continue increasing, including high rates of substance use in association with sexual behaviour, high rates of HIV infection among inner-city disenfranchised youth, and prevalent misinformation regarding risk.

**Other risk groups**

Several subpopulations that exhibit behaviour patterns carrying significant risk for HIV transmission within closed sexual networks have been identified. Of particular interest are subgroups whose sexual behaviour and relationships indicate that when HIV is introduced within a sexual network, the virus will rapidly spread. Individuals who exchange sex for money, drugs, or other material gain are at considerable risk for HIV infection because of the interrelationships among substance use, injection drug use, and multiple sexual contacts

Sex workers are at particularly high risk, with 16 per cent to 55 per cent of street prostitutes in U.S. cities testing HIV-positive. Prison inmates are also at elevated risk for HIV infection because of high rates of injection drug use and the likelihood of homosexual activity within closed sexual networks. Nearly four million U.S. migrant and seasonal workers are at risk because of living in dosed communities with HIV seroprevalence rates over 5 per cent. Chronic mentally ill adults engage in high rates of high-risk sexual practices. Psychiatric patients lack accurate information about HIV transmission and evidence high rates of HIV seroprevalence. Homeless adults with psychiatric disorders are also at substantial risk for HIV infection, with nearly 9 per cent of San Francisco homeless adults testing HIV-positive.

In contrast, groups that are at low risk for HIV infection have also been identified. Although there are isolated case reports of sexual HIV transmission between women a recent study of 960,000 female U.S. blood donors did not find a single case of HIV infection among women having exclusive sexual contact with other women. These findings were supported by a study of over 1,000 women with HIV infection, among whom only one woman reported sexual contact with women as her only risk factor.

Although the elderly tend to be sexually active as a group, persons over the age of 55 who did not receive a blood transfusion prior to 1985 are also at low risk for HIV infection. Thus, as the HIV epidemic expands, people at highest risk remain those who engage in behaviours that afford efficient viral transmission within sexual and injection-drug-using networks with high rates of HIV infection.

# 6

# HIV Sequalae

HIV infection and AIDS will touch all levels and aspects of society. The disease will affect those in the reproductive age group first, those who normally would be responsible for the nuturing of children, and the care of the elderly and extended family members. By the year 2000, the pandemic will have had a profound and lasting impact on the lives of up to 200 million, independent of adults infected with HIV. The burden of grief is enormous, as parents, children, spouses and friends experience the loss of their loved ones. Family members will be scattered, the elderly left destitute, children left homeless. Since AIDS affects adults in their economically most productives years, it may also cause serious damage to already precarious economies, undermining public sector capacity to govern and increasing the potential for social and civil unrest.

## Social Sequalae

The history of world epidemics shows that fears ultimately cause the persecution of those associated with the disease. For example, the 14th-century plague was viewed as divine punishment for sinful behaviour; the uninfected often became so terrified they blamed the epidemic on already socially ostracized groups. Many towns in Germany where plague ran rampant sought out Jews as scapegoats, putting many innocent people to death. Similarly, the cholera epidemic of the 1930s was viewed as a moral punishment for un-clean and sinful behaviour. Not until the early to middle 1900s did various forms of prejudice against cancer patients begin to give way to care and compassion, although many discriminatory practices against cancer patients still exist. The social sanctions suffered by victims of disease fit well under the broader rubric of social stigmatization.

AIDS is viewed as much more than a transmissible and lethal disease. HIV-related stigmatization is a second branch of the HIV epidemic, an epidemic of fear, prejudice, and discrimination against people with HIV infection and AIDS. Although the contributing factors may differ in different cultures, stigmatization of HIV infection occurs across societies. Several factors contribute to the stigmatization of HIV infection, including misinformation about risks of HIV transmission, prejudicial attitudes against groups most affected by the epidemic, the sexual and drug-using behaviours that transmit HIV, and fears more generally associated with sickness and death among other things. HIV-and AIDS-related stigma includes all of the adverse attitudes, beliefs, and behaviours directed at individuals perceived as HIV infected. Given below are six general dimensions of social stigmas:

a) *Concealability*: the extent to which a condition is hidden or apparent to others;
b) *Disruptiveness*: the extent to which it interferes with social interactions and relationships;
c) *Aesthetics*: the degree to which others react to the condition with dislike or disgust;
d) *Origin*: the amount of responsibility attributed for causing or maintaining the stigmatized condition;
e) *Course*: the degree to which the condition is alterable or progressively degenerative;
f) *Peril*: the degree to which the condition will physically, socially, or morally contaminate others.

Using these dimensions, Herek illustrated the stigmatization associated with HIV-AIDS. Although concealable early in its course, later stages of HIV infection and AIDS are rarely hidden from others; HIV infection interferes with social relationships; the disease physically disables and disfigures and is therefore aesthetically repellent; its origin is often, although not always, blamed on behaviours and life-style; the course of HIV infection is degenerative and not alterable; and HIV is a high-peril condition in that it poses risks to others. Thus, HIV infection represents the negative aspects of all six stigmatization dimensions.

**Bases for HIV-related stigmatization**

Prejudice against people with HIV infection and AIDS primarily stems from three distinct, although not mutually exclusive, sources. First, social stigmas result from realistic and unrealistic fears of contracting HIV. Although fears can relate to a lack of knowledge about HIV and its transmission, misinformation alone does not completely account for avoidance of people with HIV infection. Second, the groups most affected by HIV infection have been socially ostracized prior to the HIV epidemic. Social stigmas that extend beyond HIV itself therefore serve as a foundation for AIDS stigmatization. Finally, the negative course of HIV infection corresponds to cultural attitudes and fears about death and dying, and the tendency to avoid the terminally ill.

*Fears of contracting HIV infection*

Many negative attitudes toward HIV infection surfaced early in the epidemic when little was known about AIDS and its cause. Attitudes toward people with HIV infection have not, however, improved despite new information and understanding of the disease. Studies continue to show that the public lacks accurate information about HIV infection and AIDS.

For example, Herek and Capitanio conducted a random phone survey of over 1,100 men and women across the United States and found a high degree of misinformation about HIV and AIDS, and inaccurate information was associated with negative attitudes toward HIV-infected individuals.

Another random-digit-dial survey of more than 1,500 people in 44 states and the District of Columbia showed that 16 per cent believed that insects could transmit HIV.

Similar fears of casual HIV transmission, including sharing kitchen utensils and bathroom facilities, create a major source of concern among caregivers of people with

AIDS. Much of the public therefore fears contracting HIV infection through casual social contacts despite the fact that no cases of HIV transmission have occurred through these means. Misperceptions of HIV transmission potentially lead to hostility and avoidance of people with HIV infection.

Several other factors contribute to fears of contracting HIV through casual contacts. Concern about even the most remote possibilities of contracting HIV stem from its high mortality rate. The paradox, of course, is that a great deal of concern is exerted over contacts with very low probabilities of HIV transmission while people continue to freely engage in sexual behaviours that carry high risk for HIV transmission.

People are well known to inaccurately judge risks, with risks of low-probability events overestimated. Frequencies and salience of media images of a particular transmission route are a major source of risk misperceptions. For example, media coverage of six cases of HIV transmission that apparently occurred in one dental practice contributed to near social hysteria over contracting HIV from dentists, which in turn brought about guidelines from the CDC and the American Dental Association. Policy initiatives for mandatory HIV antibody testing for dentists and to limit the practices of dentists with HIV infection resulted from this one unusual case.

Fears of contracting HIV motivate avoidance and ultimately lead to the isolation of people with HIV infection. Herek and Capitanio found that 12 per cent of people surveyed would intentionally avoid a close friend if he or she learned that they were HIV positive, 16 per cent would prohibit HIV-infected children from attending schools, 20 per cent would avoid an infected co-worker, and 50 per cent would avoid a neighbourhood grocer if they knew he or she was HIV positive.

Isolating individuals with HIV infection in medical hospitals is also a common practice that stems from early policies that were based on incomplete information. Isolation of patients with HIV infection is supported by noninfected patients. Public misperceptions about HIV transmission may translate to broad-based health policies that reflect prejudicial attitudes. Although nowhere in the United States has there been a serious policy to isolate individuals with HIV infection, several states have enacted legislation to restrict the liberties of people with HIV who are known to engage in high-risk behaviours.

*Risk group characteristics*

HIV-related social stigmas are overlaid upon negative attitudes associated with behaviours and life-styles that existed before the HIV epidemic. Prejudices and fears are related to behaviour long viewed as deviant, such as homosexuality and drug abuse. Public perceptions of AIDS combine with socio-cultural perceptions of the subgroups most visibly affected by the epidemic. Discrimination against people with HIV infection has therefore arisen out of prejudice against gay and bisexual men, the sexually promiscuous, and injection drug users. Before designated as AIDS, the syndrome was originally classified as *Gay-Related Immune Deficiency* (GRID) and commonly referred to as the Gay Plague. Media images of gay activists protesting political silence about the syndrome, coupled with the first widely recognized celebrities afflicted with HIV being gay men, served to strengthen perceptions of AIDS as a gay disease.

Antigay hostility, prejudice, and intolerance became closely associated with HIV. Shortly later in the U.S. epidemic, injection drug use was associated with HIV infection. This new dimension did not reduce stigmas because drug use supports perceptions of AIDS as a disease of moral retribution. Socially condemned behaviours that afford efficient transmission of HIV create perceptions of personal responsibility for contracting the virus. Blame leads to anger and to a lack of compassion.

The greatest degree of blame for the epidemic is attributed to those HIV-positive individuals believed to have known about the risks they were taking but still chose to do so. Thus, people with HIV infection compose two socially defined groups: innocent victims who had no knowledge of their risk and are not held accountable (*e.g.*, infected infants, hemophiliacs, and transfusion recipients), and those perceived as guilty and held accountable. Thus, blame attributed to people with HIV infection corresponds to views of a just world.

Unfortunately, like other aspects of HIV infection, research in HIV-related stigmatization has underrepresented non-injection-drug-using women, heterosexuals, and ethnic minorities. Because these groups have life experiences that differ from those of gay men, there are considerable gaps in our understanding of HIV-related social stigmas. Homophobia, prejudice against injection drug users, and dismay for people perceived as sexually promiscuous inhibit the potential power of public education efforts. Misinformation that feeds prejudice is not easily corrected. Beliefs about HIV-AIDS, homophobia, and prejudices against addicts hinder policymakers from taking positive action. The links among negative attitudes, misperceptions, and misinformation further propagate HIV-related stigmas by exacerbating fears of terminal illness.

*Negative attitudes toward death*

Fears of death influence the social and medical treatment of the terminally ill. People with HIV-AIDS are socially ostracized and experience prejudices typically expressed against the terminally ill. HIV infection reminds healthy people of their own mortality and ultimate finality. Thinking of individuals with HIV infection as inherently different has the protective function of distancing oneself from the disease and therefore enables one to escape thinking about one's own vulnerability and mortality. Negative attitudes toward HIV infection reflect fears of social loss from death.

**Effects of HIV-related Stigmatization**

*Psychological effects*

Social stigmas become a source of chronic stress for people living with HIV infection. Victims of social stigmatization can become bitter, hostile, suspicious, and alienated. HIV-related stigmas contribute to anxiety, depression, and interpersonal distrust. Social stigmatization occurs across all phases of HIV disease and interferes with coping and adjustment. During asymptomatic HIV infection, when people do not suffer physical debilitation, people with HIV remain potentially discreditable. Threats of stigmatization may inhibit disclosure of HIV infection, therefore cutting off potential social support and creating another source of psychological vulnerability. Crandall and Coleman found that stigma, depression, and anxiety were highest among those whose risk behaviour histories either were not disclosed to anyone or had become completely public. Selective disclosure of HIV seropositivity to close and trusted confidants correlated with adjustment.

Internalized stigmas are another contributing factor to psychological distress. People with HIV infection commonly view the disease as punishment and believe that HIV infection has contaminated all aspects of their life. Moulton *et al.* found that the degree to which people attributed the cause of HIV infection to themselves positively correlated with psychological distress and dysphoria. In contrast, attributing HIV infection to chance or another person corresponds with lower distress.

People with AIDS frequently feel guilty about contracting HIV as well as the possibility that they might have infected others. Similarly, many HIV-positive gay men develop internalized homophobia, where hatred and fear regarding homosexuality turn inward. Gay men with AIDS held negative attitudes toward their own homosexuality and toward disclosure of their sexual orientation. People who contract HIV through heterosexual contact or injection drug use may also internalize responsibility and blame that translates into self-reprehension and distress.

*Effects on interpersonal relationships*

Loss of social support, feelings of isolation, and fear of abandonment commonly occur with life-threatening illnesses. Although seeking social support is an important coping strategy, and social relationships critically effect psychological adjustment and emotional well-being, many people with HIV infection socially isolate themselves. Like other stigmatized groups, people with HIV infection withdraw from social situations and leave themselves vulnerable to psychological distress. People with HIV infection often stop working, as well as limit their participation in social activities, cutting themselves off further from potential sources of support.

HIV-related stigmas influence the amount of social support that others willingly offer. Stigmas and fears make it less likely that individuals with HIV infection will receive support. Acceptance of one's own homosexual orientation opens up opportunities to discuss HIV-positive serostatus and, therefore, positively influences availability of support. As much as stigmas may affect available social supports, they also affect perceptions of received social support. A perceived lack of opportunities for support leaves people vulnerable to distress and maladaptive coping. Even within what at one time may have been a socially supportive network, people with HIV infection may find themselves removed from friends. It is therefore common for people with HIV infection to develop bonds among themselves, as a group with similar experiences.

Associations between HIV-related stigmatization and the quality of interpersonal relationships are reciprocally determined. Stigmas set up expectations for social rejection among people with HIV infection and can cause withdrawal from social relationships. Rejection by family members, friends, and co-workers further reinforces beliefs about being abandoned. Broken social bonds and disrupted supportive networks are therefore the product of social stigmas, through both intrapersonal and interpersonal processes.

*Health effects*

Stigmas present several potential adverse health outcomes. Concerns over discrimination and stigmatization often translate into avoiding HIV testing. Fear of harassment and job discrimination therefore precludes opportunities for early medical interventions. HIV infection can result in loss of health insurance because of the infection being deemed a pre-existing condition, lost employment, or other technicalities. Although not entirely due to social perceptions of HIV disease, discontinued health insurance benefits occur in the context of social stigmatization and therefore becomes incorporated into a broader framework of experiences.

Stigmatization also originates from within the health care system, directly affecting the delivery of medical and mental health services. People with HIV often compare themselves to lepers in the health care system, with impersonal attitudes among hospital staff and isolation within health care facilities.

**Social discrimination**

Discrimination against people with HIV infection originates from the same fears and prejudices that give rise to other forms of stigmatization. For example, foster parents of children with HIV infection fear contracting HIV and express concerns over suffering stigma and discrimination themselves for raising the child. Ridicule, interpersonal violence, housing eviction, loss of insurance, denial of health and dental care, loss of supportive services, and loss of employment are also common.

Discrimination occurs for most HIV-positive gay men, injection drug users, school-age children, and prostitutes. Crystal and Jackson found that 11 per cent of the HIV-positive gay men in their study had lost their housing because of fears and discrimination. Family members and caregivers of HIV-positive people also often suffer similar forms of social discrimination.

*Social stigmatization by medical professionals*

Studies consistently show that many medical professionals hold attitudes toward people with HIV mirroring those of society in general. Medical staff report anxiety-like reactions to HIV-positive patients and feel reluctant to offer them treatment. Wallack found that 87 per cent of physicians and nurses experience more anxiety about caring for AIDS patients than other patient groups. Nurses who care for haemophilia patients are troubled by fears of contracting the virus. Caring for people with HIV infection can be more stressful than working with other equally serious medical disorders. Several factors contribute to reluctance to provide health services to people with HIV infection. Willingness to provide services was predicted by fears of contracting HIV from patients, worries about contact with hazardous materials such as injection needles or surgical instruments, negative attitudes toward homosexuals and injection drug users, and death anxiety raised by terminally ill patients. Fears of contracting HIV infection and death anxiety interrupted the delivery of health services to patients with HIV infection. Because HIV is transmitted through blood, medical professionals who perform invasive procedures most commonly fear HIV infection. In one study, 60 per cent of medical personnel expressed concern over risks of HIV infection, with the greatest fear occurring among surgeons and emergency room physicians. Thus, fears of HIV transmission persist despite practicing well-established occupational precautionary guidelines. Concern over occupational HIV transmission among health care workers is explained by distrust of technology, instrumentation, information, and authorities. Health care workers are aware that standard precautionary procedures reduce risk but do not guarantee protection against accidental HIV transmission.

Inaccurate estimates of the relative risks of various medical procedures fuel fears of occupational transmission. Professionals may believe that HIV transmission occurs from ways in which no one has ever become infected. Even highly knowledgeable medical professionals exaggerate odds of contracting HIV infection. Fears of HIV transmission by medical procedures exceed actual risks. Risks related to medical accidents, such as needlestick injuries, are the product of three probabilities: the probability of the injury × the probability that the patient involved is HIV positive × the probability of risk of HIV transmission associated with that type of accident.

Thus, the estimated probability of contracting HIV from an occupational needlestick accident is a small fraction of 1 per cent. Under most conditions, therefore, risks through medical accidents, even relatively common accidents like needlesticks, are exceedingly low. The same factors that foster exaggerated risk perceptions in the general public cause medical professionals to overestimate their risk. Factors unrelated to fear of HIV transmission, however, influence avoidance of patients with HIV infection like homophobia and negative attitudes towards injection doing users. For example, nurses prefer to care for patients infected through blood transfusions as opposed to those infected through homosexual activity. Kegeles, Coates, Christopher *et al.* also found that between 25 per cent and 33 per cent of health care providers preferred to treat individuals infected with HIV through blood transfusion compared with HIV-positive gay men and injection drug users.

Stigmatization of HIV-positive patients by health care providers may also develop out of concerns over their own repercussions for treating HIV-infected patients. Providers may feel helpless and ineffective when dealing with HIV-AIDS patients, particularly when professionals have had minimal training and limited experiences with HIV infection. Few resources, limited support, and increased workloads associated with these difficult cases lead medical professionals to fear excessive stress and burnout.

Because most HIV-infected patients are uninsured, they may pose a financial liability to health care professionals. Finally, health care providers have expressed concern over the possibility of spreading HIV infection to their friends and family should they become infected while on the job. As many as two thirds of professionals report that friends or family members express similar concerns about contact with them should their practice include HIV-positive patients.

*Social stigmatization by mental health professionals*

Mental health professionals working in nonmedical settings do not have any occupational risk for HIV infection. Nevertheless, fears and negative attitudes are common among mental health professionals. Social stigmatization of HIV-positive individuals here again stems from homophobia, prejudice against injection drug users, and death anxiety. In a study of hospital-based social workers, 80 per cent unwilling to accept clients with AIDS into their caseloads.

Social workers feared contracting HIV infection from HIV-positive clients, suggesting widespread misinformation and prejudice. Social workers lacked empathy for HIV-positive clients and attempted to maintain distance from them. Stigmatization of HIV infection by mental health professionals appears to mirror that of medical professionals and the general public. Professionals, like the general public, distrust authoritative sources of information about HIV transmission and commit cognitive errors that result in overestimation of risk for infection. Thus, widely held social and cultural values fuel most negative attitudes toward people with HIV infection.

**Employment discrimination**

HIV infection is frequently concealed from employers. Workplace discrimination can include reduced responsibilities, isolation from co-workers or the public, lay-off, or termination. Isolation or termination causes loss of social relationships and a diminished sense of self-worth. Although job termination on the basis of illness is legal when physical limitations prohibit the performance of required duties, there is protection against discrimination for disabled individuals.

HIV-positive people in service-providing occupations are especially vulnerable to discrimination. Employers, like many people, hold irrational beliefs that HIV-positive employees will threaten the health of customers or clients. Even employers who know that HIV is not transmitted on the job may realistically fear that the public will not understand and that their business could be adversely affected if an HIV-positive employee became known.

## Psychological Sequelae

The threats of HIV infection to mental health, social relationships, and quality of life were recognized early in the AIDS epidemic. The first studies of psychological adjustment to HIV infection found significant distress and maladjustment among infected individuals. The psychological aftermath of HIV infection, however, has a range as broad as the HIV disease process itself and is as diverse as the individuals affected. Factors such as psychological disturbances predating HIV infection, comorbid substance abuse, and social disenfranchisement increase the psychological vulnerability that usually occurs with life-threatening illnesses. Acute psychotic reactions are even observed in some instances among HIV-positive people not known to be substance abusers and who did not present with central nervous system disease.

**Methodological issues**

There are several methodological constraints commonly found in this literature that should be addressed before discussing psychological reactions to HIV infection. AIDS first emerged as a world health crisis in the absence of theory, prior research, and understanding of the disease. A lack of theoretical models of human sexuality and the political issues surrounding research on sexual and drug-using behaviors further stifled systematic investigations. Because studies were initiated in response to the crisis of a new epidemic, it was impossible for research to benefit from prior empirical findings.

As the epidemic emerged, little was known about the people most affected. Years of neglect in psychological research of the urban poor, gay and bisexual men, ethnic minorities, and injection drug users created a vacuum for research on AIDS. For these reasons, the context of HIV-related emotional distress is not well understood. The first several years of psychological and social research on HIV-AIDS were therefore atheoretical, exploratory, descriptive, and methodologically limited. Three major methodological issues are discussed in this chapter: changes in context over the epidemic, sample selection, and measurement.

*Variations over the course of the epidemic*

Changes in medical terminology, advances in diagnostic procedures, scientific discoveries, and new treatments continuously shape the HIV epidemic. For example, updated case definitions of AIDS, which occurred in 1985, 1987, and 1993, have affected personal perceptions of health and illness. Changes in the 1993 AIDS case definition brought many HIV positive asymptomatic patients to be diagnosed with AIDS on the basis of impaired immunologic functioning. Many study findings prior to 1993 now provide little understanding of the experience of being diagnosed with AIDS, because the physical condition and medical status of people with AIDS has changed.

This is particularly true for studies that compared groups of asymptomatic patients with those experiencing early symptoms and those diagnosed with AIDS. It is impossible to know from the pre-1993 literature whether people given an AIDS diagnosis were responding to serious illness or to the news that they had a terminal illness, whereas today serious illness and an AIDS diagnosis can be independent events. Studies published prior to 1987 were generally conducted before 1985, before the HIV antibody test became available. Therefore, early studies are necessarily limited to symptomatic patients. Thus, the point in the epidemic when a study was conducted must be considered when interpreting its findings.

Similarly, the availability of antiretroviral therapy and medical prophylaxis has rapidly changed, and with it expectations for survival, quality of life, and optimism. For example, zidovudine at first raised hope for significantly increasing the length of survival with HIV infection. However, since then widespread use and scientific study have found that antiretroviral drugs have only limited effects, and hope has subsequently diminished.

Study designs also affect interpretations of findings. Results from cross-sectional designs are influenced by changes in understanding of the disease, treatments, and social climate. On the other hand, longitudinal cohort designs involve highly selective samples that are sensitized to measures and repeatedly exposed to diagnostic evaluations, treatment opportunities, and other aspects of long-term study participation. Another methodological issue in this literature is that, with few exceptions, studies have not assessed the prevalence of psychological distress and maladjustment prior to HIV antibody testing. Subpopulations with high base rates of psychological disturbances may present as psychologically distressed upon testing HIV-positive, whereas those who are wen adjusted before getting tested may adjust better.

**Sampling issues**

The majority of studies of psychological adjustment to HIV infection have oversampled gay men, most of whom were caucasian, well-educated, and of middle to upper incomes. Although representative of the early US epidemiology of HIV infection, these findings may not generalize to other subpopulations affected by HIV and AIDS, particularly women and ethnic minorities. Recent studies from outside of the centers of the HIV epidemic have been somewhat more diverse in sampling gender and ethnicity.

**Measurement issues**

Studies of the psychological sequelae of HIV infection contain a number of measurement problems. Like most areas of applied clinical research, studies have relied on self-report measures of psychological distress and on in-depth diagnostic interviews. However, the clinical course and symptoms of HIV disease are confounded with indicators of depression and anxiety tapped by self-report assessments and interview-based diagnostic systems.

Many constitutional symptoms of depression, including fatigue, night sweats, gastro-intestinal disturbances, loss of appetite, poor concentration, and unintentional weight loss, overlap with HIV-related illnesses. Distress measures and illness symptoms overlap most during the early symptomatic phases of HIV infection. Signs of encephalopathy, including forgetfulness, poor concentration, confusion, irritability, psychomotor retardation, decreased alertness, apathy, withdrawal, and diminished interest in pleasurable activities, also occur during early HIV symptomatic phases. Neuropsychological symptoms can mimic the clinical picture of depression and confound assessments of depression. Unfortunately, the degree to which symptoms result in misdiagnoses of psychiatric or physical illness is not known.

Overall, depressed individuals report more HIV-related illness symptoms and have lower T-helper cell counts, again pointing to the comorbidity of distress and disease and suggesting a reciprocal process between them. Assessment instruments of anxiety also overlap with symptoms of HIV infection. Autonomic nervous system reactivity that causes agitation, nausea, dizziness, tremors, perspiration, skin rashes, and gastrointestinal disturbance may be mistaken for signs of advancing HIV disease or medication side effects.

Conversely, medical illness and medication side effects may be misattributed to anxiety.

Misattribution of physical symptoms of HIV infection to anxiety may be a part of the patient's denial that can interfere with seeking medical treatment. The mirroring of symptoms between distress and physical illness can become a vicious cycle between increased anxiety and perceptions of progressing illness. Several methodological procedures can correct for the overlap between disease and distress symptoms. For the most part, researchers have considered behavioural and physical symptoms of depression and anxiety conceptually important and retained these items on assessment instruments. Other studies, however, have controlled for symptom overlap by altering instruments. For example, Kertzner et al. removed overlapping indicators of anxiety and HIV infection from the Hamilton Rating Scale for Anxiety, resulting in a measure that mostly reflected cognitive and affective dimensions.

Yet another approach has been to use statistical techniques to control for symptom overlap. For example, Kelly, Murphy, Bahr, Koob, et al. partialed both length of time since testing HIV positive and number of HIV-related symptoms out of the depression measure in multiple regression analyses. This methodology allowed investigation of predictors of depression while controlling for the potential confounds of overlapping symptoms. Through each of these methods, researchers have attempted to minimize the influence of illness-related symptoms on elevations of measures of psychological distress.

A final measurement problem has been an over-reliance on single items to assess complex constructs. For example, Joseph *et al*. used a single item from the Hopkins Symptom Checklist to measure suicidal intention. Similarly, Perry, Jacobsberg, and Fishman relied on a single item from the Beck Depression Inventory to detect suicidal ideation and intention. As an assessment of death anxiety, Catania, Turner, Choi, and Coates used one item from the Brief Symptom Inventory. The low reliability of single items therefore limits several study findings.

**Psychological distress reactions**

Multiple factors interact in HIV-related distress, including perceived responsibility for having contracted HIV, the potential for having unknowingly placed others at risk, and changes in physical appearance that may occur in late stages. HIV related depression is also fostered by a sense of pessimism and hopelessness. Knowing others infected with HIV and suffering multiple losses also exacerbate psychological distress. Cultural variations occur with respect to behavioural and physical manifestations of psychological distress, because some cultures promote expressing anxiety and depression through somatic symptomatology that may mimic symptoms of HIV infection. Psychological distress among people with HIV infection is as diverse as the epidemic itself. Reactions to HIV infection may include feelings of sadness, worry, despair, and confusion, as well as other affective, cognitive, and beha-vioural responses. Several medical events occur over the course of HIV infection that serve as markers for vulnerability to psychological distress.

Distress occurs in response to the initiation of treatment, the development of symptoms, the onset of opportunistic illnesses, the occurrence of the first AIDS defining conditions, and declines in immunologic markers. Figure 1 presents HIV-infection-related events and their potential meaning. Early in HIV infection, routine T-helper lymphocyte counts can become the focus for self-monitoring disease progression. At later times, hospitalizations have strong emotional impact, shattering denial and other coping strategies that may have been effective during asymptomatic periods. Because many events, including fluctuations in T-helper cell counts and hospitalizations, are of limited prognostic value, the evaluation of irrational reactions to events is clinically essential.

| *AIDS-related event* | *Psychological meaning* |
|---|---|
| HIV+ test result | Certainty of HIV infection |
| Decision to initiate treatment | Information seeking and sorting |

| | |
|---|---|
| Declining T-Helper cells | Monitoring of HIV activity |
| Development of early HIV symptoms | Recognition of advancing HIV disease |
| Development of early HIV symptoms -AIDS diagnosis | Entering final phases of HIV disease |
| First Hospitalization | Physical debility and increased dependence |

*Figure 1: HIV-related life events and their psychological meaning*

The result of simultaneous HIV-related events can be emotionally devastating. Individuals with high-risk behavior histories often seek HIV testing after developing symptoms. Thus, immediately upon learning that one is HIV-positive, it is also necessary to make treatment decisions. Advanced immune suppression can mean that a newly diagnosed patient will simultaneously suffer opportunistic illnesses, exacerbating an already catastrophic event. In contrast, when events of HIV infection occur sequentially over a longer period of time, distress reactions may not be of clinical significance.

The most frequently diagnosed clinical syndrome associated with HIV infection is adjustment disorder with features of anxious, depressed, or mixed mood. O'Dowd et al. identified two thirds of 183 persons with HIV infection in New York City as having adjustment disorder. Rundell, Paolucci, Beatty, and Boswell diagnosed adjustment disorder in 64 per cent of admissions to an Air Force HIV clinic.

Interestingly, a similar situation exists for cancer patients, where 68 per cent of patients with a DSM-III-R diagnosis have an adjustment disorder. It is the necessary presence of an identified stressor, such as a medical illness, for the diagnosis of adjustment disorder that is apparent in these findings. Adjustment disorder can be chronic and recurrent. Maladjustment is greatest when the source of distress is unresolvable, as is the case with HIV infection. Persistent maladjustment is also more likely among people with a history of psychological disturbances, as is the case for a large number of people with HIV infection.

*Depression*

Depression has been the most frequently studied psychiatric condition among HIV-positive patients. In addition to the enormous challenges posed by confronting a life-threatening illness, several characteristics of HIV infection have led investigators to hypothesize that patients will experience clinical depression.

Perry, Jacobsberg, Fishman, Frances, et al. reported that 43 per cent of men and 49 per cent of women at risk for HIV infection who elected to undergo HIV antibody testing had a history of mood disorders, a rate nearly seven times that of age-matched community samples. Characteristics of HIV infection may also increase risk for depression. Knowing that treatments are limited and that HIV infection is incurable leads to pessimism. Negativistic thinking is fueled by the knowledge that HIV infection will eventually lead to physical deterioration, social disruptions, and occupational limitations.

Despite these and other characteristics of HIV infection, it is not possible to conclude that depressive symptoms are entirely situational. Although depression may be a response to HIV-related stressors, depression may also result from HIV infection of the central nervous system, or may co-occur with an underlying substance abuse disorder. Like depression in general, it is estimated that 50 per cent of individuals with HIV infection who are depressed will eventually have recurrent depression during the course of their illness.

Depression has been reported, to varying degrees, in several studies of HIV-positive patients. Although less common than once believed, depressed mood is among the most frequent psychological reactions to HIV infection. Studies of HIV-positive gay men, injection drug users, and army personnel, hemophiliacs, as well as heterogeneous samples, have all found that people with HIV infection are more likely depressed than non-HIV-infected populations.

It must also be noted that depression among HIV-positive persons, measured by both self-report and interview assessments, may be inflated because of symptom overlap between depression and HIV infection. To control for this potential confound, Belkin et al. used a depression screening instrument that was void of behavioral and physical symptoms of depression. Belkin et al. found that 41 per cent of men and 54 per cent of women with HIV infection showed substantial evidence of depression, relative to 22 per cent of non-HIV-infected primary care medical outpatients screened on the same instrument.

Thus, studies using clinical diagnostic interviews as well as self-report assessments have found depression to be common among HIV-positive individuals. Although depressed mood is associated with HIV infection, some studies have found that relatively few HIV-positive patients are clinically depressed. For example, R. C. Kessler et al. reported that only 12 per cent of people with HIV infection scored beyond the psychiatric outpatient mean on the Hopkins Symptoms Checklist Depression Scale, with most scores falling between psychiatric outpatients and the general population. Likewise, O'Dowd and McKegney found that although 33 per cent of injection drug users with AIDS were depressed, the rate of depression was similar to the 35 per cent depression among HIV-negative medical patients.

A study of gay men found similar rates of depression for HIV-positive and HIV-negative men; previous history of an affective disorder was the best predictor of depression regardless of HIV sero status. In two large cohorts of gay men, approximately 20 per cent of the HIV-positive men exceeded clinical cut-offs on the CESD. Finally, J. B. W. Williams et al. found that HIV-positive gay men scored relatively low on the Hamilton Rating Scale for Depression. Williams et al. also found that depression among HIV-positive men was not significantly different from depression observed in their HIV-negative counterparts.

Therefore, although depression is common to HIV infection, affective disturbances are not universal or even usual in this population and do not necessarily reach clinical proportions. The symptoms of depression for HIV-infected persons are not substantially different from those seen in people who suffer other catastrophic life events. Depression consists of four interactive dimensions: emotional affective symptoms, cognitive symptoms, behavioural symptoms, and vegetative symptoms. People who are HIV positive and depressed likely experience all four dimensions of depression, with protracted sadness, demoralization, diminished self-esteem, sense of worthlessness, disturbances in eating and sleeping, psychomotor retardation, and social withdrawal.

Some features of depression, however, have been discussed as particularly prominent among clinically and subclinically depressed people with HIV infection. For example, one study reported depressed affect as the most frequently endorsed indicator of depression on the CESD in the Chicago MACS cohort. Bornstein et al. noted that psychornotor slowing in depression has a significant effect on concentration, attention, and memory and could lead to mistaken concerns about early HIV encephalopathy. However, depression has not been reliably associated with neuropsychological test performance decrements in people with HIV infection.

Social dimensions of depression appear particularly relevant to HIV infection. It is well recognized that social supports insulate people from depression. Because HIV infection has thus far been concentrated in groups that are on the fringe of the dominant middle class, individuals with HIV infection appear particularly vulnerable to depression. Varying degrees of stability in social relationships may influence depressive mood in important ways.

Depression can result in occupational problems, including absenteeism and declining productivity. Here again, HIV disease interacts with depression, because similar social and occupational dysfunctions ensue as a result of HIV-related stigmatization, discrimination, and physical limitations. Social disruptions related to HIV infection, such as denied access to public services and delayed health care, can exacerbate depressive reactions. HIV-related depression includes demoralization stemming from multiple interpersonal and interpersonal losses, disabilities, and prejudices.

Another feature of depression particularly relevant to HIV infection is the hopelessness of having an incurable, degenerative, and stigmatizing disease. Rabkin et al. have provided the most extensive study of hope in HIV-AIDS. Rabkin et al. found expected correlations between hopelessness and depression in a sample of HIV-positive gay men in New York City. In this study, 24 per cent of the sample obtained elevated scores on the Beck Hopelessness -Scale, classifying them with moderate to severe hopelessness. Rabkin et al. also found that hopelessness was closely related to depression, over and above HIV status and number of HIV symptoms.

This is an important finding because unlike most measures of depression, including the Beck Depression Inventory, hopelessness is primarily a cognitive and affective response and is not contaminated by overlapping physical symptoms of HIV infection. Similar findings were reported by D. Miller and Riccio in a study of hopelessness among HIV-positive hemophiliacs. Thus, hopelessness is a primary component of depression for many HIV-positive people. It should be noted that the role of hope in depression among HIV-positive women has not yet been studied and that the degree to which these findings generalize to women is not known.

Kelly, Murphy, Bahr, Koob, et al. showed that viewing chance as the locus of control for HIV-AIDS significantly predicted CESD depression scores, over and above number of HIV symptoms and length of time since testing HIV positive. Thus, a sense of having little control, albeit mostly consistent with reality, potentially contributes to hopelessness and depression in HIV infection. Several other factors co-vary with depression in HIV infection. With respect to age, for example, more severe depression occurs among younger persons with HIV infection in samples of homosexually active men and blood donors. Low self-esteem, diminished social functioning, low socioeconomic status, and limited participation in health-promoting behaviors are also associated with depression in HIV infection, although the direction of these relationships is not clear. Finally, bereavement, as would be expected, is often reflected in the depression of people with HIV-AIDS.

*Grief and bereavement*

Although grief is a normal response to loss, deaths of loved ones have potential detrimental psychological and physical effects. Two factors appear important in determining responses to AIDS-related losses: the number of losses incurred over a period of time and the HIV serostatus of the bereaved person. Multiple losses to AIDS result in severe emotional disturbance. Nearly one third of bereaved gay men in a New York City cohort experienced two or more losses in the past year, and nearly half of those men had three or more losses in that time. Such rates of death among young adults have been virtually unknown outside of war.

Bereavement over AIDS-related deaths appears most pronounced among people who are themselves HIV-positive. Given that HIV is principally spread through sexual behavior and needle sharing, people with HIV infection experience multiple losses because of the prevalence of HIV in their social networks. Witnessing the degenerative effects of HIV infection, the onset of AIDS, and the eventual death of a friend or relationship partner provides vivid images that prompt thoughts of one's own impending illness.

Observing someone with HIV infection become ill may lead to the belief that one is nearing final stages of HIV infection. People bereaved over an AIDS-related death may seek mental health services to adjust to their own AIDS-related concerns rather than to work through bereavement and grief. In a 7-year prospective study of gay men in New York City, J. L. Martin and Dean found that men who were both HIV positive themselves and bereaved over the loss of someone to AIDS consistently reported greater distress on every measure administered over the course of the entire study. Thus, multiple losses to AIDS substantially contributes to the psychological distress of HIV infection. Trends in psychological reactions to AIDS-related deaths, however, have changed over the course of the epidemic. Neugebauer et al. observed a pattern of decreasing adverse effects of loss over the second decade of AIDS among gay men in New York City. Neugebauer et al. concluded that the expanding scope of the epidemic has led to a gradual normalization and expectation for death at young ages.

*Suicidal risk*

Depression and hopelessness in response to HIV infection has led to the recognition that HIV-positive persons may be at increased risk for suicide. People with HIV infection have higher levels of suicidal ideation and more frequent suicide attempts when compared with their non-HIV-infected counterparts. Perry, Jacobsberg, and Fishman reported that suicidal thoughts, but not attempts, occurred after receiving HIV test results in over 15 per cent of individuals who tested HIV-positive.

Pergami et al. found high rates of attempted suicide among people seeking HIV testing; a history of self-inflicted harm was found for 14 per cent of people who were getting tested and who subsequently tested HIV positive, and for 22 per cent of those who were to test HIV negative. However, after receiving HIV test results, 21 per cent of HIV-positive individuals attempted suicide, compared with none of those who tested HIV negative.

In a prospective study, Perry, Jacobsberg, and Fishman used the suicidal ideation item on the Beck Depression Inventory as an index of suicidal tendency. This study found that 30 per cent of people undergoing HIV antibody testing reported suicidal ideation before being tested, whereas 27 per cent of HIV-positive and 17 per cent of HIV-negative individuals continued to consider suicide 1 week after receiving their HIV test results. Perry et al. found that suicidal ideation occurred in 16 per cent of both HIV-positive and HIV-negative people two months following test result notification. Thus, thoughts of suicide in relation to HIV testing may be greatest before result notification and within the first weeks of receiving results.

Studies have reported that suicides attempted by people with HIV infection occur relatively early in HIV disease, with risk for suicide most elevated among people with early symptoms of infection. AIDS patients were comparable in suicide risk to non-HIV-infected medical patients facing other life-threatening illnesses.

The onset of symptoms may be an important factor in suicidal ideation. Individuals diagnosed with AIDS who are not currently ill, either because their diagnosis was based on T-helper cell counts or because an AIDS-defining condition was successfully treated, may also be at increased risk for suicide because of increased energy to commit the act. Belkin et al. and Donlou et al. both reported close associations between suicidal ideation and HIV symptom intensity and chronicity. In both studies, physical symptoms mediated relationships between depression and suicidal tendencies, with people most likely to think about suicide when simultaneously having physical symptoms of HIV infection and clinical depression. Along with the physical decline of a progressive illness, the threat of long-term dependency leads to increased risk for suicide.

Rabkin, Wilson, and Kimpton found that individuals who expressed a wish to die, although not necessarily to commit suicide, almost always did so under the threat of serious debilitating illness, particularly when faced with an impending hospital admission. Similarly, Belkin *et al.* reported that the association between physical symptoms of HIV disease and suicidal ideation was mediated by the number of days that a person had been bed-bound. In this study, physical symptoms and immobility predicted thoughts about suicide.

For some, thoughts of suicide may also intensify at later points in HIV infection. Rather than being in response to the knowledge of being HIV positive, later considerations of suicide may reflect despair and hopelessness in the face of debilitating illnesses.

The risk for suicide in symptomatic HIV infection and AIDS is between 17 and 66 times higher than for non-HIV-infected comparison groups. A lack of more recent studies, however, limits generalizing these findings to the current state of the epidemic. Common predictors of suicidal tendencies in HIV infection parallel well-established predictors of suicide risk in general. Risk for suicide is greatest among people with HIV infection who have preexisting or coexisting cognitive and affective disturbances, substance use disorders, and poor social supports.

Consistent with non-HIV-infected populations, O'Dowd *et al.* reported that an inpatient psychiatric history was significantly associated with suicidal tendencies across stages of HIV infection and that risk was greatest among those with a prior history of attempting suicide. O'Dowd *et al.* also found that 90 per cent of HIV-positive people who attempted suicide indicated that their first attempt was unrelated to their HIV infection status. Furthermore, similar to non-HIV-infected samples, methods of attempting suicide are highly diverse in HIV infection.

Outside of documenting its prevalence, few studies have investigated the dimensions underlying suicidal risk in HIV infection. Schneider, Taylor, Hammen, Kemeny, and Dudley investigated predictors of suicidal ideations among 100 HIV-positive and 112 HIV-negative men in the Los Angeles MACS cohort. Notification of positive HIV test results, onset of symptoms, number of close friends diagnosed with HIV, knowing someone who died from AIDS, and perceived risk of developing AIDS significantly predicted intentions to attempt suicide. Not having a close friend or confidant, and feelings of loneliness, also predicted suicidal ideations.

With advancing disease, people also may refuse treatment and seek to control the course of their life and death. Psychological despair of advancing disease may therefore inhibit accepting medical interventions and life-sustaining supports. Caregivers may also be asked to help hasten death. One study found that 12 per cent of caregivers of gay men who died of AIDS in San Francisco acknowledged increasing medication doses to hasten death for the person they were caring for.

*Anxiety*

Anxiety disorders and nonclinical anxiety reactions are among the most frequent responses to HIV infection. As noted earlier, people with high risk behavior histories have pervasive worries of being HIV positive. More than 48 per cent of individuals who decline to receive their HIV antibody test results indicate that they would rather not know their HIV zero status because if they were HIV positive they would worry excessively and be unable to cope. Among HIV-positive gay men, R. C. Kessler et al. reported that 12 per cent of their cohort scored above normal levels on a measure of obsessive-compulsiveness. Among HIV-infected hemophiliacs, Dew *et al.* found that 45 per cent of their sample showed greater anxiety than an HIV-negative comparison group. A clinic chart review of depressed patients with HIV infection showed significantly more use of anti-anxiety medications than among a non-HIV-infected depression comparison group matched on sociodemographic characteristics, suggesting frequent comorbidity of depression and anxiety in HIV infection.

Anxiety, like depression, is composed of cognitive, affective, behavioral, and somatic symptoms. Physical symptoms of anxiety stem from autonomic nervous system reactivity, including gastrointestinal, psychomotor, visual, and dermatological disturbances. As discussed earlier, physical symptoms of anxiety can be misattributed to the HIV disease. Comorbidity of somatic symptoms of anxiety and symptoms of HIV infection therefore makes it difficult to disentangle the etiology of physical symptoms.

People with HIV infection feel vulnerable to disease, body disfigurement, prejudices, and becoming dependent on others. There is often concern about eventually developing physical disabilities, social rejection, and isolation. Finally, because HIV is transmissible, HIV-positive individuals feel pressure to protect others from infection while simultaneously protecting themselves from rejection and isolation.

The uncertainties of HIV infection contribute substantially to anxiety, particularly at the onset of early symptoms. In addition, the lack of curative treatments for HIV infection leads to mistrust of medications. Because most antiretroviral medications are taken several times a day, they too serve to constantly remind asymptomatic persons that they have HIV infection.

The progressive and degenerative nature of HIV infection is expected to result in death anxiety. People with HIV infection indicate that the prospect of dying is a major source of anxiety found that 85 per cent of HIV-positive gay men reported worries and concerns related to death, relative to 64 per cent of HIV-negative gay men. Death anxiety is greatest among men experiencing symptomatic HIV infection and increases with the length of time since a person tested HIV positive. Worries about physical decline and fearing dependence on others for basic needs are closely associated with the dying process, and these concerns supercede fears of death itself. As is the case with depression, it should be noted that anxiety can stem from previous histories of affective disturbance. Anxiety varies over the course of HIV infection, and so results depend on when assessments are conducted and which instruments are used.

*Somatization and hypochondriasis*

Somatization provides an example of how HIV infection can be intermeshed with psychological distress. Somatization is the tendency to amplify somatic symptoms of psychological distress and attribute them to physical illness in the absence of corroborating organic pathology. Symptom expectations can produce vague and diffuse physical complaints. In HIV-related somatization, minor physical discomforts associated with distress can heighten concerns about becoming ill. Misperceptions of innocuous's sensations may feed and exacerbate distress, intensifying stress responses that are open to further misinterpretation.

Physical health commonly preoccupies people who recently received a positive HIV test result. Repeated body checking and palpating for swellings, discolorations, blemishes, and other physical changes indicative of HIV-related illnesses can take on an obsessive character and can become maladaptive and disabling. Preoccupations with physical functioning and compulsive symptom checking may develop from premorbid histories of obsessive-compulsive behaviors among both HIV-positive, and non-HIV-infected medical patients.

HIV-related somatization can be initiated or aggravated by non-HIV-related illnesses, such as a cold or the flu. Symptoms of relatively innocuous illness can lead to perceptions of progressing to AIDS. Early symptoms of HIV infection, such as persistent fever or diarrhoea, can bring about somaticizing reactions. However, physical signs of HIV disease appear less important in somatization than attributional processes. Ostrow, Monjan, et al. found that gay men with HIV infection who reported swollen lymph nodes experienced significant psychological distress, regardless of whether enlarged lymph nodes were actually detected upon physical examination. R. C. Kessler et al. demonstrated that physical illness mattered less in HIV-related somatization than perceptions that HIV disease was progressing.

Perry, Ryan, Ashman, and Jacobsberg found that although markers of immune system functioning are not related to concurrent psychological distress, knowledge of T-helper cell counts and intrusive thoughts of somatic functioning did predict distress. In addition, people notified of declines in their immune system functioning become preoccupied with physical illness compared with people with stable immune systems. The use of T-helper cell counts as a benchmark for immune system functioning may also become a means for self-monitoring disease progression. When T-helper cells decline, patients may erroneously expect illness symptoms to quickly follow, and these expectations increase somatic anxiety.

HIV-related somatization appears similar to a condition referred to as *transient hypochondriasis*, a subclinical form of hypochondriasis, characterized by multiple and diffused somatic complaints attributed to undetected medical illnesses. Several aspects of transient hypochondriasis suggest that it may occur in HIV infection. Transient hypochondriasis tends to develop in the context of a life-threatening and terminal medical condition and is related to perceptions that treatments are ineffective. Distortions of physical symptoms tend to focus on a specific ailment. Finally, people most susceptible to transient hypochondriasis tend to have fewer coping strategies than those who are free of these symptoms.

However somatization and physical preoccupation are not universal to HIV infection. Thus, not all patients with HIV infection become preoccupied with physical functioning and symptom checking. Many probably do not recognize actual illness symptoms because they lack awareness of their meaning or are unaware of proper methods of selfdetection.

*Anger and guilt*

Anger and guilt are not regularly assessed in studies of psychological responses to HIV infection. In one of only a few studies investigating anger in HIV infection, McCusker et al. found that HIV-positive gay men were angrier than their HIV-negative counterparts. Anger, frustration, uncertainty, and social rejection contribute to angry reactions to HIV infection. As expected in reactions to sexually transmitted diseases, guilty feelings are a part of HIV infection. Self-blame, shame, and self-devaluation are among the first emotional responses to an HIV-positive test. These emotions most often stem from beliefs about having engaged in behaviours that resulted in infection, beliefs that the HIV infection is a form of moral retribution or punishment, and the social disapproval of others. Guilty feelings also arise after surviving lovers and friends who die of AIDS. Finally, guilty feelings may arise about having possibly infected others before or after testing HIV positive.

Anger and guilt both come from attributions of blame for HIV infection. Anger can be directed outward toward the person believed to have transmitted the virus to the infected person, medical caretakers unable to cure the disease, or society for failing to respond with urgency and compassion. Anger directed inward is similar to guilt and can stem from beliefs about having taken irresponsible risks, failing to recognize risky situations, or falsely trusting what appeared to be safe situations. Guilt is also fostered by social stigmas attached to sexual and drug use behaviors and may stem from discrepancies among behavior, moral beliefs, and social judgments. Anger and guilt are therefore emotional reactions that warrant careful consideration in clinical evaluations.

## HIV-related Ddistress Reactions

The literature on the psychological sequelae of HIV infection suggests that depression, anxiety, and somatization are the most prominent and intensely experienced psychological reactions to HIV infection. However, it is not possible to discern from studies whether these emotions are the most commonly experienced or merely the most frequently studied. Psychological reactions to HIV infection are consistent with those known to occur in response to other life-threatening circumstances.

Like HIV infection itself, psychological reactions are both chronic and phasic. Depression, anxiety, and somatization ebb and flow over the course of HIV infection, subsiding at some points and later surfacing in response to both internal and external events. The psychological and social demands of HIV infection change over the course of HIV disease. For example, psychological distress commonly occurs with notification of HIV-positive test results and subsides shortly after an adjustment period. Distress often recurs in conjunction with knowledge of drops in T-helper cell counts, the onset of HIV-related illnesses, and the death of a friend or partner to AIDS. Suicide risk increases, decreases, and changes meaning with repeated episodes of illness. An emotional roller coaster therefore best describes the catastrophic life events that occur over the course of HIV disease, with reactions changing unpredictably at each phase.

*Emotional reactions*

It is useful to describe the psychological dimensions of HIV infection in context of phases of HIV disease progression. Although there are several cohorts of HIV-positive people, only a few studies have reported changes in psychological functioning over the natural history of HIV infection. Psychological reactions are usually reported at one point in time, such as notification of HIV test results, asymptomatic periods, the onset of early symptoms, or during AIDS.

An approximate chronological representation of psychological sequelae follows the three major phases of HIV infection: absence of detectable symptoms, onset of early symptoms, and late illness. This layout of psychological sequelae assumes a sequential unfolding of the disease where people learn that they are HIV positive while still asymptomatic. However, people who learn their HIV status after developing symptoms of HIV-related illnesses are likely to have different reactions.

In such cases, each phase of disease yields more complex and intensified emotions. Therefore, rather than a linear progression, psychological reactions to HIV infection represent cycles of emotions usually initiated by HIV-AIDS-related events Although certain reactions infection, are not tied to particular points in HIV infection, the stages of disease provide a useful framework for conceptualizing psychological reactions.

*Asymptomatic phases*

Psychological reactions tend to be intense early in HIV infection, regardless of whether a person expects beforehand that he or she is HIV positive. Receiving a positive test result sets off a cascade of psychological responses that are best characterized as an acute distress reaction, including confusion, bewilderment, and emotional turmoil. Initial reactions to testing HIV positive include psychological numbness and disbelief. Cognitive dysfunction, psychomotor slowing, and feelings of fear, sadness, guilt, and anger are also common.

Atkinson et al. reported that most people with HIV infection who develop generalized anxiety disorder report the onset of symptoms at the time of HIV diagnoses testing. Maj reported that as many as 90 per cent of recent diagnoses of HIV infection result in acute distress. Initial responses to HIV-positive test results therefore mirror other catastrophic stress reactions. Acute distress following diagnosis with HIV infection may include symptoms of depression and somatization. Perry, Fishman, *et al.* found that more than one third of people with early HIV infection showed signs of immediate emotional distress, and one third of this group met diagnostic criteria for *DSM-III-R* clinical diagnoses.

Hopelessness, maladaptive behaviours, health-compromising behaviours and increased potential for suicide have all been observed early in HIV infection. Initial reactions to testing HIV positive precede long periods of psychological adaptation, eventually progressing toward acceptance. Early in the adaptation process, denial is a short-term compensatory mechanism. Denial may include repeated HIV testing and numerous calls to physicians and counsellors. Even upon intellectually accepting HIV seropositivity, emotional disbelief often persists.

Prospective studies show that distress declines over repeated assessments. Rabkin et al. found that symptoms of depression and generalized anxiety significantly declined over a 6-month inter-assessment interval. Cleary, Van Devanter, et al. also reported reduced depression 2 weeks following HIV test result notification, with similar declines in distress following diagnosis reported by other investigators. Most compelling, however, has been a prospective study in New York City that showed severity of depression in HIV-positive individuals to significantly decline 6 months after notification of HIV test results.

Overall psychological distress one year after receiving results for asymptomatic HIV-positive individuals did not significantly differ from their HIV-negative counterparts. In another study, HIV-positive asymptomatic patients responded more favourably to antidepressant medications than did people with early and late symptomatic HIV disease, suggesting that HIV-related depression, at least early in the course of infection, responds well to treatment.

*Early symptomatic phases*

The onset of HIV-related symptoms gives new meaning and urgency to being HIV positive. The first signs of illness can cause a resurgence of depression, anxiety, somatization, and other mood disturbances. Early symptoms tend to prompt generalized anxiety, despair, tension, physical preoccupation, and substance use relative to both asymptomatic and late symptomatic periods. The first physical signs of disease can signal the progression of infection, creating thoughts of soon developing AIDS. Symptoms may also fuel beliefs that medications and other treatments have not impeded the progression of the virus.

In addition to first onset of symptoms, the frequency of illnesses elicits psychological reactions. Numbers of symptoms significantly correlate with emotional distress and subjective impressions of declining physical health.

Depression assessed by self-report instruments correlates with HIV symptoms, even when affective and somatic symptoms of depression are assessed independently.

One study showed that people with symptomatic HIV infection scored significantly higher on the Beck Depression Inventory and the State-Trait Anxiety Inventory than both HIV-positive asymptomatic and HIV-negative people. Ostrow, Monjan, et al. reported that individuals with HIV-related symptoms were five times more likely to be depressed.

In contrast with relationships between symptoms of HIV infection and depression, two studies have failed to identify associations between number of HIV symptoms and feelings of hopelessness. This lack of association may be accounted for by the absence of overlap between symptoms of HIV infection and hopelessness. Detecting one's own HIV-related symptoms is directly related to psychological distress. Although severity of symptoms correlates with distress, immune markers for HIV progression have not been consistently related to measures of depression.

Perceptions of symptoms alone do not, however, explain dysphoria with advancing HIV disease, suggesting that multiple factors contribute to the association between illness and distress. Finally, early symptoms of HIV infection rarely cause physical disability and are usually followed by a return to asymptornatic phases and improved psychological functioning.

*Later symptomatic phases and AIDS*

Psychological distress typically returns with an AIDS diagnosis. Following an initial reaction, people living with AIDS are actually less distressed than people at both asymptomatic and early symptomatic phases of infection. These findings differ from those reported in studies of other chronic illnesses, where severity of depression usually increases with severity of medical illness. With other terminal illnesses, depression increases over time because the course of disease tends to be persistently debilitating. In contrast, HIV infection is characterized by long asymptomatic periods followed by symptom onset and return to asymptomatic phases.

With a diagnosis of AIDS may come a sense of relief because a person now knows the extent to which HIV infection has progressed. People with AIDS usually have had time to adjust to earlier symptoms and illnesses. The distress that accompanied earlier symptoms of HIV disease may serve to prepare a person for AIDS.

Long-term survivors with AIDS indicate that the most intolerable aspects of HIV disease include the prospects of protracted pain, declining mental abilities, loss of vision, urinary incontinence, and loss of privacy and personal control. Cognitive disturbances from late-stage involvement of HIV in the central nervous system, potentially resulting in delirium and dementia, further complicate psychological functioning in later phases.

Depression, anxiety, somatization, anger, and guilt characterize the emotional roller coaster of HIV infection. These emotions change rapidly over the course of HIV infection in conjunction with uncertainty about the course of illness. Distress results from testing for HIV antibodies, receiving HIV test results, making life-style adjustments to an HIV-positive status, searching for symptoms, observing others along the spectrum of disease, and fearing the progression of one's own disease.

## NEUROPSYCHOLOGICAL SEQUELAE

The human immune system is the principal site of HIV infection. Numerous other organ systems become infected by the virus. HIV brain infection and AIDS-related opportunistic illnesses of the central nervous system pose some of the most feared HIV-related health problems. Studies conclusively demonstrated that HIV itself crosses the blood-brain barrier and infects brain tissue. Early on, a large number of people with AIDS were thought to develop severe cognitive impairment. The diagnostic label AIDS dementia complex introduced in 1987, served to describe the clinical constellation of neuropsychological symptoms in cases of AIDS.

AIDS dementia complex is diagnosed in 3 per cent of adults and 14 per cent of children with AIDS. It is believed that most HIV-positive people will develop HIV infection of the central nervous system and that between 30 per cent and 60 per cent of all AIDS patients develop symptoms of central or peripheral nervous system disease. In addition, AIDS patients can have opportunistic infections of the nervous system, including toxoplasmosis, cryptococcal meningitis, progressive multifocal leukoencephalopathy (PML), and non-Hodgkin's lymphomas.

*Table 1:*
*Clinical manifestations of HIV-related dementia*

| Domain | Early manifestations | Late manifestations |
|---|---|---|
| Cognitive | Reduced attention and concentration, increased forgetfulness | Generalized dementia |
| Motoric | General slowing, clumsiness, disrupted walking | Paraplegia |
| Behavioural | Apathy, agitation | Mutism |

HIV infection of the brain and opportunistic illnesses of the nervous system must be distinguished. Originally, AIDS dementia complex was defined by cognitive and behavioural deterioration in the absence of an AIDS defining condition of the central nervous system. The parameters for a diagnosis of AIDS dementia complex were self-evident: AIDS reflects the morbidity of neuropsychological impairment relative to other complications of HIV infection; dementia denotes acquired and persistent declines in cognitive functioning observed over the course of late-stage infection; and complex reflects a triad of cognitive, motor, and behaviour dysfunctions.

*Table 2:*
*Clinical staging of AIDS dementia complex*

| *Stage* | *Symptoms and characteristics* |
|---|---|
| 0 (normal) | Normal mental and motor function. |
| 0.5 (subclinical) | Either minimal or equivocal symptoms or motor dysfunction characteristic of HIV-related dementia, or mild signs but without impairment |

| | |
|---|---|
| | of work or capacity to perform activities of daily living; walking and strength are normal. |
| 1 (mild) | Unequivocal symptoms, neuropsychological test performance, or functional, intellectual, or motor impairment characteristic of HIV-related dementia but able to perform all but the most demanding work or daily living tasks; can walk without assistance. |
| 2 (moderate) | Cannot work or maintain demanding aspects of daily life, but able to perform basic activities of self-care; may require assistance in walking. |
| 3 (severe) | Major intellectual incapacity or motor disability, including carrying on conversations, performing daily living tasks; requires walker or personal support in walking, usually motor slowing and clumsiness of arms. |
| 4 (end stage) | Nearly vegetative; intellectual and social comprehension and responses are at very low levels; nearly or absolutely mute; paraplegic with incontinence. |

Like organic mental disorders in general, the essential feature of AIDS dementia complex is a loss of intellectual abilities of sufficient severity to interfere with social or occupational functioning. Although it occurs at all ages, AIDS dementia complex has a greater likelihood of afflicting children. In addition to loss of functions from dementia, children with AIDS experience several developmental delays, motor disturbances, and structural abnormalities of the brain. Table 2 presents the diagnostic staging scheme used for AIDS dementia complex.

**Diagnosis and classification**

Classifications of central nervous involvement of HIV infection have undergone several revisions. For a number of reasons, however, AIDS dementia complex is now viewed as an incomplete description of the neurocognitive effects of HIV infection.

First, although AIDS dementia complex describes a loss of cognitive and motor functioning not attributable to opportunistic infections, malignancies, or systemic HIV disease, dementia does not correctly characterize HIV-related central nervous system disturbances because the cognitive, motor, and behavioural triad does not invariably exist. Second, HIV infection of the brain occurs early in the course of HIV disease, inconsistent with the notion that central nervous system involvement is only associated with AIDS. Finally, earlier and less severe neurological symptoms associated with HIV infection do not approach levels of dysfunction that characterize dementias.

Several new diagnostic labels are now replacing AIDS dementia complex, including HIV-associated neuro-behavioural deficit, and HIV-related or HIV-induced organic mental disorder. The most widely used nomenclature was introduced by the Working Group of the American Academy of Neurology AIDS Task Force.

The system distinguishes two subclasses of HIV-related disorders: HIV associated minor cognitive/motor disorder and HIV associated dementia complex. HIV associated minor cognitive/motor disorder is diagnosed in patients with mild functional impairment, including minimal disruption of their social relationships, occupation, or everyday living. Severe neuropsychological impairment is diagnosed as HIV associated dementia complex, denoting progressive HIV encephalopathy.

The major distinction between the minor and severe subclasses is the degree of functional impairment. HIV associated dementia complex constitutes a combination of clinical symptoms consistent with disturbances of both subcortical and frontal lobe functioning, including cognitive slowing, memory impairment, and behavioural disinhibition.

Available evidence strongly suggests that HIV infection of the brain predominantly affects subcortical brain structures. Damage to the basal ganglia, three large subcortical structures that play critical roles in the functioning of motor systems, results in involuntary movements such as tremors and reduced motor speed without paralysis.

### HIV encephalopathy

Structural damage to the brain because of HIV disease is well established, but clinical signs of higher-order cortical dysfunction, such as verbal responsiveness, aphasia, or emotional reactions, rarely occur. HIV-related encephalopathy involves nonspecific disturbances including clouding of consciousness, dysfunctions in short-term memory, and psychomotor slowing. HIV infection can involve diseases of the spinal cord where dysfunction of the lower extremities is greater than cognitive impairment. Other conditions include peripheral neuropathy, diseases of the peripheral nerves causing both sensory numbness and pain in up to 35 per cent of people with AIDS; and myopathy, slow and progressive weaknesses of the arms and legs.

Although neurological symptoms overlap with other AIDS-related conditions, particularly in later HIV disease, HIV associated minor cognitive/motor disorder and HIV associated dementia complex occur independently of other manifestations of HIV infection. Unfortunately, many of the mechanisms of HIV-related nervous system dysfunction remain poorly understood. HIV-related neuropsychological disturbances do not appear invariably progressive. Symptoms can be static or somewhat reversible, but the determinants of any particular course of disease are unknown. We also do not know whether minor and severe forms of impairment are the same disease entity expressed in different degrees or whether people with minor forms of cognitive decline inevitably progress in severity.

**HIV-related disease of the nervous system**

HIV was isolated from the brain tissue of people with AIDS very early in the U.S. HIV epidemic. Autopsies of people who died from AIDS consistently found that 70 per cent to 90 per cent of cases showed significant central nervous system disease, with structures most affected by HIV involving information transfer across brain regions including central white matter, the thalamus, areas of the brain stem, and basal ganglia.

In addition to postmortem studies, brain imaging research has identified structural damage. Both computed tomography (CT) and magnetic resonance imaging (MRI) have shown that a substantial number of AIDS patients have cerebral cortical atrophy (widening of cortical sulci), scattered brain lesions, and ventricular dilation.

Electrocephalograhy (EEG) has also identified abnormalities in both slowed Alpha rhythms, associated with states of relaxed wakefulness, and diffused Theta waves, normally associated with sleep in adults. However, structural damage and electrical disturbances in AIDS are not directly linked to functional impairment; some people show clinical signs of dementia without apparent HIV encephalitis, whereas others show gross abnormalities on CT and MRI scans but do not indicate problems in functioning. AIDS may also involve spinal cord disease, including vacuolar myelopathy, potentially resulting in spasms of the extremities and significant leg weakness. The peripheral nervous system can become involved with polyneuropathy, which causes painful burning or numbness in the feet and lower legs, or inflammatory demyelinating polyneuropathy, resulting in slowed nerve conduction.

HIV appears to enter the central nervous system shortly after viral transmission. HIV antigens are found in the cerebrospinal fluid soon after infection, and some longitudinal studies have detected HIV in the cerebrospinal fluid of asymptomatic cases within 6 to 24 months following HIV seroconversion. HIV infection of the central nervous system principally occurs in monocyte-derived cells, including macrophages and microglia, cells sharing the same origin as T-helper lymphocytes and carrying out immunological functions in the brain.

HIV does not, however, directly infect neurons or oligodendrocytes (cells that form insulating myelin sheaths that wrap around axons). HIV infection of macrophages in the brain does, however, both cause the loss of neurons and damage cell dendrites, effectively disabling neurons. Table 3. summarizes the areas of the brain most commonly affected by HIV and associated symptoms.

HIV-related neurological damage may have several mechanisms, including autoimmune responses, where cell destruction is caused by immune system attacks on HIV-infected immunological cells. Synergy of HIV with other pathogens may cause additional damage. However, most neuronal damage seems to be caused by toxins, either created by viral components of HIV or released from HIV-infected neighbouring cells.

Neurotoxic products of HIV include the viral envelope glucoprotein *gp*120, which disrupts neurons by causing imbalances in intracellular chemistry. Uninfected macrophages respond to HIV envelope proteins by releasing cytokines, a cascade of which interferes with interneuron communication. Brain cells infected by HIV, particularly the macrophages and microglia, release additional neurotoxins that compromise metabolic activities of neurons. Diffuse encephalopathies caused by metabolic and toxic disturbances are also identified by MRI scanning conducted with AIDS patients.

*Table 3:*

*Areas of the brain most commonly affected by HIV*

| *Structures* | *Symptoms* |
|---|---|
| Frontal lobes | Apathy, depression, trouble concentrating, loss of organizational skills |
| Limbic system and temporal lobes | Memory loss and language impairment |
| Basal ganglia | Impaired eye movements, involuntary movements, tremor |
| Brain stem | Disturbed gait, eye-movement dysfunctions, visual disturbances |
| Demyelination | Delayed information processing, slowed responses, impaired fine motor skills, incontinence |

Concurrent with primary HIV infection of the brain, damage often results from systemic diseases, opportunistic infections, and malignancies within and outside of the nervous system. In addition, reduced cerebral blood flow early in HIV infection can cause encephalopathy. Co-infection with other viruses, including HTLV-I, HTLV-II, and cytomegalovirus, may also contribute to brain damage.

Finally, neurologic symptoms may stem from iatrogenic factors, such as direct effects and side effects of treatments for HIV infection and associated ailments. For example, most antiretroviral medications, including zidovudine, ddC, and ddI, can cause neuropathy and even seizures in extreme cases. Like other aspects of HIV disease, multiple sources of damage co-occur and become superimposed because of underlying immune suppression.

Multiple etiologies and interrelated symptoms cause complex neuropsychological impairments in AIDS cases, as well as a variety of neuropsychological disturbances across the HIV disease spectrum. Before reviewing specific neuropsychological impairments related to HIV associated minor cognitive/motor disorder and HIV associated dementia complex, it is important to note several methodological constraints in this literature.

**Methodological issues**

HIV-related neuropsychological impairment research shares many of the problems encountered by early research on other forms of neurological disease and dementias. Studies commonly use diverse assessment batteries, ranging from brief mental status screening examinations to full neuropsychological batteries. Research has often failed to include external behavioural indices of daily functioning to corroborate neuropsychological testing data. Finally, non-neurological factors may cause direct and indirect effects on test results.

*Confounding factors*

Studies of HIV-related neuropsychological impairment have generally failed to control simultaneous causes of disrupted test performance. There is today substantial evidence that depression does not seriously threaten the interpretation of neuropsychological test findings from most people with HIV infection. Many studies fail to identify meaningful associations between measures of depression and functional impairment, performance on standardized neuropsychological batteries, screening measures of cognitive functioning and attention, and tests of memory. Relationships between depression and neuropsychological testing may be attenuated because of the restricted range of minimal neuropsychological impairment during asymptomatic HIV infection and the severe impairment of later phases of HIV associated dementia complex. Other potential confounds in this literature threaten internal validity. Concomitant HIV-related opportunistic illnesses, past and current prescription and illicit drug use, sleep deprivation, and nutritional status may potentially confound neuro-psychological studies.

In addition, education and socioeconomic status may influence neuropsychological test performance, particularly in studies of gay men with higher education and of injection drug users, whose education and socioeconomic status are typically low. Antiretroviral medications may confound studies because they disrupt neuropsychological performance through fatigue and reduced concentration.

On the other hand, zidovudine, particularly at higher doses, may reduce cognitive symptoms of HIV associated dementia complex and therefore improve neuropsychological test performance. In either case, studies of neurological functioning of people taking zidovudine and perhaps other antiretroviral medications could be confounded by effects and side effects of these drugs.

*Sample selection and sample sizes*

Majority of studies on neuropsychological sequelae of HIV infection have investigated predominantly white gay men who have high levels of education, are from higher socio-economic statuses, and are members of cohorts followed in U.S. epidemic centers. Although some studies have targeted injection drug users, few have represented heterogeneous samples of people with HIV infection, and few have included women. Also limiting most studies outside of longitudinal cohorts is ignorance of when participants seroconverted, making it impossible to track effects of HIV on the central nervous system over time.

Additional sampling problems result from methods used for defining symptomatic and asymptomatic comparison groups. For example, Janssen et al. included men with constitutional symptoms of HIV infection in a group classified as asymptomatic, even though constitutional symptoms would have defined these same men as symptomatic in studies using the CDC staging system.

This literature also tends to draw conclusions from small samples, often with less than 30 participants. Studies with small sample sizes have also tended to use large batteries of neuropsychological tests, conducting multiple statistical comparisons without correcting for chance associations.

*Impairment*

The prevalence of neuropsychological deficits in a given sample is a function of the criteria used to define impaired neuropsychological test performance. Studies using lenient criteria to define impairment, such as scores falling within one standard deviation of the mean of a control group, will necessarily differ in prevalence rates from studies using more stringent criteria, such as greater than two standard deviations above a control group mean. More extensive test batteries also yield higher rates of impairment because of the greater likelihood of identifying performance deficits.

Stringent criteria and less extensive test batteries are therefore less sensitive to subtle neuropsychological changes. To address these problems, some studies have used multiple performance criteria for defining impairment, internally controlling for differences among criteria. Thus, rates of neuropsychological impairment at various points along the HIV disease spectrum are directly affected by definitions of test performance.

The literature on neuropsychological sequelae of HIV infection is limited by the characteristics of comparison and control groups. For example, groups of HIV-positive and -negative people are often confounded by history of substance abuse. Furthermore, tests selected for study inclusion necessarily limit the scope of neuropsychological functions investigated.

Finally, studies usually lack non-psychometric data to corroborate neuropsychological test findings. Such external data are essential because neuropsychological test performance does not necessarily translate to impaired occupational, social, and everyday functioning.

**Neuropsychological manifestation**

HIV enters the central nervous system shortly after infection and many individuals with AIDS suffer cognitive decline, but little is known about the mechanisms and course of HIV-related neuropsychological disorders. Available research can, however, describe neuropsychological decrements at early, asymptomatic, and later phases of HIV disease.

*Early HIV infection*

Although most people do not experience cognitive or motor symptoms early in the course of infection, a small number of newly infected persons have some signs of neurological impairment. Acute meningitis and meningoencephalitis occur soon after HIV crosses the blood-brain barrier. When they occur, early neurological symptoms usually overlap with other acute symptoms. Early nervous system infection has symptoms common to non-HIV-related meningitis, including fatigue, headache, sensitivity to light (photophobia), pain around the eyes and facial areas, and leg weakness. The prevalence of early neurological symptoms differs across HIV subgroups, particularly age groups. Infants and young children demonstrate early nervous system involvement more often than adolescents and adults, with progressive encephalopathy in children beginning as early as 2 months.

Young children with HIV infection usually fail to reach developmental milestones, such as sitting up and walking, or lose abilities they once had achieved. Children with HIV infection otherwise show the same features of neuropsychological impairment observed in adults. The course of central nervous system involvement varies in children and, as in adults, can be either progressive or stable.

*Asymptomatic HIV infection*

Much research, discussion, and controversy has been devoted to possible central nervous system dysfunction before significant immune suppression and opportunistic illnesses. Several studies with small sample sizes and extensive testing batteries have demonstrated HIV-related neuropsychological impairment prior to other HIV-related illnesses. Early neuropsychological dysfunction would suggest that HIV can cause insidious damage to the central nervous system prior to symptomatic HIV disease.

Using a one-standard-deviation difference from a control group mean as a criterion for neuropsychological impairment, Bornstein et al. classified 26 per cent of HIV-positive men as neurocognitively impaired, relative to 15 per cent of HIV-negative men. Bornstein et al. showed that degrees of neurocognitive impairment for the HIV-positive sample were twice the magnitude of those observed among HIV negatives. The study also found that neuropsychological impairment was not accounted for by clinical depression and that neuropsychological test performance agreed with self-reported ratings of functional limitations.

Thus, studies that find neuropsychological deficits in asymptomatic HIV infection suggest that only a subgroup, and probably a small group at that, evidences such decline. The MACS cohort provided data from 727 HIV-positive asymptomatic gay men, 84 men with symptoms of HIV disease, and 769 HIV negative men. Using an extensive neuropsychological battery, including the Trail Making Test, Digit Span, a verbal fluency test, the Grooved Pegboard Test, the Symbol Digit Modalities Test, and the Rey Auditory Verbal Learning Test, the study did not identify any significant differences between HIV-positive asymptomatic and HIV-negative men.

Using a two-standard-deviation difference from the HIV-negative group mean as a criterion for impairment, Miller et al. classified 6 per cent of HIV-positive men as impaired relative to 4 per cent of HIV-negative men. When the criterion for impairment was relaxed to one standard deviation from the control group mean, Miller *et al*. classified 37 per cent of HIV-positive and 34 per cent of HIV-negative men as neurocognitively impaired.

Miller et al. also failed to find relationships between immunologic markers and neuropsychological functioning. Subdividing men on the basis of duration of HIV infection also did not-show-any associations with impairment. These findings strongly suggest that neuropsychological deficits in asymptomatic individuals are rare and that changes that do occur are usually modest. The degree to which these results are generalizable to women, however, is not known.

Additional research has failed to find neuropsychological impairment in otherwise asymptomatic HIV-positive people. Egan et al. found no significant cognitive impairment prior to the onset of other HIV-related symptoms in a large cohort of HIV-positive injection drug users.

Other studies using more extensive neuropsychological batteries and experimental memory tasks have failed to distinguish asymptomatic HIV-positive from HIV-negative persons, and studies that have identified central nervous system electrophysiological and structural changes in HIV-positive individuals, such as EEG abnormalities and cerebral atrophy, have not consistently related such abnormalities to clinical impairment. Little evidence, therefore, supports the notion that HIV associated dementia complex is a progressive disorder that has an early onset and evolves during asymptomatic periods.

An absence of detectable cognitive decline over asymptomatic HIV infection further suggests that HIV-related neuropsychological impairment follows the development of substantial immune suppression and usually coincides with opportunistic illnesses, although not necessarily opportunistic illnesses of the central nervous system.

Therefore, a competent immune system may delay the onset of HIV-related cognitive disruptions, encephalitis, and opportunistic illness. However, these conclusions remain tentative because some studies, mostly with small sample sizes and extensive batteries, have identified a small subgroup of asymptomatic HIV-positive individuals with cognitive deficits. In contrast with the controversy over cognitive and motor impairment in asymptomatic phases of HIV infection, there is greater acceptance of the more frequent neuropsychological deficits in later phases of HIV disease.

*Later HIV infection and AIDS*

Neuropsychological dysfunctions of HIV infection are most likely to occur at times of severe immune suppression. Studies have found neurocognitive deficits in 40 per cent to 50 per cent of people with symptoms of HIV infection and 33 per cent to 87 per cent of people with AIDS. As many as

15 per cent of AIDS cases demonstrate abnormal brain structures on CT and MRI scans.

Studies of the clinical symptomatology of HIV-associated neurological impairment suggest that one third of cases eventually develop severe impairment, one third show mild disturbances, and one third experience few or no neurocognitive symptoms. Even when neuropsychological impairment does occur, only a minority of HIV-positive people progress to dementia. Thus, although many individuals with later HIV infection do not demonstrate serious cognitive decline, a sizable proportion of AIDS cases do have some degree of neurological impairment.

A broad range of neurocognitive disturbances occur in later-stage HIV infection. The earliest symptoms include diffused and nonspecific symptoms such as lethargy; social withdrawal; psychomotor slowing, attention, concentration, and retrieval deficits; derailed train of thought; increased difficulty with complex tasks; forgetfulness; clumsiness; and complaints of slowed thinking.

Severe cognitive disturbances of HIV associated dementia complex most often occur late in HIV infection and include declines in social, occupational, and daily functioning, confusion; disorientation; motor losses; and eventual degeneration into a vegetative state. Most commonly, declines occur in information-processing speed and efficiency; impaired memory and learning, and motor disabilities. Cognitive slowing is, however, the most widely observed feature of HIV-associated neurocognitive impairment.

In addition to slowed cognitive processing speed, attention and concentration deficits also occur among some individuals with HIV infection. E. M. Martin, Sorensen, Robertson, Edelstein, and Chirurgi found that HIV-positive men performed less accurately on a subtle visual attention task relative to HIV-negative men. Another study using the same sample reported by E. M. Martin, Sorensen, Robertson, *et al.* showed further evidence for disrupted attention processes using the Stroop colour—word naming task. HIV-positive men had more difficulty than HIV-negative men with controlled cognitive functions on a Stroop task that relies on effortful, voluntary actions that place greater demands on attention.

Additional evidence from divergent neuropsychological measures has also suggested that cognitive and perceptual information-processing disturbances occur at later stages of HIV infection. HIV infection, particularly during later symptomatic phases, also involves deficits in learning and memory. People with HIV infection perform less accurately than HIV-negative control groups on tests of long-term and short-term memory and on verbal learning tasks.

HIV-positive injection drug users also have difficulty with the Finger Tapping Test, an index of fine motor speed. Motor slowing, leg weakness, and loss of mobility can occur in the absence of other cognitive and intellectual dysfunctions.

The risk for neuropsychological impairment increases as HIV disease progresses. Twenty-five per cent of people with AIDS develop clinically significant cognitive impairment within 9 months of their first AIDS-defining condition, and another 25 per cent show impaired functioning within 1 year of diagnosis. Rather than starting out slowly and gradually progressing during asymptomatic phases, HIV-associated neuropsychological impairment seems to follow the onset of systemic HIV manifestations, and its progression usually occurs rapidly.

Although both longer duration of infection and accelerated rates of T-helper cell declines are associated with neuropsychological impairment, deteriorated immune functioning does not reliably predict neurocognitive dysfunction. Because progression of the central nervous system disease does not necessarily follow immune suppression, both immune and neurological declines are correlated but not causally linked. Cognitive disturbances coincide with immune suppression, making it likely that neuropsychological impairment will occur with illnesses. Later HIV infection therefore involves simultaneous vulnerability to HIV-related symptoms, HIV related neurological disorders, and opportunistic illness.

**Opportunistic illnesses of the central nervous system**

Advanced immune suppression leads to increased

susceptibility to infections and malignancies of multiple organ systems, including the nervous system as shown in Table 4.

*Table 4:*
*AIDS-related diseases of the central nervous system*

| *Manifestation* | *Causal agent* |
|---|---|
| Opportunistic viral infections | Cytomegalovirus |
| | Herpesimplex I & II |
| | Herpes zoster |
| | Papovavirus (PML) |
| Fungal and protozoan infections | Toxoplasmosis |
| | Cryptococcus |
| | Candida |
| | Mycobacterium |
| Malignancies | Primary lymphoma |
| | Metastatic lymphoma |
| | Metastatic Kaposi's sarcoma |
| Cerebrovascular conditions | Haemorrhage |
| | Infarction |

Diagnoses of AIDS-related central nervous system opportunistic illnesses are made through CT and MRI scanning, attempts to medically treat neurological symptoms, and brain biopsy. Among the less frequent initial AIDS diagnoses, nervous system disorders often develop during late stages of AIDS.

*Cytomegalovirus*

This infection is highly prevalent, with 95 per cent of HIV-positive gay men carrying antibodies for cytomegalovirus. Although an infrequent manifestation, cytomegalovirus can cause meningoencephalitis, resulting in clouding of consciousness and other disabling symptoms. Cytomegalovirus infection causes several other neuropsychological disturbances. More commonly, cytomegalovirus infects the retinas (CMV retinitis), a serious threat of partial and complete blindness. Cytomegalovirus can also cause demyelination of brain white matter and a subacute encephalitis. Cytomegalovirus may synergistically interact with HIV and other viruses to cause an array of nervous system disorders.

*Progressive Multifocal Leukoencephalopathy (PML)*
This demyelinating disease is caused by activation of a latent papovavirus infection. Progressive deterioration of white matter occurs because the papovavirus attacks oligodendrocytes, resulting in loss of nerve fiber insulation. Changes in mental status, memory loss, motor weaknesses, loss of vision and other sensory functions, and decreased mobility are common consequences of PML. Symptoms of PML develop gradually and significantly reduce AIDS survival time.

*Toxoplasmosis*
The protozoan *Toxoplasma gondii* principally affects the central nervous system as a generalized encephalopathy as well as by causing massive brain lesions. Toxoplasmosis is the most common central nervous system infection in adults with AIDS. Toxoplasmosis encephalopathy includes headache, fever, confusion, lethargy, changes in personality, and delirium. Focal neurologic damage resulting from brain lesions can cause seizures and specific functional deficits. In general, cerebral toxoplasmosis progresses rapidly and seriously threatens permanent brain damage. However, once diagnosed, there are several available medications that effectively treat toxoplasmosis and provide relatively fast symptom relief.

*Cryptococcal meningitis*
Caused by the fungus cryptococcus, an encapsulated yeast, Cryptococcal meningitis is the most common central nervous system fungal infection in AIDS, affecting up to 25 per cent of cases. The symptoms of Cryptococcal meningitis are similar to those of other meningitides, including neck stiffness, headache, photophobia, lethargy, changes in mental functioning, confusion, and sometimes nausea and vomiting. Symptoms can range from mild to severe and can result in encephalitis, causing symptoms that mimic depression.

*Lymphoma*
Central nervous system lymphomas occur in 5 per cent of AIDS cases. Although the brain is rarely the site of primary lymphoma, people with AIDS are nearly 100 times more

likely to develop primary central nervous system lymphoma than the general population. Symptoms include headache, lethargy, and damage to cranial nerves, as well as focal damage caused by specific sites of tumour growth.

HIV-related conditicns may become disseminated to the central and peripheral nervous systems, although most of these occurrences are relatively rare. Herpes simplex viruses I and II can cause encephalitis and meningitis, with acute symptoms of headache, fever, seizures, and abrupt behavioural changes.

In addition to its characteristic painful outbreaks of rash, herpes zoster virus can also cause encephalitis. Candidiasis, a common fungal infection in HIV, can cause brain abscesses in people with AIDS. Coccidioidomycosis and histoplasmosis, also fungi, can cause chronic meningitis. Mycobacterium infection can cause meningitis and brain abscesses. Neurosyphilis may develop or recur with suppressed immunity and is more difficult to treat than primary syphilis. Spread of Kaposi's sarcoma to the central nervous system is also possible, although rare. In addition to infections and malignancies, people with AIDS can suffer strokes because of changes in cerebral vascular walls and blood flow, as well as cerebral haemorrhaged resulting from HIV-related changes in blood clotting factors. Finally, it should be noted that many causal mechanisms of HIV-related diseases of the nervous system are still unknown, particularly diseases affecting the peripheral nervous system.

**Neuropsychological assessment**

Neuropsychological testing in HIV infection is most useful for evaluating subjective reports of decline in cognitive functions, including but not limited to attention, concentration, abstraction, reasoning, visual-perceptual skills, problem solving, mental and motor processing speed, and language. Neuropsychological evaluations inform clinicians of cognitive deficits and can disconfirm mistaken beliefs about losses in cognitive abilities. Factors such as expectancies, anxiety, depression, and systemic illness can contribute to reports of the presence or absence of early neuropsychological symptoms.

Because most cognitive changes in HIV infection are subtle, clinical mental status exams lack adequate sensitivity for reliable assessment. Therefore, comprehensive neuro-psychological evaluations that assess multiple mental faculties, although time consuming, labour intensive, and expensive, remain the most effective method for evaluating cognitive capacities. Several authorities have suggested comprehensive neuropsychological assessment batteries that provide optimal sensitivity to neurocognitive deficits associated with HIV infection.

Clinical findings from a neuropsychological battery usually lack sufficient sensitivity and specificity to diagnose HIV-related neuropsychological impairment. Neuro-psychological testing is most limited early in the course of HIV-related central nervous system disease. When present, early symptoms are usually subclinical and cannot be reliably detected by standard clinical instruments. In addition, although neuropsychological tests can suggest focal lesions, underlying disease processes cannot be determined. The interpretation of neuropsychological tests therefore requires consultation with neurologists and infectious disease specialists.

Differential diagnosis of cognitive dysfunction and affective disorders can pose another obstacle to neuropsychological assessment, particularly in earlier phases of infection. Even when symptoms of depression and anxiety are somewhat distinct from those of mild neurocognitive impairment, negative emotions can disrupt neuro-psychological test performance. Neurological conditions are often accompanied by overlapping symptoms with psychological distress, including indifference, apathy, social withdrawal, emotional blunting, and lethargy.

*Table 5*

*Neuropsychological test battery recommended by a workshop sponsored by the National Institute of Mental Health*

| Cognitive function | Assessment instrument |
|---|---|
| Premorbid intelligence | WAIS-R Vocabulary<br>National Adult Reading Test |
| Attention | WMS-R Digit Span |

| | |
|---|---|
| | WMS-R Visual Span |
| Processing speed | Sternberg Search Task<br>Simple and Choice Reaction Time<br>Paced Auditory Serial Addition Test |
| Memory | California Verbal Learning Test<br>Working Memory Test<br>Modified Visual<br>Reproduction Test |
| Abstraction | Category Test<br>Trails Making Test A and B |
| Language | Boston Naming Test<br>Letter and Category Fluency Test |
| Visual-spatial ability | Embedded Figures Test<br>Money's Standardized Road-Map<br>Test of Direction Sense<br>Digit Symbol Substitution |
| Construction ability | Block Design Test<br>Tactile Performance Test |
| Motor abilities | Grooved Pegboard<br>Finger Tapping Test<br>Grip Strength |
| Psychological distress | Diagnostic Interview Schedule<br>Hamilton Depression Rating Scale<br>State-Trait Anxiety Inventory<br>Mini-Mental Status Examination |

People with asymptomatic HIV infection may report neuropsychological impairment when test results fail to identify even subtle cognitive deficits. Thus, subjective complaints, neurological signs, and brain imaging often do not correspond with laboratory findings. Neuropsychological evaluations in HIV infection require substantial expertise. Interdisciplinary approaches help to fully evaluate cognitive functions in HIV infection and to assure careful medical follow-up.

**HIV-associated functional incapacities**

Physical disabilities that may result from neurological complications of HIV infection range from complete absence of impairment to severe disability. People with central nervous system HIV infection, determined through either examinations of cerebral spinal fluid or radiological imaging, are often completely asymptomatic of neuropsychological impairment. In HIV associated minor cognitive/motor disorder, most complex daily living skills are usually minimally disrupted. Asymptomatic HIV infection usually does not involve cognitive and motor dysfunctions. Early symptoms of HIV infection may include slowed information-processing speed and deficits in verbal memory, but neither of these cognitive domains is affected to the degree of impairment seen in everyday functioning.

Apathy, mental slowing, social withdrawal, and avoidance of complex tasks may occur and pose problems in differential diagnosis with clinical depression, especially as HIV-related illnesses emerge. HIV associated dementia complex and most opportunistic infections and malignancies of the central nervous system pose serious threats to daily functioning in later phases of HIV infection. Impairment can be progressive and affect multiple cognitive and motor abilities.

Opportunistic illnesses may cause diffuse damage or focal lesions. Cognitive and motor disorders related to HIV infection are most likely to co-occur with systemic manifestations of HIV disease and opportunistic illnesses outside of the nervous system. Cognitive and motor impairments also limit coping and adaptation, further complicating efforts to adjust psychologically to HIV disease.

The prospect of losing mental and sensory abilities is one of the most frightening aspects of HIV disease. People who expect to develop cognitive dysfunctions often become hypervigilant and monitor their day-today activities and performance of even simple tasks. Typical forgetfulness or lack of concentration under stress can be misinterpreted as the beginnings of dementia.

Although neuropsychological testing helps to evaluate subjective complaints of cognitive decline, most tests do not detect subtle symptoms. In addition, individuals with HIV infection are usually aware of the potential for neuropsychological impairment and may have known others who have developed neurocognitive dysfunctions. Thus, expectations for HIV-related neuropsychological symptoms create anxieties that amplify normal lapses in cognitive functioning.

HIV-positive individuals, their families, and others in their support networks often benefit from education and counselling about the risks of cognitive decline. HIV patients should be aware that significant deterioration in mental abilities rarely occurs before systemic illness and that many people with HIV infection do not ever decline in neurocognitive functioning.

Counselling may educate about how symptoms of depression, anxiety, and medication side effects can mimic HIV related neuropsychological symptoms. HIV-positive individuals should be informed of the distinctions between HIV-related encephalopathy and opportunistic illnesses of the central nervous system, as well as the different treatment options available for each.

# 7

# Retrovirus Survival: Threat to Mankind

Retroviral movement appears to be largely a function of environmental instability since the main force for retrovirus survival is adaptation to environmental change. Such change may concern the microenvironment of a single host or the macroenvironment of the host community, or a combination of both. The process seems to start at the macro level, where the main factor is the availability of susceptible hosts. After all, if an accustomed host is decimated, a virus dies with the host unless it happens to gain a foothold in a new species. The new host must be susceptible and close at hand, especially if close contact is needed for transmission. These dynamics are entirely random and take place over many virus generations.

In the case of chimpanzee SIV (SIV cpz), it can be inferred that this virus passed to humans—but not often or persistently—long before chimpanzees were ever endangered. Passage occurred simply because of opportunity. Now and then a chimpanzee bit a hunter and left a small population of SIV in a human host. Perhaps at first SIV cpz replicated poorly in humans, so such a population usually failed to cause infection. But now and then an odd strain would gain a foothold due to chance advantages in its makeup or circumstances. It infected a hospitable cell and produced progeny in the hunter or in someone to whom he passed bodily fluids.

Of that progeny, the odd strain or two survived and in turn produced progeny in which a few survived, and so on. Eventually, after many virus generations and passages from human to human, a virus population evolved in which the majority could survive in humans. At this point we say that "the virus has adapted," which seems to imply viral determination, but viruses cannot determine anything. They simply do or do not survive.

Many human-to-human passages were no doubt needed before chimpanzee SIV evolved into HIV-0 and HIV-1. Only when conditions were optimal for their dissemination among humans did HIV-0 and HIV-1 become relatively stable viral populations with a genetic makeup readily distinguishable from the chimpanzee SIV. Their evolution as human viruses began in the nineteenth century when human-chimpanzee contact began to increase. Subjected to more hunting and disturbance of food sources, chimpanzees eventually became endangered.

Chimpanzee SIV was equally endangered (albeit oblivious) but had more options than its host. The virus could profit from the fact that, in its area of endemicity, the decrease of chimpanzees was paralleled by a handy increase of humans. Humans are physiologically close to chimpanzees and about equally susceptible to SIV, so adaptation was relatively easy. This general scenario can be applied to HIV-2, although its host was not endangered.

In a sense, viruses are simply opportunistic, so SIV jumped to humans just because they were susceptible and available. Any virus, wherever it finds itself, simply tries to survive and spread.

No matter how or why a virus changes hosts, we know it suddenly confronts a new set of cells to infect. These cells look somewhat familiar but are not perfectly accommodating. Perhaps the virus is drawn to the right cell receptor and can interact to infect the cell with modest efficiency but cannot reproduce too well. Gradually it adapts during the subsequent replication cycles.

For a virus, the meaning of life is survival and spread. It seeks only efficient reproduction and transmission in the host population at hand. Virus-host adaptation is a balance between virus virulence and host resistance. Both host and virus must survive long enough to produce offspring.

However, the virus must survive only that long whereas, in general, the host must survive to produce and then raise the offspring.

For the AIDS endemic to happen, humans had to remove the accustomed host of SRV from its natural surroundings and place it close to unaccustomed animals that were extremely sensitive to the virus: the Asian macaque. SRV did what came naturally, and not for the first time either. Much earlier, this virus was born when an SRV ancestor found itself in an entirely new family of animals.

SRV is actually a rodent retrovirus that acquired a monkey retrovirus envelope so it could spread efficiently in primates. Two endogenous retroviruses—a mouse virus and a monkey virus—were involved in this event. A mouse bite probably transferred a few mouse cells to a monkey. The contact of mouse and monkey cells could have activated an endogenous virus carried by the mouse cells. It shed virions that entered certain monkey cells.

Meanwhile, the contact of mouse and monkey cells also activated an endogenous monkey virus. It shed virions that entered the same cell as the mouse virions. The two viruses mated, and the mouse virus ultimately picked up a monkey envelope. This enabled it to interact with a key molecule on the surface of a particular host cell.

SRV shows how a mouse virus, needing to spread among monkeys, took advantage of viral sex to gain, by chance, a gene just for that purpose. The environmental pressure on the mouse virus in a monkey cell environment is its limited ability to enter and multiply in its new microenvironment, the monkey cell. The acquisition of a monkey envelope is all that it needs to become a monkey virus.

The cell receptor is the center of the universe for a virus: it permits cell entry, without which the virus cannot multiply. If it cannot multiply, it cannot survive in that particular environment. The receptor used by SRV and other D-type monkey viruses is used exclusively by primate viruses with one exception: an endogenous virus of small cats.

Clues to the monkey virus parent of SRV may come from a close look at other D-type monkey viruses. Of the monkeys that carry those viruses, can we find one whose habitat overlaps with the talapoin?

The evidence suggests the go-between was a mandrill, as will be explained. The BaEV of baboons, a C-type virus, is usually endogenous and totally inert. However, being quite newly integrated into the baboon genome, it retains its own complete genome in at least some baboon cells. This complete genome can be activated to generate exogenous virus. Other monkeys carry BaEV, but only baboon BaEV can be activated. This is important to our study because, although sex and recombination are remotely possible when one or both partners are endogenous, the process is far more likely—and far less cumbersome—when at least one is exogenous. Ideally a mouse virus picking up a monkey virus envelope needs both its parent viruses to be infectious particles when they meet.

The study has demonstrated that in an individual baboon only a few (if any) cells carry complete BaEVs. But in a baboon that carries such BaEVs, activation by invasion of foreign cells can generate virions able to infect and reproduce. The process typifies the way an endogenous virus can become an exogenous virus in response to environmental pressure. The invader cells can come from other monkeys, from humans, even dogs and bats—or a mouse bite. In other words, baboon BaEV is xenotropic.

Most African monkeys have been thought to carry BaEV, but our work has not confirmed this. When family tree of African monkeys was checked for BaEV viruses that include envelope genes (the key for entrance to the monkey world), only a select group of monkeys qualified. Essentially, BaEV is present only in baboons and other Papionini monkeys and in the four subspecies of African green monkey. This shows remarkable coincidence with SIV, with two very important exceptions.

Unlike SIV, BaEV is not found in chimpanzees and humans, nor is it found in guenons other than African green monkeys. Still, it seems clear that two monkey families—guenons and Papionini—govern most of the retrovirus evolution among primates, since they bring together endogenous viruses like BaEV and exogenous viruses like SRV, STLV, and SIV. To study virus adaptation to new primate environments, we have only to look at the habitat of these two families. Habitat was obviously a factor in the spread of SIV between sabaeus monkeys and sooty mangabeys. The work convincingly shows it was equally a factor in the distribution of BaEV. Whereas one group of mangabeys clusters genetically with olive and chacma baboons and another group clusters with mandrills, the BaEVs of all mangabeys cluster with the BaEVs of mandrills. The BaEVs of baboons cluster with the BaEVs of African green monkeys, although the monkeys themselves are not genetically close.

Clearly the virus clusters follow habitat more than species separation. BaEV seems to branch into forest viruses and savanna viruses. The former have concentrated on forest primates like mangabeys and mandrills. The latter have focused on savanna primates like baboons and African green monkeys. Since the talapoin is a forest monkey, we must assume that SRV derived its primate envelope from an endogenous BaEV of some other forest monkey: a mandrill or a mangabey. One of these could well be the missing link between baboons and talapoins, and geography favours the mandrill.

All known monkey viruses seem to predominate in one habitat or the other. The simian foamy virus is most widespread, infecting Asian, African, and New World monkeys and higher primates such as gorillas, chimpanzees, orangutans, and humans. It may be the most ancient of monkey viruses since it infects all its hosts without the slightest detrimental effect.

Simian foamy virus is the ultimate happy retrovirus. It never meets a primate it doesn't like. This retrovirus finds all primate hosts equally attractive and never encounters a primate environment that is hostile to its dissemination and spread. Its hosts are also happy (so far) because this virus does not need to adapt in ways that cause disease or death. Only a hostile environment forces the need for increased virus load for more efficient spread. When a monkey virus encounters a monkey of the preferred host species, no adaptation upon transmission is required since multiplication is optimal. But when a less preferred but susceptible host is encountered, virus multiplication is usually minimal at first. In the body of this new host, the virus will begin to evolve toward a new optimum, and the fittest viruses will survive.

These survivors will subsequently go on to the next host. HIV shows how this process can involve heightening the virus load, causing AIDS and the death of the host. BaEV and SRV show a different way to enhance virus spread. Instead of heightening the virus load like HIV, a virus can acquire a better envelope. This option was used in the case of cross-species transmission from mouse to monkey.

All these observations indicate that the micro-environment of a virus—the preferred cell and its hospitality to virus entry and multiplication—is closely linked to the macroenvironment, the host that houses the preferred cell. In fact, the host provides more than housing. It serves the virus as a means of transport to the cell. From a retrovirus perspective, the host is a vast conglomerate of cells that exist only to support various activities that get the virus to its desired cell. These activities must enable the virus to pass from one individual to another, enter the body by a certain cell type, travel by a certain route to its target cell type (i.e., where it can multiply), then interact with the cell receptor to enter and cause infection.

Unfortunately for the virus, the host has an immune system to fight foreign intruders. When running smoothly, this system does not distinguish between good and bad but only between self and non-self. Otherwise it would damage the host, as it does in auto-immune disorders like rheumatoid arthritis. The system ignores all elements that are part of the host while attacking all foreign proteins. These include antigen, the protein (or perhaps several) unique to each invader that provokes the immune system to generate the antibody specific to that invader.

Unfortunately for us, our immune system may be effective at the onset but finally is ineffective against HIV.

Despite an immune response that includes antibodies and T cells to fight HIV, the HIV-infected individual almost invariably develops AIDS and dies from the inability to fight off normally innocent viruses, bacteria, and parasites. This inability is immunodeficiency or immunosuppression. In theory, disease should be prevented by HIV-specific immunity, which ideally should also clear HIV from the system.

This suggests strongly that the HIV virus is able at each phase of infection to reach new susceptible cells without much obstruction from anti-HIV immunity. From the virus point of view, host immunity hampers adaptation to new host environments. The more effective host immunity, the more restricted the virus in seeking the best way to survive.

In HIV infection, host immunity seems to be a small obstacle for the virus. The HIV virus loads generally remain extremely high throughout the course of infection, and only a tiny percentage of infected individuals escape immunosuppression and death. Based on these observations, one can predict that in AIDS, the virus-host adaptation to an equilibrium happens fast, since virus and its desired cell meet virtually unimpeded. The absence of effective anti-HIV immunity makes it very easy for HIV particles to reach their goal because the road is unblocked, except by small speed bumps. All they need is the urge to arrive at the right cell, and this is driven by the chemical affinity of the viral envelope for a particular receptor.

Members of the HIV family share many features and strategies in addition to their affinity for meeting place. But viruses outside the family can also rendezvous (and ultimately mate) with HIV if only they share this affinity for the same cell type in the same type of host. This one common interest can bring potential partners to the same place, attracted by the cell receptor.

As any virus moves through a new host, it scans the total cell population and all the receptors offered to its envelope. It looks for the special cell type or types offering the molecule that fits the viral envelope. The molecule and its corresponding envelope protein are like a lock and key.

Some keys fit only a single lock. Others fit multiple locks and, conversely, some locks respond to multiple keys. The third case is analogous to cell types that can accommodate more than one type of virus. As we watch for HIV to mate with another retrovirus, the third case is most important. Whether it invites multiple viruses by one or several receptors, this kind of cell provides a rendezvous for recombination.

It is easy to see that for the best chance of meeting, two retroviruses should share more than a taste for the same target cell. They should also share port of entry into the body. Once inside the body, viruses infect the first available cells of the right type. So if one virus enters through the mouth and the other through the anus, they are unlikely to come together. They will head for the same type of target cell but at opposite ends of the body. Viruses with different ports of entry rarely meet without development of generalized infection. This puts both viruses into the bloodstream.

Viruses spread opportunistically into any hosts that give them entry and allow them to replicate. Retroviruses continuously adapt to changes in their microenvironment. The most dramatic selective pressure for adaptation occurs when the virus finds itself in a new host, as when SIV cpz jumped to humans and became HIV-0 and HIV-1. It is in such instances that phenotypic mixing and viral recombination are most likely to occur.

In the modern world of population and environmental change, retroviruses are ever more threatened with the loss of natural hosts and the need to find new hosts, including us. There is perhaps some logic in our vulnerability to primate retroviruses since our activities are the major threat to rain forest animals not only in Africa but in all parts of the world.

The larger-sized monkey species are more vulnerable to habitat disturbance than smaller species. In addition to body size, diet plays a role. If a monkey depends for its survival on fruits, it is more sensitive to habitat disturbance than a monkey that relies on leaves. Of course there are always exceptions. In Asia it turned out that fruit-eating macaques are very opportunistic and that some of them, like Indonesian macaques (*Macaca fascicularis*), are more common in disturbed forests than in undisturbed forests. Several macaques seem to prefer disturbed forest, resembling humans in this respect.

Chimpanzees on the other hand thrive poorly in disturbed forest because they rely on fruit (to a greater extent than the more versatile Asian macaques).

Since habitat disturbance is not always harmful, one suspects it is not the most important environmental threat to nonhuman primates. Nor is it the greatest threat to the retroviruses that depend on these animals. Both the animals and their viruses are far more threatened by direct assaults: attacks on one primate by another.

Human and nonhuman primates eat other primates. In addition, humans capture nonhuman primates for export around the world as pets, zoo animals, or laboratory models. If we focus on the western equatorial rain forest, where many retroviruses met their first human host, we find communities of talapoins, chimpanzees, mandrills, gorillas, and a few colobines, as well as humans. All are part of the ecosystem that modifies retrovirus host availability. This ecosytem is nothing more than a food chain: humans eating humans (in the not-too-distant past), humans eating monkeys, monkeys eating other monkeys. Such a system offers ample opportunity for the cross-species transmission of viruses.

Humans can be infected by eating a monkey, but infection is more likely to result from a monkey bite during a hunt. For two reasons this danger was greater in earlier times when hunting was done with bow and arrow. First, the hunter had to get closer to the animal to shoot. Second, a wounded animal was more likely to be alive and biting when approached for capture. With guns, the hunter can shoot from a greater distance and is more likely to make a deadly hit.

The chance for prey to fight back is now dramatically reduced, but this only applies to hunting for food. Animals hunted for capture must be taken alive, so they can still bite their captors. When large monkeys or apes are taken, hunters commonly kill the mothers, but the babies can bite. Their panicked defense can cause injuries (and perhaps retroviral infection) but is less dangerous than the defense of adult animals. Young apes are not as large or as strong as adult apes, and they rarely carry the viruses that threaten us. So guns have decreased the bites of monkeys hunted for food but have increased the bites of monkeys hunted for export. And habitat disturbance may make hunting easier for humans, further increasing their chance of being bitten.

The risk to humans has also probably risen. Theoretically, there is no reason why some still undiscovered primate virus might not eventually appear in humans. Depending on the level of adaptation needed to achieve efficient spread, such crossover could conceivably lead to new epidemics of fatal disease. Of course, if predation or habitat disturbances drive monkey retroviruses to new hosts, these hosts may not be human but other monkeys. Habitat disturbance has many subtle and unexpected effects on neighbouring animals of all kinds.

A shrinking habitat may force two or more species of monkeys to live in a smaller area. This could cause them to fight more for food and territory, and perhaps to prey more on each other. For example, chimpanzees have long been predators of red colobus monkeys and several guenon species but have relied primarily on fruit. Disturbed habitats offering less fruit may cause them to eat more meat.

Cross-species transmission of primate retroviruses could happen again. One involved local entry into the unaccustomed host population and subsequent dissemination over the globe. The other involved export of the natural host to a new environment occupied by unaccustomed hosts. Both cases plead strongly for stability in the natural host populations of primate retroviruses, to prevent future outbreaks of human disease.

Stability in these animal populations can only be achieved by leaving them intact. Whatever we think of "animal rights," for our own safety we must avoid human encroachment on these communities. We must also avoid the export of natural primate retrovirus hosts to unnatural environments where they can encounter susceptible species. Individuals and social groups who are at low risk for diseases like AIDS must realize that the risks affect everyone. They affect people who have never set foot in Africa or a gay bathhouse; never received a blood transfusion; never seen a prostitute, or engaged in promiscuous sex. They threaten people who will never themselves be infected with HIV. When a retrovirus harms its host species, it harms not only the infected individuals but also the uninfected, mainly by curbing population growth. If too many disease victims die at or before reproductive age, their loss is also the loss of their potential offspring.

An example of minimum damage is the epidemic of adult T-cell leukemia in southwestern Japan. The prime mode of transmission is by ingestion of breast milk, so individuals are infected before reproductive age. This by itself is threatening, especially since fertile women are affected. However, with HTLV, the threat is alleviated because although both men and women are infected, only women can transmit the disease. Men do not contribute to the spread of the virus, and unless women are unusually mobile, they infect only a few children. This keeps the infection very localized and, since few individuals actually develop adult T-cell leukemia, the death rate is very low. Taken together, these factors mean that the population effect of HTLV infection is virtually nil, despite a mode of transmission that allows for dramatic effects.

In contrast, HIV causes maximum damage. Being sexually transmitted, it obviously infects individuals at or before reproductive age. It infects both sexes and is transmitted by both sexes. Infected women can infect their offspring. If passed among strictly homosexual men, HIV- 1B has minimal effect on population growth because these men are less likely to reproduce than heterosexual people. However, many homosexual men are actually bisexual. Indeed, most Asian or African women infected by HIV are infected during their early years of sexual activity, their most fertile period. This is because HIV (mainly subtypes 1A and 1E) is endemic in the whole population, including sexually active males. Consequently, potential parents of either sex may die before they can reproduce or raise children. They may produce infected offspring who themselves will never live to reproduce.

Of course, HIV infection of fertile adults threatens more than population growth. It threatens not only the future but the present because a population ravaged by AIDS is increasingly a population of grandparents and grandchildren. The death of the people in between, the parent population, hurts not only the birth rate but the society in general. Many vital resources are eliminated because the parent population is also the population providing the resources.

Survival of the uninfected population is therefore closely linked to the survival of the infected population. The larger the infected population and the higher the death rate, the more devastating is the effect on the whole retrovirus-susceptible group or species.

# 8

# Strategies for Preventing AIDS

The greatest hope for combating HIV/AIDS in the foreseeable future is that of helping people to choose safer behaviour so that they will be less likely to contract and spread HIV. But can governments affect the very private and intimate behaviours that spread HIV/AIDS? And if it can, what are the priority actions that governments should take to prevent the epidemic, so as to maximize the impact of scarce resources?

The first aim should be to influence individual choices directly within the existing economic and social context by changing the costs and benefits of various types of behaviour, making safer behaviour a more attractive choice.

However, individual behaviour is shaped and often constrained by the economic and social context; some individuals choices are very constrained. A second, complementary approach is to change the economic and social conditions that make it difficult or impossible for some people to protect themselves from HIV. The benefits of this approach typically extend far beyond HIV prevention. It is therefore often difficult to assess the cost-effectiveness of measures to affect the economic and social environment, but they are likely to improve the efficacy of direct interventions to individuals.

Which activities are most justified for government action and, among them, which should be priorities? There are three activities in which governments have an indispensable role in ensuring the efficiency and equity of prevention programs: providing public goods related to prevention, such as the collection and dissemination of information about the epidemic; reducing the negative externalities of risky behaviour by promoting safer behaviour among people who are most likely to contract and spread the virus; and promoting equity by ensuring that the most destitute are not denied access to the means by which they may protect themselves from HIV.

These activities will reduce the spread of HIV most quickly and will benefit everyone in society, including those with low-risk behaviour and the poor. Private individuals would not invest in them in sufficient quantity to slow the epidemic. In addition to satisfying these criteria of public economics, government-sponsored preventive activities should be cost-effective. We will review some important factors that influence the cost-effectiveness of government actions and propose a set of public priorities for preventing HIV according to the stage of the HIV/AIDS epidemic.

While governments, in collaboration with private actors, have implemented many worthwhile programs, some of which have had demonstrable impact, there is a need for renewed effort to implement the activities that are likely to be most cost-effective from the government perspective in preventing the epidemic.

Perhaps the major impediment to more effective, efficient, and equitable prevention is a lack of political commitment, first, to collect and disseminate the data on HIV prevalence, risk behaviour, the effectiveness of programs, and their costs, and, second, to work constructively with those at highest risk of contracting and spreading HIV to prevent infection. These are important issues that national governments, international donors, and non-governmental organizations need to act on urgently.

### Influencing Individual Choices

A substantial body of economic research, much of it in developing countries, has shown that actual and perceived costs and benefits, some of which can be affected by government policies, significantly influence private decisions about marriage, childbearing, and contraceptive use. It is therefore reasonable to assume that sexual behaviour that spreads HIV can also be influenced by public policy.

Similarly, studies have shown that under the right conditions drug users change their injecting behaviour to reduce the likelihood of being infected with HIV. Four types of policies are likely to yield positive results with regard to the HIV epidemic: providing various types of information, reducing the costs of using condoms, reducing the costs of using sterile injecting equipment, and attempting to raise the costs of engaging in commercial sex and injecting drug use.

Knowledge about the levels of HIV infection in the population—how HIV is transmitted, and how to avoid contracting it—can induce some people who engage in high-risk behaviour to adopt safer sexual and injecting practices or to refrain from casual or commercial sex and injecting drug use altogether.

Moreover, there is considerable evidence that people engaged ill high-risk activities are more motivated to learn about HIV than others, since they are more likely to become infected and suffer the consequences. Surveys conducted by the Global Programme on AIDS in 1989-90 found that respondents who had engaged in risky behaviour knew more about modes of transmission and the severity of AIDS than those who had never engaged in risky behaviour.

Researchers have identified a number of interrelated factors that affect the way in which people use knowledge to assess the costs and benefits of risky behaviour and internalize them. These factors include the extent to which they understand how HIV infection would affect them personally, now risky they perceive their own behaviour to be and they have the skills necessary to negotiate safer behaviour with partners and to resist social pressures. Interventions that address these issues can result in substantially more behaviour change than knowledge alone. These interventions can take many forms, from public information campaigns using mass media to training and education programs conducted face-to-face.

Nevertheless, many knowledgeable people who have the skills to reduce their risk and have internalized the dangers will continue to engage in risky behaviour. Given the devastating personal cost of contracting HIV, why isn't the danger of being infected sufficient to cause people to forgo all risky activities? One reason is that the costs of reducing risk are clear and immediate while the benefits are uncertain and distant. Whether people are willing to incur these up-front costs to reduce the risk of future sickness and premature death from AIDS depends on their assessment of the probability of infection from a specific act and the discount rate applied to future years of healthy life.

Assessing the probability of infection is not easy, since most people do not know the HIV infection, status of their partners or even the extent of their partners' current or past risky behaviour. It is hardly surprising that, for people in the thrall of passion, addiction, or difficult economic circumstances, the immediate and certain costs of reducing their risk of contracting HIV will sometimes appear greater than the uncertain future benefits. Moreover, even if people making decisions about their private behaviour take into full account the potential costs to themselves, they are likely to greatly undervalue the costs of their behaviour to society in terms of secondary infections that unintentionally may result.

For these reasons, although better information on the risks will induce people engaging in high-risk behaviour to reduce their somewhat, they will still engage in riskier behaviour than society would prefer in the interest of curbing the AIDS epidemic. Additional measures will be necessary to change the costs and benefits of risky behaviour and its alternatives in ways that encourage safer behaviour.

**Lowering the cost of condoms**

The costs of condom use include not only the price of the condom but also the potential inconvenience and embarrassment of obtaining and using one, and, for some people, reduced sexual pleasure. Policies that lower these costs, by lowering the price of condoms, improving their availability, and increasing their social acceptability, would be expected to increase condom use and reduce HIV transmission. Condom social marketing programs aim to achieve all of these objectives.

These programs are often targeted at low-income households, where the price of condoms is more likely to inhibit demand. Following the introduction of condom social marketing programs, sales have increased dramatically. In many of the countries condoms were virtually unavailable or unknown prior to the program. Most condom social marketing programs are subsidized by international donors and many, such as the program in India, receive government subsidies. Some governments have also lowered condom prices by reducing import tariffs and sales taxes on condoms and latex rubber.

Some governments, NGOs, and condom social marketing programs also have launched for condom promotion focused specifically on commercial sex. Some of these programs distribute condoms to sex workers for free. Several NGOs have succeeded in raising condom use among sex workers and have shown decrease in cases.

Policies to increase condom use among people who have unprotected sex with many partners are a potentially powerful means of reducing the size of the HIV epidemic and thereby of providing significant benefit to the entire society.

**Lowering the costs of safe injecting behaviour**

Since HIV greatly increases the personal cost of injecting with shared equipment, we would expect to see substantial behavioural change, provided there are low-cost ways for injecting drug users to avoid becoming infected. Not all injecting drug users are addicted, but for those who are, quitting is rarely a low-cost option. It can be extremely painful, can take a long time, and is often not successful: within a year or two of completing drug treatment, 70 to 80 per cent of people treated for heroin use typically resume injecting. Although treatment often does not result in permanent cessation of drug use, it can sometimes result in less risky behaviour, lower injecting rates and less needle sharing among those who resume injecting. Thus, by providing information on the risks of HIV transmission and lowering the costs of drug treatment programs, it may induce some injecting drug users to stop injecting altogether and others to adopt safer practices. Many are likely to continue risky injecting behaviour unless the costs of safer injecting behaviour—primarily the costs of obtaining sterile equipment or bleach—are sufficiently low.

But in many countries safer injecting behaviour can be very costly to the injecting drug user. Research suggests that difficulty in obtaining sterile injecting equipment is the most important reason that injecting drug users share equipment.

One inexpensive way for governments to lower the cost of safer injecting behaviour is to remove legal barriers to the purchase and possession of sterile injecting equipment. When armed with knowledge of the risks and provided with, easy access to sterile equipment, injecting drug users in many countries have rapidly adopted safer behaviour.

Needle exchange programs, by providing new sterile injecting equipment in exchange for used syringes, minimize needle sharing and remove contaminated needles from circulation. Many NEPs also supply free condoms to help prevent the spread of HIV to the sexual partners of injecting drug users, as well as education about reducing high-risk behaviour and referral for drug treatment. NEPs have been widely adopted in Australia, New Zealand, and many Western European countries with great success in reducing transmission of HIV as well as other blood-borne infections, like hepatitis B and hepatitis C.

A recent study compared trends in HIV prevalence among injecting users in a sample of 81 cities in North America, Europe, and Asia and the South Pacific. In the 52 cities without NEPs, HIV prevalence among injecting drug users increased by 5.9 per cent per year, on average, while it declined by an almost equal per cent annually (5.8 percent) in the 29 cities that had NEPs. Nonetheless, political opposition to needle exchange programs remains a potent force.

A recent study estimated that a national NEP in the United States would have prevented from 4,000 to 10,000 HIV infections between 1987 and 1995 among drug users, their sexual partners, and children; if such a program had been implemented in 1996, it could still have prevented from 5,000 to 11,000 infections over the next five years. Can harm reduction strategies also work in low-income countries? The answer appears to be yes. Although there is less experience with harm reduction strategies in developing countries, the remarkable success of a needle exchange program in Nepal suggests that such programs should be attempted more widely.

Where resources for needle exchange are lacking, bleach distribution may offer a less expensive alternative. Bleach is not only cheaper, it is also less controversial than needle exchanges, and, when used correctly, highly effective in killing HIV on infected equipment.

Furthermore, improved availability of bleach is virtually the only option for harm reduction among injecting drug users in prisons, since prison authorities are unlikely to distribute needles because they can be used as weapons. However, bleach is not always readily available.

Bleach programs produce the greatest gains. Programs that reduce the cost of safer injecting procedures often arouse fears that they will encourage people to initiate drug use or discourage addicts from seeking treatment. If efforts to reduce the cost of safer injection behaviour did encourage illicit drug use, this would have to be weighed against the benefits of reduced HIV transmission.

Fortunately, there is substantial evidence indicating that this is not the case. Two evaluations of NEPs in six industrial countries failed to find any evidence that the programs raised the number of injecting drug users or that they increased the number of properly discarded needles. We have seen that lowering the costs of safer sex and safer injecting behaviour can encourage less-risky behaviour and reduce the transmission of HIV. But both prostitution and use of illegal and addictive drugs impose substantial negative externalities on society in terms of sexually transmitted and blood-borne diseases, crime, the costs of law enforcement, and incarceration.

It is not surprising, therefore, that programs that attempt to promote safer behaviour among sex workers, injecting drug users, and other people who engage in high-risk behaviour may be politically unpopular, especially if they are perceived to be condoning prostitution or drug addiction. An alternative approach that often has broad popular appeal is to discourage such activities through punitive measures and stepped up enforcement of existing laws. From the standpoint of economic theory, such attempts to raise the cost of potentially risky behaviour could discourage it, provided that costs can be raised sufficiently.

However, because sexual activity and injecting drug use are private activities, enforcing prohibitions is costly and difficult in practice. Moreover, as we discuss below, such attempts may have unintended consequences that may exacerbate the epidemic. Numerous studies have shown that prohibition and punishment of commercial sex causes sex workers to shift their place of business and to change the way they solicit clients to avoid prosecution. Singapore, for example, attempted to eradicate prostitution by closing "red-light" districts in commercial areas; brothels soon appeared in residential areas.

Enforcement problems aside, punishing commercial sex is also not very efficient in preventing HIV, because the virus is transmitted not by commercial sex per se but by unprotected intercourse with multiple partners, regardless of whether one party pays the other.

Thus, even if commercial sex could be eliminated by these measures, HIV could persist and spread through casual sex networks, although perhaps less rapidly. Moreover, it is reasonable to expect that the more effective is the curtailment of commercial sex, the more casual sex networks will expand.

An alternative to prohibiting and punishing commercial sex is to legalize and regulate it. Although this approach sometimes arouses considerable political opposition, it can make sex workers and their clients easier to monitor and to reach with information, condoms, and STD treatment.

The likely result is a legal, high-priced market, presumably with lower transmission of HIV, and an unregulated, low-priced Market, which authorities cannot easily monitor and where transmission of HIV will presumably be higher. Moreover, mandatory health screening of prostitutes, even in the regulated brothels, is not always enforceable. The net impact of legalization and regulation is also difficult to predict and will depend on how much regulation raises the price of sex in the legalized sector and the extent to which programs are successful in encouraging safer sex in the illegal, unregulated sector.

Arguments for and against raising the costs of drug use through prohibition and punishment are broadly similar to those for prohibiting commercial sex. Again, it is important to note that neither drug use per se nor injecting per se spreads HIV; rather, it is the sharing of unsterilized equipment that does so. Many who use illicit drugs do not inject, and often those who inject do not share needles. So efforts to eliminate illegal drug use, while they might be rationalized on other grounds, are potentially a very inefficient and costly way of reducing the unsafe injecting behaviour that spreads HIV.

Nonetheless, the already substantial political appeal of drug enforcement efforts is likely to be strengthened by the close association between use of injected drugs and HIV. It is therefore useful to consider the likely impact on HIV of the two main strategies for eradicating illegal drugs: restricting supply, by attempting to halt the drug trade, and reducing demand, by punishing drug users or forcing them into treatment. The most politically popular way to attempt to reduce drug use is to reduce the availability of drugs. However, drug interdiction may simply rearrange the problem or make it worse. For example:

- — Addicts may switch to other substances.
- — May shift from smoking to injecting, which requires a smaller dose to produce euphoria but greatly raises the risk of HIV.
- — The drug trade may shift to other areas where people not previously exposed to drugs may begin injecting.

Because most injecting drug users are chemically dependent, prohibition and threats of punishment are notoriously ineffective in reducing their demand for drugs.

A survey of 450 injecting drug users in Manipur State in India, where addicts are imprisoned, found that only 2 per cent regarded the threat of imprisonment as a reason to stop injecting drugs; half of the addicts surveyed had previously been in prison. And far from reducing HIV transmission, imprisonment may have the opposite effect. Unable to obtain syringes, prisoners who inject drugs frequently resort to shared, improvised equipment, such as ballpoint pens, which would be very difficult to sterilize, even if bleach were available. Mandatory drug treatment is likely to be even less successful in ending drug use than voluntary treatment, since patients entering such programs presumably have very little desire to change their behaviour.

Efforts to raise the cost of injecting drugs through drug interdiction or the punishment of injecting drug users may increase rather than decrease risky injection behaviour. Although the data on the impact of such efforts on HIV incidence are fragmentary, the available evidence suggests that harm reduction programs, including information about HIV, sterile injection equipment or bleach kits, and referral for voluntary treatment programs will be more effective and less costly in reducing risky injection behaviour than drug interdiction or incarceration of addicts.

### Easing Social Constraints to Safe Behaviour

A second approach to reducing the spread of HIV aims to change the social and economic factors that shape—and sometimes constrain—individual choices about risky behaviour. Measures pursued by this approach have many other benefits besides reducing the HIV epidemic and they are already on the agenda of most developing country governments. The benefits are sometimes more difficult to quantify because of their broad impact, which extends far beyond HIV prevention. However, these measures are highly complementary to policies that directly affect the costs and benefits of risky behaviour.

#### Altering social norms

Social norms and peer pressure that encourage men to use the services of prostitutes or that venerate men with many female "conquests," while placing a high value on female chastity create the conditions for an explosive HIV epidemic. The challenge for policymakers in countries with social patterns that are very conducive to the spread of HIV is to encourage safer behaviour, without stigmatizing those who engage in unsafe behaviour in ways that make them more difficult to reach with public health interventions.

Norms on marriage and childbearing can also affect the spread and prevention of HIV. The tradition of a man selecting a bride who is five or ten years younger than himself spreads HIV from one generation to the next. Finally, efforts to encourage condom use among married couples for HIV prevention will be especially difficult in societies where people want large families and a woman's social status and economic well-being are heavily dependent on the number of children she has.

While sexual conservatism may be one of the best protections against HIV at the societal level, adherence to norms is never complete. An HIV epidemic can nevertheless occur, and conservatism can result in stigma of those who become infected or who are in social groups associated with high-risk behaviour, making it more difficult to support safer behaviour.

**Improving the status of women**

The lower social and economic status of women reduces their ability to insist upon male sexual fidelity and to negotiate safe sex. These problems can be particularly acute in societies where women's inheritance rights, property and child custody, rights in divorce, and even the right to own land and other property are limited. In some instances, a wife's mere suggestion that her husband use a condom can provoke physical abuse. Even where the situation is not this stark, women's lower literacy, lower incomes, and low economic independence give them less access to HIV prevention information, fewer resources to purchase condoms and treat conventional STDs, and less ability to leave a relationship that puts them at risk of contracting HIV. For all these reasons, many more women than men face situations in which they are unable to protect them from HIV.

Women who sell sexual services often face particularly constrained choices. Unemployment, divorce, desertion, and the breakdown of the extended family are among the factors that can lead women to offer sex for money. One-half of sex workers interviewed in Calcutta cited extreme poverty as the reason for entering sex work, and 22 per cent cited "family disturbances".

Ending legal restrictions on women's rights, encouraging social equality, and raising economic opportunities for women not only make it easier for women to avoid HIV, they are also important in fostering development. Policies that specifically help women include increasing girls' school enrolment; guaranteeing equal employment opportunities; outlawing and severely punishing slavery, rape, wife abuse, and child prostitution; and guaranteeing inheritance, property, and child custody rights.

A growing economy is also an important ingredient for increased economic opportunities for women. Of course, improving the status of women will also open new opportunities to choose risky behaviour; a few women may do so. However, it is reasonable to expect that the vast majority of women, given expanded choices, would seize the opportunity to choose safe behaviour and avoid HIV infection.

**Reducing poverty**

Poverty and low socio-economic status also constrain the decisions people make about risky behaviour. Those with low incomes, for example, may not be able to afford to treat STDs or to buy condoms. Poor families may see commercial sex as a lucrative occupation for young and poorly educated daughters. People with less education may have less access to information about the dangers of high-risk behaviour or be less able to understand prevention messages. This explains why those most likely to contract STDs and other infectious diseases within a society are the poor and uneducated.

However, studies have proved that people with higher socio-economic status have higher HIV infection rates. The first reason is that men with higher education and income will find it easier to attract and support additional commercial and casual sexual partners. For example, analysis of data from the WHO/GPA sexual behaviour surveys found that in five African sites, as well as in Thailand,

Manila (the Philippines), and Rio de Janeiro (Brazil), the more education a man has, the more likely he is to have had a casual, nonregular sexual partner. A second reason is that men and women with more education and higher incomes are likely to travel more and thus have more opportunities for a variety of sexual contacts.

Several studies of sex workers have found that women with higher incomes were more likely to use condoms and had lower levels of HIV infection. In three cities in Sao Paulo, Brazil, for example, sex workers who charged higher prices had fewer clients, were more likely to have always used condoms in the past year, were less likely to have injected drugs, and consequently were less likely to be infected with HIV and other STDs than were low-priced sex workers.

Despite the links found between higher socioeconomic status and HIV infection in some areas, government policies to raise incomes and schooling and reduce poverty should lower the economic constraints to engaging in safer behaviour and reduce the incidence of HIV over the long term. These policies are often pursued because they have far-reaching social benefits; they are also highly complementary to short-term interventions to encourage safer sexual and injecting behaviour and will likely enhance the impact of these interventions.

## GOVERNMENT PRIORITIES IN PREVENTING HIV

This section proposes a broad prevention strategy for governments at all stages of the epidemic to maximize the impact of limited government resources in curbing the spread of HIV. In keeping with the principles of public economics, governments should finance or directly implement interventions that are essential to stopping the spread of HIV because private individuals or firms will not have sufficient incentive to finance on their own—namely, provision of public goods, reduction of the negative externalities of behaviour that spreads HIV, and protection of the poor from HIV infection.

Programs that address these issues will improve the efficiency and equity of government prevention efforts.

Program effectiveness will be improved if governments act as soon as possible and if they succeed in preventing infection among those most likely to contract and spread HIV. The intention is to identify the minimum set of activities that all governments should be engaged in to improve the efficiency and equity of prevention programs, and a rational order in which to expand them. This strategy should be broad one, based on underlying principles of public economics, epidemiology, and cost-effectiveness. It remains for individual countries to identify the specific combination of programs, policies, and interventions to pursue this strategy in a cost-effective way.

However, even within these guiding principles, the cost-effectiveness of HIV prevention programs is likely to vary considerably according to the setting. Programmatic choices are necessarily country-specific because the costs and effectiveness of interventions, as well as the characteristics and accessibility of those most likely to contract and spread HIV, vary widely across the globe.

**Public economics and government priorities**

Government policies can potentially address three types of market failures that occur with respect to the prevention of HIV. The first problem involves the underprovision of public good-specifically, the lack of incentives for the private sector to collect and disseminate information crucial to the prevention of the epidemic. The second involves the negative externalities of high-risk behaviour: people deciding whether or not to take steps to protect themselves from HIV are likely to consider the costs to themselves of becoming infected but may not consider the cost of secondary HIV infections that may result if they become infected. The third type of market failure involves equity: very poor people are less able to protect themselves against HIV than others.

*Providing public goods*: The collection and production of information about the prevention and control of HIV is almost entirely a public good. Essential information includes data on the levels and trends of HIV and STD infections, the prevalence of high-risk behaviour, and the costs and benefits of prevention programs.

*Reducing the negative externalities of behaviour that spreads HIV*: Unprotected intercourse with multiple partners and unsafe injecting practices raise the risk of infection for everyone, even for those who do not engage in high-risk behaviour. People who practice risky behaviour are likely to take some steps to reduce their risk of contracting HIV because of the enormous personal costs if they become infected. However, because they react primarily to the increased risk to themselves, their response will not reflect the full costs—that is, the negative externalities—of unintentionally spreading HIV to the rest of society.

Many people who do not practice high-risk behaviour would be willing to pay those who do practice it to adopt safer behaviour in order to contain the epidemic and thus lower everyone's risk of contracting HIV. Government is the only mechanism through which this can happen. Thus, there is a strong justification for government to subsidize safer behaviour among people who engage in high-risk behaviour in order to protect everyone—either by preventing primary infections among those who engage in high-risk behaviour or, when such individuals are already infected, by preventing the infection from spreading to others. The principles of public economics and epidemiology are therefore in agreement that governments should give high priority to the prevention of infection among people most likely to contract and spread HIV.

The extent of negative externalities of risky behaviour can be measured by the number of secondary infections that a person would generate if infected with HIV. By this definition, the riskier an individual's behaviour, the more secondary infections he or she is likely to generate, and thus the greater the negative externalities of his or her behaviour. The reproductive rate of HIV among such individuals is likely to be much greater than 1, sustaining the epidemic. They are vulnerable to the negative externalities generated by others' risky behaviour.

In countries where government has a broad mandate to provide health services to everyone, and where resources are adequate, expanding government-financed preventive interventions to the low-risk population should not be ruled out. However, even in these cases, governments should first ensure that programs achieve adequate coverage of those most likely to contract and spread HIV, starting from those with the highest-risk behaviour, since this is the most efficient way to protect everyone.

There are situations, however, in which interventions for the entire population are essential to the success of programs aimed at reaching those most likely to contract and spread HIV. For example, although information that helps people with low-risk behaviour to further reduce their risk will have very little impact on the overall epidemic, they need to understand how HIV is transmitted and—more important—how it is not transmitted. Inaccurate information or even accurate information presented in ways that create feelings of fear and vulnerability can incite discrimination against those who are at high risk of contracting and spreading HIV and people who are HIV-positive or living with AIDS.

This is not only unwarranted and unjust, but it may also compromise the ability to launch the prevention programs most likely to slow the spread of HIV. Information that fuels fear of HIV-infected people has been a serious problem in nearly all countries where there has been extensive early publicity about the epidemic.

*Helping poor people to avoid HIV*: Government's first step should be to lower the costs of safe behaviour for the poor by improving the functioning of markets, for example, by eliminating tariffs on condoms and restrictions on condom advertising. If prevention is still too costly for the poor, subsidies may also be warranted. In countries where particular groups face significant barriers to acquiring information because of illiteracy, different languages, or`lack of access to newspapers, radio or television-subsidized information for the disadvantaged groups will not improve their access to prevention.

Besides subsidized information about HIV, the most important preventive measures are those that make it easier for poor people to obtain condoms, treatment for STDs, and access to safe blood. However, unless there is substantial overlap between the poor and those with high-risk behaviour, subsidized HIV interventions for the poor will address equity but will not be sufficient to contain the epidemic, particularly in its early stages.

**Cost-effectiveness from a government perspective**

Cost-effectiveness analysis is a tool for deciding among alternative courses of action when resources are scarce. It seeks to determine how to achieve the maximum effect within a given budget or, viewed differently how to achieve a desired effect at the lowest possible cost.

Measures for which individuals would have paid on their own are not a priority for a government's limited funds. Rather, governments should first spend their limited resources on interventions that are cost-effective in the conventional sense and that would not occur in the absence of government involvement—that is, cost-effective interventions that provide public goods and reduce the negative externalities of high-risk behaviour. This strategy will ultimately prevent the largest number of subsequent infections among all subgroups in the population, including the majority who do not engage in high-risk behaviour. Some governments have the mandate to intervene broadly in the health sector and to assume responsibility for providing curative and preventive health care for all citizens, irrespective of whether government spending is efficiency enhancing. However unless the costs of changing behaviour among those most likely to contract and spread HIV are extraordinarily high, promoting behaviour change among them is likely to be the most cost-effective in terms of preventing infection in the general population.

Several factors that affect the cost-effectiveness of alternative, publicly financed by HIV/AIDS prevention programs, do not necessarily enter into cost-effectiveness calculations for private individuals. There are also a number of issues specific to the cost-effectiveness of HIV interventions that need to be taken into account.

*Public benefits include averted secondary infections*: In calculating the benefits from prevention programs, it is important to consider not only the benefits received by the person directly affected, but also the number of secondary infections that are averted. Secondary infections measure, in effect, the extent to which negative externalities are being addressed by programs. Failure to include secondary infections among the benefits of public health programs will result in serious underestimates of the benefits of prevention in groups that are very likely to contract and spread HIV. Even the number of people in these groups tends to be small so far as the total population is concerned, the number of secondary infections per person tends to be large.

*Public and private prevention efforts*: Public programs will be more cost-effective if they raise additional demand for risk-reducing behaviour without "crowding out" private sources of inputs. For example, in societies where condoms are already widely available at low cost, subsidized condom projects that are not specifically directed toward those most likely to contract and spread HIV may simply shift the financing of existing condom sales from private pockets to public ones, with no impact on the epidemic. Whether the resulting redistribution enhances equity depends on the income distribution of condom purchasers relative to the general population.

The effectiveness of public programs should therefore be measured as the difference between outcomes with and without the program. HIV/AIDS prevention has other external effects: many HIV/AIDS preventive interventions have additional positive effects that might be overlooked if cost-effectiveness calculations considered only the impact on HIV/AIDS. For example, condom programs also prevent other STDs, which are spread in the same ways as HIV and generate similar negative externalities.

HIV education in the schools and encouragement of condom use among adolescents who engage in sex will complement efforts to postpone sexual activity, reduce teenage pregnancy and abortion, and as a result improve school completion rate, among girls. Harm reduction programs among injecting drug user, generate demand for drug rehabilitation programs and reduce transmission of hepatitis B and C and other blood-borne diseases. Although these benefits are difficult to quantify, they should not be overlooked. Involving other factors can improve cost-effectiveness: while governments must support prevention efforts among those who are most likely to contract and spread HIV, governments are not necessarily the most effective agent to design and implement such programs.

Enlisting and subsidizing NGOs to help in the design and implementation of interventions can greatly improve the cost-effectiveness of public programs, particularly if the NGOs are staffed by or representative of people at high risk of contracting and spreading HIV. The cost-effectiveness of all interventions can also be improved through other government measures, such as relaxing legal prohibitions and minimizing the stigma that people in high-risk subpopulations often face, so that NGOs can work more effectively.

In the baseline scenario, before any intervention, we assume that only 20 per cent of sex workers and 5 per cent of men having sex with casual or commercial partners use condoms consistently, that is, in every act of intercourse. We also assume that none of the women in steady relationships are using condoms.

The simulations show the impact of instantaneously raising consistent condom use among sex workers to 90 percent, and among the other two groups to 20 percent. These levels were selected because the authors believed that they are realistically achievable in some countries. In other countries, it may be possible to exceed the levels of condom use simulated here. Among those who use condoms, the failure rate through breakage or misuse is assumed to be 5 percent.

The simulations also show the impact of increased STD treatment on HIV prevalence. The baseline scenario assumes that 25 per cent of all STD cases that produce symptoms are effectively treated and that there is no specific screening or treatment program for sex workers. The simulations show the impact of increasing the share of symptomatic STDs treated to 75 per cent in the general population and, in a separate scenario, the impact of implementing a monthly screening and treatment program that covers 90 per cent of sex workers. In the latter intervention, it is assumed that 5 per cent of sex workers are not cured.

Despite the different underlying patterns of sexual behaviour, the impact of specific interventions shows some striking consistencies across populations:

— Achieving 90 per cent condom use among sex workers results in a dramatic drop in HIV prevalence in all three populations where there is commercial sex, even though sex workers comprise only a very small share of each population (0.25 per cent or fewer women). STD screening and treatment for sex workers is far less powerful.

— Increased STD treatment among the general population is less effective than raising condom use among those with many partners. This is not surprising, since people with high-risk behaviour generate a disproportionate number of STD cases, and condoms prevent transmission of both HIV and STDs. STD treatment among the general population and condom use by women in stable relationships have the largest impact in the populations with concurrent casual sex.

— The impact of greater condom use among women in stable relationships is very small, and in the serial monogamy population it has almost no impact on the epidemic. In the population where the epidemic is driven by commercial sex, condom use by Monogamous women slightly accelerates a decline in HIV prevalence, while in the other two populations it merely slows the growth of a still-expanding epidemic.

— In the epidemic fuelled by commercial sex alone, all of the interventions produce an absolute decline in HIV prevalence; in the epidemic fuelled solely by casual sex, none of the simulated interventions is sufficient to cause an absolute decline.

— In the population with concurrent commercial and casual sex, prevalence declines in response to 90 per cent condom use among sex workers; 20 per cent condom use by men in casual sex keeps prevalence from rising. Other interventions in this population merely slow the expanding epidemic.

— In the population practising serial monogamy, increased condom use by sex workers is the only intervention that results in an absolute decline in HIV prevalence.

There is always spillover between interventions intended for people with different rates of partner change, so any particular intervention is likely to change behaviour in more than one group of people but to differing degrees. Further, combined interventions to multiple groups will have greater impact than single interventions; for example, working only with sex workers to raise condom use will be less effective than simultaneously working with both sex workers and their clients. However, these simulations show that greatest share of the impact will be achieved through the interventions that succeed in changing the behaviour of those with the highest rates of partner change.

Although the overall pattern of sexual behaviour in the population does affect the impact of interventions, prevention of infection among those with the highest rates of partner change has a large effect irrespective of the underlying patterns of sexual behaviour in the population. Assuming that it is not a great deal more expensive to increase rates of condom use among those with high rates of partner change—sex workers or other—focusing condom subsidies and promotion efforts on changing their behaviour is likely to be highly cost-effective.

Studies of the cost-effectiveness of HIV interventions in developing countries are rare and not transferable. Fewer than half a dozen studies have documented the costs and effects of preventive interventions in developing countries. Most evaluation studies measure impact by changes in intermediate behaviours that are believed to affect risk-such as the increase in condom use, or knowledge about HIV prevention, or the number of people receiving sterile syringes.

The number of HIV infections averted is then extrapolated on the basis of assumptions about the relationship between the behaviour and HIV incidence. However, the lack of good data on sexual behaviour and on the relation between sexual behaviour and incidence makes these benefits very difficult to assess. Virtually no studies, except those based on simulations, have measured the impact of interventions on secondary cases where they are thought to exist. None to our knowledge have taken into account the external benefits of interventions or the issue of complementarities between interventions.

While cost-effectiveness studies can be very useful in deciding among alternative interventions in a given setting and stage of the epidemic, their conclusions are usually not easily transferable to other settings. Ideally, we would like to know the costs and effects of alternative interventions implemented in the same setting, but this has rarely been done.

Interventions focused on those most likely to contract and spread HIV should be more cost-effective from the public perspective, because preventing infection in a person with risky behaviour prevents many secondary infections among individuals with whom they mix—some of whom practice high-risk behaviour and some of whom practice lower-risk behaviour. In fact, the extent to which ongoing programs affect those who practice high-risk behaviour is often unknown.

Although it is highly desirable to focus public interventions on those who are most likely to contract and spread HIV, identifying and reaching these individuals can be difficult, especially where legal sanctions and social stigma cause these people to want to avoid being discovered. The costs of reaching those most likely to contract and spread the virus can have a significant impact on the cost-effectiveness of intervention.

Since individuals with high-risk behaviour cannot be easily identified, programs need to focus interventions on people with characteristics that are highly correlated with risky behaviour. However, some sex workers consistently use condoms, and some government employees who have many partners do not. Intervening to change the behaviour of people with specific characteristics like age, sex, occupation, or geographic area is not a perfect way to reach those with high-risk behaviour.

The lack of perfect criteria for focusing interventions on those with the highest-risk behaviours is one source of leakage of program resources. This reduces the cost-effectiveness of interventions if resources go to people with lower-risk behaviour.

On the other hand, leakage may improve cost-effectiveness if resources go to people with even riskier behaviour than those targeted. Surveys of sexual behaviour, such as those conducted by WHO/GPA and DHS, can help to overcome these problems by establishing the characteristics and geographic location of those who have unprotected sex and high rates of partner change. Unless programs are carefully designed and implemented, targeting prevention programs to groups with specific characteristics may stigmatize members and lead to discrimination, making future prevention efforts more difficult and less effective.

There must be a broad prevention strategy that assigns priority to activities based on the principles of epidemiology, public economics, and cost-effectiveness. Whatever the stage of the epidemic, this strategy calls for a strong emphasis on prevention activities starting with those at highest risk of contracting and spreading HIV and covering as many others as available resources allow.

As the epidemic expands, it will increasingly require efforts to prevent infection among people with relatively lower levels of risk, which will raise the cost of prevention activities. If the epidemic is to be contained, this expansion of activities must not weaken the fundamental commitment to work with those most likely to contract and spread the virus.

Provision of public goods or ensuring their provision by regulation is an important role for government at all stages of an HIV/AIDS epidemic. Governments should invest in the information-collecting infrastructure they need to monitor the epidemic and to identify where high-risk behaviours are practised and how to reach those at highest risk. In a nascent epidemic, understanding levels of HIV and STD infection in the subpopulations most likely to contract and spread HIV, the underlying patterns of sexual behaviour, and the nature of the links to lower-risk subpopulations are critical pieces of information for assessing the probability of a more extensive epidemic.

As the epidemic progresses, governments need to monitor, in addition, the spread of HIV to populations at lower risk and to support evaluation of the costs and effectiveness of alternative interventions. The need to reduce the negative externalities of high-risk behaviour, as well as the insights of epidemiology, argue for heavily subsidizing safer behaviour among those most likely to contract and spread HIV in countries at all stages of the HIV/AIDS epidemic. It is not necessary to wait for HIV to take hold to make widespread knowledge, 100 per cent condom use, and quick recognition and treatment of other STDs the norm among those more likely to contract and spread HIV, such as sex workers, bar maids, long-distance truck drivers, the military and police, millers or factory workers living away from home, and homosexual and bisexual men with multiple partners.

The case for rapid action is even stronger in the case of injecting drug users because of the potential for very rapid increases in HIV prevalence in this subpopulation, and the subsequent spread of HIV to others, including their sex partners (some of whom may be sex workers) and their children. In a nascent HIV epidemic, such highly focused actions may be sufficient to dramatically slow the spread of the virus.

In countries with concentrated and generalized epidemics, preventing HIV among those with the highest chances of contracting and spreading the virus is still essential to slowing the epidemic. However, behaviour change among with less-risky behaviour who may nonetheless inadvertently spread the virus will be necessary to reverse the course of the epidemic.

With respect to ensuring equity, in countries with nascent epidemics, government can protect the poor best by acting early and decisively to prevent an epidemic. In countries with generalized epidemics, the risk of infection has risen for everyone and poverty should not restrict access to preventive services. Government can ensure that the poor have access to the knowledge, skills, and means to prevent HIV.

The cost-effectiveness of interventions aimed at people with different levels of risky behaviour will also change as HIV spreads from those who practice more risky behaviour to those at relatively lower risk. Interventions for those most likely to contract and spread HIV are still likely to be highly cost-effective. In countries where HIV has spread widely in the general population, the cost-effectiveness of preventive interventions for lower-risk populations, such as subsidies for STD treatment, provision of safe blood, and reproductive health and AIDS education in schools, improves. However, these programs do not generate many externalities: their benefits accrue mainly to the person who uses them. While such interventions will prevent HIV infections and save lives, they will not do so as efficiently as interventions focused on those more likely to contract and spread HIV and they will often not be sufficient to reverse the course of the epidemic.

Furthermore, the costs of providing these services to the entire population at low risk of spreading HIV are potentially very large. In light of the substantial individual benefits of these services, people who are not poor will usually be willing and able to pay for them. In countries with scarce financial resources, the priority should be first on guaranteeing equity in access to these services by the poor.

Not all developing countries face equal resource constraints in pursuing this strategy. In the lowest-income countries, prevention should start among those whose behaviour generates or is likely to generate the higher reproductive rate for HIV; subsidized prevention to others with lower HIV reproductive rates that are still greater than 1 can be extended as resources permit.

Middle-income countries may have the resources, even in the earliest stages of the epidemic, to finance interventions for a much larger share of those for whom the HIV reproductive rates would be greater than 1. They may also have the resources to subsidize to a greater extent services for the poor and to extend prevention subsidies to subpopulations that are unlikely to spread HIV to others.

At an operational level it is impossible to determine the actual or potential reproductive rate of HIV for any group of individuals. However, using information about the average number of partners, condom use, and injecting behaviour from surveys and epidemiological surveillance, subpopulations in a given country can be ranked from those with the highest-risk behaviour those most likely to contract and spread HIV to those with the lowest-risk behaviour.

Once the highest-priority subpopulations have been effectively reached, programs can be expanded to cover those with progressively less-risky behaviour, provided that sufficient resources are available. Indeed, if sustained behaviour change is achieved in the highest-priority groups, the relative priority assigned to other groups will increase.

Of course, no ranking of this sort can apply to all countries, or even to a single country over time. To overcome problems in locating the people most likely to contract and spread HIV at any given point in time, it is essential that policymakers and program managers finance collection of the necessary information for cost-effective use of the scarce resources available for HIV prevention.

Countries at the nascent stage of the epidemic have a unique opportunity to act early, to make a few key investments, and largely prevent an HIV epidemic. Not all countries with low levels of infection will necessarily go on to experience an HIV epidemic, even without government action. However, our inadequate understanding of the distribution of different behaviours in the population and the links between different subpopulations make it difficult to predict which among the countries will be so lucky and which will not.

Furthermore, even in countries where high-risk behaviour is relatively rare, patterns of sexual and injecting behaviour can change with economic and social conditions. Interventions at the nascent stage are the most effective and will likely involve far less total cost than if implemented after HIV has saturated subpopulations with high-risk behaviour.

These recommendations are not meant to limit the scope of government involvement if there are ample resources and public will to undertake even more. Rather, our intention is to point out the minimum set of activities that all governments should be engaged in to improve the efficiency and equity of prevention programs and a rational order in which to expand these activities if HIV spreads or more resources become available.

The overwhelming impression left by the AIDS in the world-wide survey and national AIDS control plans started by many countries, is that many countries have launched a collection of AIDS prevention activities without clear-cut priorities; indeed, many programs do not focus on preventing infections among people most likely to contract and spread the virus. The lack of understanding the importance of spreading virus, domestic political considerations and the preferences of international donors for particular programs are probably also responsible. Nevertheless, in such an environment, limited resources are likely to be stretched very thin, and the cost-effectiveness of public expenditure on prevention is likely to be low.

The limited evidence available suggests that as much as one-quarter of all developing countries have yet to initiate systematic monitoring of HIV prevalence. A background study for AIDS in the world-wide classified countries into four groups according to whether HIV sentinel surveillance sites were planned (but not yet operating), limited, many, or extensive.

The good news is that countries at the generalized stage of the epidemic were most likely to have many or extensive sites, while those at the concentrated and nascent stages were most likely to have limited sites. However, one in five developing countries at the nascent stage of the epidemic reported no sentinel surveillance sites, and for another 14 per cent the extent of sentinel surveillance was unknown. If we add all the countries reporting only planned sites to those countries for which information about sites was inadequate to determine their extent, we find that 27 countries—more than one-fifth of countries at all stages of the epidemic—were not reporting any operating HIV sentinel surveillance sites in January 1995.

Even in those countries that have some form of sentinel surveillance, information on HIV prevalence among those most likely to contract and spread the virus is often lacking.

Although delays in the receipt of reports probably account for some missing data, available information was insufficient to classify 31 developing countries by stage of the epidemic, usually because of a lack of information on those presumed on average to practice riskier behaviour—sex workers, injecting drug users, men who have sex with men, the military, and STD patients.

Among the 123 developing countries attempted to classify, 43 countries (35 per cent) had no information on HIV prevalence in any group with presumed high-risk behaviour during the last 5 years. While it is more convenient to monitor HIV trends among blood donors and women attending antenatal clinics, regular monitoring of HIV Prevalence early in the epidemic among those who practice high-risk behaviour is much more important.

In addition to ensuring more and better monitoring of HIV prevalence, governments urgently need information on patterns of sexual behaviour, condom use, and drug-injecting behaviour. The heterogeneity of behaviour and the extent of mixing between people with high and low-risk behaviour determine the baseline shape of the AIDS epidemic. Countries at all stages of the epidemic need information on the prevalence and distribution of risky behaviours among representative samples of men and women to understand the likely path of the epidemic and how the epidemic can be minimized.

However, this information remains scarce. Fewer than 20 developing countries are known to have undertaken sexual behaviour surveys, such as those sponsored by GPA or DHS, that could provide such information.

Evaluations of HIV prevention programs often fail to measure the costs of interventions or their impact, reporting instead on indicators of process and implementation. Information on costs and impact is important not only for assessing the most efficient allocation of resources, but also for demonstrating the effectiveness of interventions to change behaviour among those most likely to contract and spread HIV and the spillover benefits to the low-risk population. Developing countries need better information on the costs and effects of pilot interventions, which interventions affect whose behaviour, and at what cost.

Most countries have a few interventions that focus on people most likely to contract and spread HIV, but most of these programs achieve only limited coverage. To arrest the epidemic, the coverage of preventive measures directed toward these groups needs to be expanded considerably. Although many people practising high-risk behaviour are difficult to reach for prevention, some people whose circumstances may put them at higher risk of HIV infection are part of "captive" populations that can be readily identified: the military, police, and prisoners. Because governments usually have much easier access to these organized groups than to injecting drug users, sex workers, or others with many casual partners. It should be possible for governments to reach nearly all members of each of these groups with preventive interventions only.

The Civil-Military Alliance to combat HIV and AIDS conducted a survey of prevention activities among the militaries of 50 countries, about half of which were low and middle-income countries. Although individual country results are not available (countries were assured that responses would be confidential), the aggregate data clearly reveal that prevention programs in the military often fall short of complete coverage.

Low coverage of other groups of people presumed to practice riskier-than-average behaviour can be seen in a small survey of UNAIDS Country Programme Advisers conducted for this report. The survey asked the advisers who work in 32 developing countries to identify groups of people with high-risk behaviour and to comment on the extent to which programs focused on prevention in these groups; the approximate percentage of each group covered; and the extent of government encouragement and finance of these programs.

Although the results reflect the assessment of the advisers rather than the national AIDS program managers and cannot be generalized beyond the countries surveyed, they nonetheless reveal tremendous scope for improving outreach to those who are most likely to contract and spread HIV. Respondents named adolescents as the subpopulation most likely to be the recipient of an intervention, financed either by government or the private sector.

All countries had at least one program focused on youth, even though in many of the countries it is not clear to what extent adolescents engage in risky behaviour. About nine out of ten countries reported a public or private program focused on sex workers, while about seven out of ten countries had a program focused on injecting drug users; a slightly lower proportion of countries had programs that focus on the military and on men who have sex with men.

However, respondents estimated that these programs on average covered only about one-half of the relevant group with high-risk behaviour. Coverage was highest for adolescents and the military, and lowest for men who have sex with men and injecting drug users.

The UNAIDS Country Programme Advisers also reported that governments were least likely to finance and most likely to impede prevention programs targeted to men who have sex with men and injecting drug users. Although six out of ten governments funded prevention programs for adolescents, only about one-third did so for the military and for sex workers. Two advisers indicated that the government in their country promoted prevention for the general population of heterosexuals, but neither encouraged nor discouraged programs for those most likely to contract and spread the virus.

While some prevention programs have attempted to encourage safer behaviour among those most likely to contract and spread HIV, coverage is generally low. The fact that governments may have logistic and political difficulties in reaching groups such as sex workers and injecting drug users, while understandable, does not detract from the urgent need to assure the fullest possible coverage of these groups. Often these obstacles can be overcome through government funding and support of NGOs.

Moreover, in many countries coverage is low even among "captive" populations, such as the military; where this is the case, governments have an opportunity to inexpensively reach these groups with information and other prevention interventions. Effective interventions with broad coverage of those with high-risk behaviour will go a long way toward preventing infection among others engaging in high-risk activities and among the lower-risk population.

The effectiveness of government programs in ensuring access to prevention for the poor has rarely been evaluated. However, improving equity of access to condoms is one of the major objectives of condom social marketing programs and free government distribution of condoms.

Condom availability and use in general have expanded considerably, partly as a spontaneous response to HIV and partly as a result of social marketing and other public, private, and donor-sponsored programmes. As of 1996, 60 developing countries had functioning condom social marketing programs, although not all were on a national scale. The extent to which these programs disproportionately help poor people to obtain condoms is not clear. As we have seen earlier in this chapter, in most countries, people with higher incomes and education are more likely to use condoms. Providing subsidized condoms to low-risk individuals who would have purchased them at market prices, would neither improve equity nor reduce the epidemic.

Likewise, while condom use has risen in both the subsidized and commercial market, it is still not clear the extent to which subsidized programmes have squeezed out private sales. This is likely to be an important issue in older condom social marketing programmes, after their initial effect on popularizing condoms and generating greater demand has worn off.

A second way in which these programs promote equity is by encouraging condom use among those most likely to contract and spread HIV, forestalling or slowing the epidemic before it reaches the poor. Unfortunately, relatively little is known about the extent to which condom social marketing programs are used by those with the highest rates of partner change—which is the key to their effectiveness in slowing the epidemic. Surveys of sexually active adults confirm that people are far more likely to use a condom for sex with a casual or extramarital partner than a steady partner or a spouse. But they do not show whether these programmes reach people with the highest rates of partner change. Do these programs lower the costs of condom use sufficiently to bring about high-use rates among sex workers, soldiers, truck drivers, and other people with many partners? By selling through nontraditional outlets like bars and hotels, condom social marketing programs are probably much more likely to reach people with risky behaviour than are conventional programs that distribute condoms through health clinics.

The condom program may also fail to reach those with the highest rates of partner change. For example, sex workers and young, sexually active men do not frequent by visit health or family planning clinics. Furthermore, women who need condoms for STD prevention may be reluctant to obtain them from community health or family planning clinics, even if free of charge, because of inconvenience, an unreliable supply, or a desire for anonymity. These problems can be overcome if condoms are promoted specifically for HIV and STD prevention and if they can be readily and cheaply obtained in nontraditional outlets readily accessible to people in situations that tend to be conducive to casual and commercial sex. One way for governments to stimulate demand for condoms for disease prevention is to end restrictions on condom advertising. But even when there are no legal barriers, open promotion of condom use can be extremely controversial if it is seen as encouraging promiscuity. Messages must convey useful information and at the same time be directed to the appropriate populations so as to avoid offending influential leaders and segments of the public.

# 9

# Community Development and AIDS Prevention

The HIV/AIDS epidemic in India is still in its early stages. Yet an estimated one million Indians are already infected with HIV. Urgent action is called for by government and nongovernmental organisations. The South India AIDS Action Programme (SIAAP) is responding to the threat of AIDS by helping to inform and mobilize their NGO and community organisations, and providing services to some of the most vulnerable groups carrying HIV/AIDS.

In October 1988, the PANOS Institute, U.K. commissioned Shyamla Nataraj, at that time a Madras-based freelance journalist with little interest in or knowledge of AIDS, to write about a group of 30 women sex workers who had been diagnosed HIV-positive and were being detained by the police in Madras. Because of official fears of publicity, it took Shyamla six months to gain access to the women, and when eventually she did, it was a very emotional and shocking experience.

Unable to drop the matter after writing her article, she sought legal advice and decided to take the Government of the State of Tamil Nadu to court for unlawful detention of the women. Shyamla eventually won the case and the women were released in July 1990. While the court case was still being contested, however, Shyamla had been travelling around South India to investigate what support services were available for people with HIV/AIDS, but had found none at all. She became increasingly worried about what would happen to the women if and when they were finally released from detention.

Legal action alone, she realized, was of little use without a supportive social infrastructure. She was also struck by the almost complete lack of AIDS awareness at all levels of society, including among NGOs and community groups. Upon returning to Madras she established a link with the Voluntary Health Services Centre in Madras, who agreed to provide her with a bank account for channelling funds and to rent her an office. After several anxious months the project finally received financial assistance from the WHO Partnership Programme (in collaboration with the PANOS Institute) and the Ford Foundation.

## NGO Workshops

Shyamla had begun linking up with existing NGO networks in South India, especially those of the Voluntary Health Association, the Association of Voluntary Agencies and the Social Welfare Board of Tamil Nadu State. In February 1991 she organized the first one-day, district-level workshop for NGOs in the Tirunelveli District Tamil Nadu. By September 1991, while still awaiting funding, she had organized twelve district-level workshops, with more than 200 NGOs participating. She had also developed a calendar and booklets, in English and Tamil, containing basic information about AIDS, and distributed copies of these to the NGOs participating in the workshops. For most participants these workshops were the first time they had ever received any information about AIDS, apart from occasional stories in the mass media. They reported that the experience helped them to clear up their misconceptions and fill important gaps in their knowledge.

In March 1992 SIAAP organized a five-day training workshop for 60 representatives of 45 NGOs from all over the State of Tamil Nadu. The topics covered included in-depth HIV/AIDS information, communication skills and funding. The participants also explored ways of networking more effectively among NGOs doing AIDS-related work in South India.

### FOLLOW-UP SUPPORT

The workshops so far organized have shown that NGOs, however well-motivated, need considerable help in planning AIDS intervention programmes. The NGOs that have participated in the workshops come from a wide range of ideological backgrounds and have different organizational capacities. Some are very cautious about becoming involved in new, potentially sensitive or controversial issues—such as HIV and AIDS —outside their existing areas of activity.

Most NGOs agreed that sexually transmitted diseases (STDs) were a common problem in their communities, but they felt unable to talk openly about the topic, or to provide diagnostic and clinical services to those affected, or even to forge links with organizations providing such services. Condom promotion was rare: most NGOs involved in health care concentrated on family planning methods which required women to take responsibility for contraception.

Few NGOs had much experience of collecting and analysing information to enable them to assess their programme needs. Many had difficulty in identifying possible intervention strategies for STD/HIV, control and prevention, tending to stick to approaches with which they were already familiar.

Programme monitoring and evaluation were almost nonexistent. Most importantly, NGO staff were unaccustomed to talking with their clients about sex and sexuality, and needed help in developing communication skills in this area. SIAAP received its first opportunity to provide follow-up support to an NGO when, in April 1991, the Madras Christian Council of Social Services (MCCSS) asked for help in setting up an AIDS education programme in some of the slums where they had been working. SIAAP helped MCCSS to design and conduct a survey to assess the needs of the slum communities, to develop an appropriate intervention strategy and programmed, and to recruit and train staff.

It soon became clear that in order to integrate the AIDS programme into the work of the organization, all the MCCSS staff needed information and training on HIV/AIDS. SIAAP worked with MCCSS staff to help them overcome their reluctance to talk about sex and to encourage non-judgemental attitudes. The work with MCCSS was very valuable for SIAAP's own staff as well, giving them the chance to actually experience what they were suggesting other NGOs should do.

### Lorry Drivers Project

In August 1991 SIAAP appointed G. Kumaresan (Kumar) to plan and implement a project aiming to protect long-distance lorry drivers and their sexual partners against HIV infection and other STDs. As in many other parts of the world, long-distance lorry drivers in South India are a group at high risk of contracting HIV infection and other STDs. Spending most of their working life on the road, away from their families, most drivers regularly engage in sex with partners other than their wives. Kumar brought with him two years experience of an HIV/STD prevention programme in Madras.

Originally the programme had tried distributing condoms to female prostitutes, but it soon became clear that the women were in no position to insist on their use. A more effective strategy was to concentrate on the prostitutes' clients. Shifting the responsibility to the clients also avoided the implication— too often conveyed— that prostitutes are uniquely responsible for spreading HIV and other STDs, and that their clients are merely victims. Kumar began the SIAAP initiative in October-November 1991 with a survey of long-distance lorry drivers who passed through Puzhal checkpoint.

The survey found that over 1,000 drivers and cab assistants passed through the checkpoint every day. Interviews with 200 drivers found that almost 90 per cent visited prostitutes but few used condoms. More than 90 per cent had suffered from an STD, and all were keen to learn how to avoid contracting STDs, including AIDS, in future.

SIAAP opened its health education booth at Puzhal in January 1992. A health educator meets with drivers individually in the booth to talk about HIV and AIDS and other sexually transmitted diseases. He also provides at least ten drivers a day with a pack of five condoms, after demonstrating their correct use on a model of a penis. Group discussions are also held. These always elicit a few laughs and help to bring down barriers against condom use. Once a week a video is also shown, mixing AIDS information with entertainment.

The booth is well accepted because it focuses on something its clients really want: prevention and treatment of STDs. Condoms are promoted not only for the prevention of AIDS and other STDs, but also as a family planning device. Kumar believes that about 75 per cent of condoms distributed are used for the purpose intended —most of the remainder are used for more ingenious purposes such as stopping oil leaks in lorry engines.

In April 1992, for the first time, the booth advertised that a medical team would come one evening and carry out STD testing. Over 30 customers turned up. Those with positive results were informed on their next stop, and sent for treatment at a clinic in the city. Since approximately the same population of drivers uses this route, over time the results of STD testing will give a reliable indication of the impact of the programme.

The possibility of offering HIV testing is still under consideration—so far only one driver has expressed an interest in being tested. The SIAAP health education booth, in itself, will have only a small impact on the spread of HIV and AIDS in South India. Its importance is that it represents a new strategy of AIDS control and prevention in South India, based on an acceptable approach to an occupational group at high risk of contracting the disease.

The project has yet to create sufficient demand for condoms to sell them at cost, but it has developed an approach that can be replicated by other organizations on other trucking routes, at bus stations, in ports, and wherever the long-distance lifestyle encourages sexual straying. Already five NGOs have asked SIAAP to help them set up similar projects in other parts of South India.

## WOMEN IN PROSTITUTION

Virtually no HIV/AIDS intervention programmes for women, as a group, in India. The few programmes that do exist are targeted specifically at women engaged in prostitution. The women tend to be regarded, however, as pools of infection rather than as human beings with their own problems, needs and rights.

The emphasis is usually on containing the spread of HIV infection into the community, rather than on providing care, support services and information to the women concerned. Recognizing the basic injustice and practical inadequacy of such an approach, SIAAP has started working with some of the women engaged in prostitution in the city of Madras.

In a conscious effort to move away from the usual stereotyped approach to sex workers, SIAAP tries to put the women themselves at the centre of the programme. SIAAP was aware that women sex workers viewed their own health as only one concern amongst many. Their main felt needs were for security in the face of the oppressive legal and social system within which they operate, and facilities for the care and education of their children. SIAAP therefore decided to address these two felt needs alongside specifically health-related issues.

In the next phase of the project, SIAAP plans to make counselling and STD services available as well. SIAAP also plans to arrange for school sponsorship for the women's children, In addition, SIAAP is working with a group of women activists and lawyers to examine ways of removing or restructuring the existing laws on prostitution, so that the women are not at the mercy of the entrenched, male-dominated control structure.

## VOLUNTEER TRAINING

SIAAP established a volunteer training programme in order to help equip people with the knowledge, skills and self-confidence they need to communicate with their peers about HIV and AIDS, in December 1991. By April 1992 three training workshops had been run for 25 volunteers. The first group consisted mainly of students, but subsequent groups have included a wider cross-section of the population first on basic information about HIV/AIDS, then moving on to more complex issues, and finally onto means of communicating about AIDS.

The potential of various means of communication is explored—posters, videos, oral presentations, discussions, one-to-one interactions, skits and street plays. Participants are encouraged to think about what forms of communication are most appropriate for their own peer education activities. Although the feedback so far has been very encouraging, the programme does not take place on a regular basis. Training sessions are organized only in response to specific requests from potential volunteers.

### STD SURVEY

Working in the slums of Madras brought home to SIAAP staff the need for STD services as well as AIDS education. The presence of an STD greatly increases the chances of HIV transmission between sexual partners. Without effective STD services, AIDS education in itself can have only limited value. SIAAP therefore believes that the diagnosis and treatment of STDs should be a key part of any strategy of AIDS control and prevention.

Yet there was very little reliable information about the actual prevalence of STDs and the diagnostic and treatment services available. SIAAP therefore engaged Dr. Roman Solomon to carry out a study to provide this information. The study found that men were generally well aware of the dangers of STDs and sought medical attention (including penicillin injections) after risky sex. Women, however, went for treatment of STDs only if they had a visible problem, and then almost invariably to private practitioners.

Very few women sought treatment for STDs at government hospitals and health centres, due to the lack of female STD specialists, the absence of privacy, the judgemental attitudes of doctors, the scarcity of specialist STD clinics and the cost of travelling to the few clinics available. NGOs working in the slum areas tended to concentrate on basic MCH services, referring STD cases to the general hospital. The study identified the urgent need for

STD diagnostic and treatment services to be provided in the slums, preferably by a mobile clinic capable of covering a larger population than one located in a hospital or health centre. SIAAP is currently exploring ways of trying to meet this need.

The scope and volume of SIAAP's work have increased dramatically since its humble beginnings, in January 1991, as a project with a one-year time span. Now it is registered as a Trust—a fully fledged NGO with the right to apply for and receive funds directly. SIAAP now has three main roles. First, it functions as a resource centre, helping NGOs to integrate HIV/AIDS prevention and control into existing community development programmes by providing information, training, technical support and materials. Second, it facilitates networking among NGOs in South India so that they can learn from one anothers' experiences and also assist one another in various ways. And third, it implements its own community-based activities: the projects for lorry drivers and women in prostitution, soon to be followed by the telephone information service and the drop-in centre.

The pressure to expand in order to provide urgently needed services also has financial implications. SIAAP's initial funding has been from foreign donors. The staff and members of the SIAAP Trust would prefer the programme's activities to be funded entirely from local sources—including government agencies, charitable organizations, the private business sector, individual donors and community groups.

They recognize, however, that this ideal may not be attainable in the near future. It is unlikely that the AIDS epidemic will wait for self-sustaining development to be achieved. Although some of SIAAP's future activities may well be funded by local donors, others will probably still be dependent on external support.

In the space of less than two years, SIAAP has helped to give NGOs in South India a headstart in planning AIDS control and prevention programmes that are integrated into existing community development activities. It has also developed an innovative programme providing AIDS-related information and services to two occupational groups at high risk of HIV infection.

# 10

# Human Survival: Vaccines to Disarm HIV

When a virus encounters a new host, it will remain if it can establish itself rapidly enough for transmission. Even if adaptation is long and difficult, the virus will remain as long as it can maintain at least some level of spread in the new population. If the host environment accommodates the newcomer well enough, an optimal equilibrium can be found between virus survival and host survival. This equilibrium may not be harmless to the host. If it is, it may not stay that way forever. The issue of harm to the host will arise when efficient spread requires destruction of cells crucial to host well-being and/or when it requires a virus load too high to be handled by host immunity.

When we see these viruses harm Asian monkeys, we assume they once harmed their natural African hosts. We see that several passages of SIV can increase virulence so that it infects more readily and kills faster. It may assume that continued passage would increase virulence to a point, then reverse the development, resulting eventually in an attenuated virus. This cannot be proved.

Whatever their virulence in the past, viruses like SRV and SIV can thrive generation after generation without doing harm to their accustomed host. When SRV and SIV are faced with insufficient numbers of this host and simultaneously meet an abundant new host, they jump, spread, and cause the eventual death of individuals in the new host population.

The fact that SIV or SRV in macaques can serve as a model for AIDS gives us some evidence that SRV or SIV cannot easily spread among Asian monkeys without harming them. But there are SIV strains that cause no harm to macaques whatsoever. We do not knowIt is not known whether their proportion in relation to harmful strains or how either kind would affect macaques in nature because neither would ever encounter macaques in nature. Looking from monkeys to humans, while HIV tends to kill us, HIV-1 has no detrimental effect on about one percent of infected individuals. And HIV-2 has no detrimental effect on about 90 percent of the people it infects.

In contrast, HIV-1 spreads strongly in humans compared with the chimpanzee SIV. Though harmful to humans, it is harmless in chimpanzees in the wild. So far we have no evidence from historical accounts that HIV-2 has ever been more harmful to humans—certainly never as harmful as HIV-1 is today. This suggests that from the virus point of view, the current level of HIV-2 spread is optimally adapted to the local West African environment. This is not to say that under different environmental conditions, such as HIV-2 now meets in India, the virus will not behave differently.

Since HIV-2 seems happy with circulation that is not widespread, we must rethink "widespread" from a virus point of view. To us, it has a global connotation, but to a virus, a small area may be wide enough. Currently, HIV-2 can sustain itself by infecting about one percent of West African humans, especially since SIV provides backup, continually crossing over from West African monkeys to start new strains of HIV-2.

This SIV needs little help from its human variant to sustain the family. Monkeys are its main reservoir, and what little is contributed by HIV-2 is incidental to family survival. In contrast, humans are the main reservoir of HIV-1. Though the virus may have come to us from chimpanzees, it appears to be rare in those animals today. No other host for HIV-1 is known among primates or any other animals. The virus seems to rely for its survival completely on human dissemination, and humans have spread it beyond its original boundaries.

Normally it would have remained limited to its original homeland in the western equatorial rain forest, but humans increasingly travel the world. They now carry HIV (and all human pathogens) far and wide. The chances are close to zero that a human virus infection will remain confined to its natural ecological niche, as do the infections of most animals (unless those animals are transported by humans). So HIV- 1 might have been happy with circulation in a very local human population, but we ourselves have carried it far beyond its natural evolutionary pathway

Another way to contrast HIV-1 and HIV-2 is to look at their genetic closeness to related viruses. The SIV of sooty mangabeys is so closely related to HIV-2 that some monkey strains are hard to tell apart from human strains. This means that SIV can shift to a human host as HIV-2 with very limited adaptation, perhaps none at all. The virus can just do its usual thing: when it finds itself in a human, it can replicate without much problem. It reproduces a little less than in a sooty, perhaps, but can comfortably sustain itself. One may say that this SIV is optimally adapted not merely to one species of monkey or primate but to a whole community of human and nonhuman primates. It is adapted to the shared habitat of humans and monkeys in West Africa.

Multiple adaptations lead to virus flexibility in terms of hosts, which leads to virus survival at low cost to the population at hand.

The spread of SIV/HIV-2 as well as BaEV argues for this line of reasoning, though SRV offers an exception. SRV is apparently quite comfortable infecting only talapoins, even though humans are handy. It has been noted that the virus load in SIV-infected but healthy sooty mangabeys is as high as the load of HIV-1 and HIV-2 in individuals who are developing AIDS (but much higher than in individuals not developing AIDS). Although this point is still debated in the scientific community, it appears to suggest that the level of circulating virus is indeed related to effective spread, but varies in its effect on the host species.

Clearly, the sooty mangabey can remain healthy with an amount of virus in its body that makes humans very sick.

Progression to disease after HIV-1 or HIV-2 infection depends more on our genetic makeup (as a species and as individuals) than the makeup of the virus. Obviously, we would greatly benefit if HIV-2 could outcompete HIV-1 in the human population, but this seems unlikely. Studies conducted in Dakar, Senegal, by the Harvard group headed by Phyllis Kanki and Max Essex show that, under similar conditions, heterosexual spread of HIV-2 is much slower than HIV-1.

There data suggest that HIV-2 is less infectious and therefore less capable of maintaining itself than HIV-1 in a human population. Sexual transmission of HIV-2 is rare, and its perinatal transmission is even more rare compared with that of HIV-1. Since sexual and perinatal transmission are the most common routes in Africa, HIV-2 will lag far behind HIV- 1 in a shared environment on that continent. Not only is HIV-2 slower to infect than HIV-1, but it is much slower to cause disease. In short, in a competitive situation, HIV-1 spreads well and usually makes the host sick. HIV-2 hardly spreads at all and causes disease, if ever, only several decades after infection. An individual is undeniably better off with an HIV-2 infection than with an HIV- 1 infection. In fact, in places like West Africa, where both viruses circulate, HIV-2 offers some protection against HIV-1. The Kanki and Essex group have shown that individuals infected with HIV-2 are less likely to be infected with HIV- I than those who are not infected with HIV-2. They found that only after HIV-2 infection has caused a decline in $CD_4^+$ cells can HIV-1 infection get a foothold.

However, this means that HIV-2 protection is only temporary and, once dual infection occurs, disease progression is faster than with either infection alone. Finally, we must remember that HIV-2 is an AIDS virus: it will ultimately cause AIDS and death when it manages to cause infection and disease. Its temporary protection against HIV-1 is nevertheless a good sign. It suggests that a weak AIDS virus has the potential to protect against a much stronger one, even when the two are as distantly related as HIV-2 and HIV-1.

Limited evidence pointing in the same direction comes from the rare individuals infected with HIV-1 who are long-term nonprogressors. These are individuals who escape impairment of the immune system for more than ten to fifteen years. Most of them can thank their own unusually good immune response and/or HIV target cells that are unusually poor at propagating the virus. But a tiny fraction of them (less than half a percent of all individuals infected with HIV-1) must thank their luck in catching an attenuated HIV-1 strain.

The big problem is that although attenuated HIVs may protect individuals, such strains are not likely to end the AIDS epidemic by outcompeting the more dangerous HIVs in the general population. This at least is true of the naturally attenuated strains we have seen so far. Whether HIV-1 or HIV-2, naturally attenuated strains simply do not spread efficiently. To do so, they would have to increase their production. This would probably make them more virulent, putting us back where we started.

Is there any way that a retrovirus can spread well while doing its host no damage? We all know the answer by now. It can, but only in the right host. African green monkeys and sootys, as well as talapoins, can cope with high levels of circulating virus without experiencing the slightest sign of harm from their SIV or SRV strains. It seems likely, but cannot be proved, that when these populations were first exposed, most infected monkeys died. If so, a few males and females must have been able to survive infection. They produced offspring also able to survive infection, and eventually the monkey population—the ecological niche—was dominated by hosts that could coexist peacefully with the virus.

Another kind of coexistence has been seen among certain mice. The story starts early in this century when researchers developed AKR mice, a strain that is extraordinarily likely to get cancer of the thymus.

In the end, this cancer causes the death of virtually all affected mice about a year after birth. Though discovered in laboratory mice, this intricate phenomenon also occurs in a certain type of feral mouse. In this wild population it is offset by another phenomenon: an intriguing case of retroviral protection against retroviral disease. It was detected in studies by Murray Gardner, Christine Kozak, and Stephen O'Brien of the University of California at Davis and the National Institutes of Health at Bethesda and Frederick, Maryland.

In the late 1960s, Gardner captured many types of wild mice in southern California. Testing them for infection with cancer-causing retroviruses, he found most types free of them, but one population was not. Gardner had captured this population on a farm near Lake Casitas. Now called Lake Casitas mice, they were found to be infected with murine leukemia virus (MuLV). Over a period of observation, almost one-third of the animals developed disease: 18 percent had lymphoma and 12 percent had paralysis of the hind limbs. Later two strains of MuLV were identified, one causing the cancer and the other, paralysis. Since the infection rate was so high and about a third of the infections were lethal, long-term survival of the Lake Casitas mouse population was surprising. Even though MuLV-induced disease occurs only after sexual maturity, the infection and its detrimental effects would be expected to decimate these mice and eventually to wipe them out. This was especially true since MuLV is primarily transmitted by milk ingestion.

A substantial proportion of Lake Casitas mice never became infected with MuLV despite its endemicity. This proportion was resistant even to direct injection of purified virus, whereas the rest of the mice were vulnerable. A virus-host balance had somehow been established in which the virus survived in the vulnerable population (which eventually got sick and sometimes died), while the host population survived in its resistant members. If all Lake Casitas mice were vulnerable, they would eventually die out, taking the virus with them, but virus and host had reached a kind of detente.

During more than twenty years of observation, the Lake Casitas mouse population was seen to remain MuLV-infected at a stable level of just over 50 percent. MuLV-induced disease remained the main cause of death among these mice, but the virus did not overwhelm the population. Nor did the number of MuLV-resistant mice grow to threaten virus survival.

This story shows that a retrovirus can sustain itself very effectively in a population that is partly susceptible to infection and partly resistant. The virus could sustain itself because it was passaged to the next mouse generation during feeding of the newborns, before disease debilitated any infected mice. Gardner wondered exactly how the protective phenomenon worked. He found the answer by breeding AKR females with Lake Casitas males with and without MuLV infection. His question was, did mating with a MuLV-resistant male produce offspring resistant to the blood cancer or leukemia seen in all the AKR mothers?

The answer was that when the father was completely resistant, that is, he had two MuLV-resistance genes, one on both chromosomes. However, when the gene was resistant but had only one MuLV-resistance gene, the offspring were split. Half were resistant and half were not. What was this gene that protected some Lake Casitas mice against MuLV infection?

As we know, a retrovirus enters a susceptible cell because the proteins on the viral envelope can attach to a receptor molecule on the cell surface. The moment cells are infected by a retrovirus, they become resistant to infection by retroviruses that use the same receptor. They are shielded by viral interference since their receptor molecules are saturated with bound envelope molecules. In the MuLV-resistant Lake Casitas mice, the receptor molecules were found to be saturated.

However, no sign of prior infection was seen. The mice were postulated to have an endogenous and crippled version of MuLV that expressed an MuLV envelope on the surface of susceptible cells. And indeed it was finally shown, by Hidetoshi Ikeda and Haruhiko Sugimura of the University of Tokyo as well as by the American group of Christine Kozak, that MuLV-resistant mice carry a truncated and noninfectious fragment of MuLV in all their cells.

The bottom line is that, at this point, all Lake Casitas mice are infected with MuLV. About half have the exogenous virus that makes them sick; the others have the endogenous virus that keeps them well. Apparently, this situation benefits not only the mice but the virus; at least it does not threaten the virus. It shows that optimal host-virus interaction need not lead to the complete harmlessness of the virus in a given host population.

It seems to suggest a strategy against AIDS: the genetic engineering of humans to give them endogenous HIV that would express an envelope protein to fool exogenous HIV. Unfortunately, there are major problems with this model. First of all, HIV never infects the human embryo, so it could never become endogenous to humans. Even if it could, the treatment is too laborious (and AIDS already too widespread) to render all humans in the world resistant.

If somehow this could be accomplished, we would not be resistant to all possible HIV strains but only to the most typical strains. Natural selection would then favour a typical strains that could threaten us in new ways. Needless to say, we cannot copy the Lake Casitas model by making only half the world resistant.

HIV-1 is in a class by itself. The most dangerous of all AIDS viruses, it was pressured to jump from chimpanzees or colobus monkeys to humans. Its arduous route has involved splitting into subtypes, adapting, and spreading according to whatever conditions it met. By now, some subtypes appear optimally adapted to anal transmission, others to vaginal transmission. Either way, all HIV-1 subtypes eventually cause AIDS, and they do so more rapidly than HIV-2. HIV-1 appears to have no other major reservoir than humans, and, so far, its optimal spread could be achieved only with virus variants that are ultimately fatal. No rapidly spreading and replicating HIV-1 strains have been identified that do not cause disease. This indicates that HIV-1 will not become harmless to its human host simply through natural selection for the best-spreading variant. On the other hand, HIV-1 continues to search for more efficient viral dissemination. It spawns more and more recombinants, particularly in Africa but also in Asia. HIV-1 subtype E, the virus that spreads most efficiently in Asia, is a stable envelope recombinant: a subtype A virus with a new coat. Subtype A appears to mate frequently with subtype C, another variant rapidly spreading in Asia.

The virus seems to keep looking for the best configuration of its genes for optimal spread in the human population at hand, by the transmission route at hand. Its search may represent an opportunity for human survival. Perhaps one of its many recombination events will fortuitously yield a rapidly spreading HIV- 1 that is harmless to us. Unfortunately, no evidence suggests that this lucky event is imminent, or even very likely. Somehow we must push HIV-1 evolution in the right direction.

Our best long-term strategy against AIDS is to develop a live vaccine. It must be an HIV-1 strain that is harmless (or relatively so) but spreads well enough in the human population to assure strain survival. It must also outcompete more harmful strains. It must be a strain that can take over and drive HIV-1 into oblivion, as HIV-1 now threatens to do with HIV-2 in West Africa. Such a strain is not likely to occur naturally. We have seen that naturally attenuated HIV strains do not spread well enough to outcompete dangerous strains.

We must develop conventional vaccines that consist of HIV proteins, or antigens, that spark our immune system to defend us better. Science will continue to seek treatments that lower the level of virus. Ideally they will not only limit disease in the treated individual but limit viral potential to infect new hosts. However, we cannot be over-optimistic. Such therapies are on the horizon but will most likely involve drugs that will be far too difficult and costly to provide to the whole world, particularly to the people at highest risk: those living in poor areas without education or health services. Right now, brief treatment of pregnant women can often reduce perinatal HIV infection of newborns. It is not only costly but must be delivered just at the end of pregnancy.

A constantly shifting combination of drugs is needed to keep up with shifts in HIV resistance. Even with the best combination, infections will keep spreading, and HIV may well develop multidrug resistance, making treatment harder and harder. Already drug-resistant mutants have begun to circulate that hamper the two-part goal of reducing disease and reducing infection of new hosts.

The conventional type that elicits immunity may never completely prevent HIV infection. However, once infection occurs, such a vaccine could lower the circulating virus load, preventing spread of infection and progression to AIDS. This idea is feasible but, so far, no vaccines consisting of individually produced viral proteins have been tested in humans. Their development has been severely delayed by the lack of an HIV-1 animal model, a living humanlike system in which to observe vaccine effects.

Such an animal is still lacking, but we now have the next best thing. Classically, immunity to the all-important virus envelope leads to prevention of infection, or at least disease. Based on this concept, a virus was recently constructed, in the laboratories of Bill Narayan in Kansas City and Joe Sodroski with Norm Letvin in Boston, that wraps the genetic material of SIV in an HIV-1 envelope. Known as SHIV, it is SIV disguised as HIV-1.

Passages in monkeys have shown these hybrid viruses to be able to replicate and cause disease. Produced by in vitro fertilization, they are man-made recombinants never found in nature. They have opened the way to test quickly all kinds of viral envelope vaccines for their efficacy in protecting against infection and disease development. The HIV-1 envelope of these hybrids will be recognized by T cells and antibodies that attach to its distinctive proteins. If a preparation of HIV-1 envelope proteins protects rhesus macaques against infection or disease caused by SHIV, the same preparation most likely will also protect humans against infection and disease caused by HIV-1. We now have the means to find a safe and effective vaccine. We have the methods to monitor the shifting movements of HIV-1 strains. We know which viruses to watch and fear the most: HIV- 1C and E in Asia and HIV 1A and C in Africa. But having a vaccine and knowing where to use it do not automatically get it to the people who need it the most. Distribution remains a frustrating problem. Regardless of where the AIDS epidemic started, the people now at highest risk are the most deprived in the world.

A futuristic solution is to introduce HIV proteins in the food chain. The idea of edible vaccines was pioneered by Charles Arntzen of Cornell University in Ithaca, New York. Such vaccines would be simple and nonthreatening. Compliance would be assured since food is familiar, generally welcome, and often crucial for survival. The vaccines would be self-administered by those in need, not administered by outsiders often regarded with fear and suspicion. In collaboration with Arntzen, we have succeeded in producing potatoes that contain HIV proteins. In fact, their genetic material has been augmented with genes that express HIV proteins. But this is only a start. Such proteins must be expressed at a higher level, and, instead of potatoes, they must be expressed in something like a banana: a food with broad climatic range that is natural to Africa, Asia, and South America; a food that can be eaten without cooking.

Then, once the reengineered banana is eaten, the trick is to elicit immune response to the HIV proteins it smuggles into our system. Normally, foreign proteins are tolerated by the digestive tract so we can ingest and absorb nutrients. We would never survive if our immune system saw food as non-self and attacked everything we eat. So how can we get antibodies to attack the HIV proteins in bananas and not bananas as a whole or food in general? One strategy involves the genetic reengineering of the entire banana plant so that HIV proteins are not only expressed but encased in some kind of toxin. When the fruit is eaten, the digestive system will react to the toxin and trigger an immune response. The rest of the banana will be accepted as usual.

But if everything fails, we may still need a living vaccine, an HIV strain that will work for us. This evolutionary path might be our best long-term answer to AIDS. Such a strain, if introduced into a population at risk for HIV-1 infection, might offer individuals protection against HIV-1 and, ideally, would outcompete HIV-1 in the population. But this kind of evolutionary project demands answers to many big questions.

First of all, it is not yet certain that the disease-causing effect of HIV-2 can be separated from its efficient spread and replicative capacity. The same is true for HIV-1 strains: all subtypes that spread efficiently appear also to cause disease. Second, though we have SHIV, we still lack an animal model for HIV-1 or HIV-2 as they appear in nature; this is because in nature no other primate or animal of any kind gets sick from HIV infection. Third and most frightening, only vigorous and well-replicating new HIV strains will protect against today's aggressive HIVs—but what if these new strains get out of hand? Can a vigorous and harmless virus be constructed without even the slightest chance of back mutation into a harmful virus?

This living vaccine must also spread from one host to another by sex or some other natural route. If a live, attenuated vaccine strain cannot spread naturally in the global community but can only replicate after injection in the body of a single host, its chances look poor from an evolutionary point of view. It probably cannot outcompete its naturally spreading and aggressive counterparts. And how can vaccine by injection reach all those millions in Asia and Africa who are currently at risk for HIV-1 infection?

For every man, woman, or child injected with the harmless strain, many more individuals would be infected with the harmful strains. A concerted worldwide effort would be required to vaccinate every single person at risk for AIDS at such speed that the wildtype HIV-1 strains would suddenly find no unprotected humans to infect. The virus must be locked out so abruptly and securely that it has no time or place to adapt for survival.

A big task lies ahead. We must know the AIDS virus very well to tame it, and already our knowledge gives us promising options. But we must recognize that science will find no quick or final solution to HIV or AIDS. Science alone cannot control this virus. Now that the HIV family has found the human family, it will always be with us in some form. All people must know HIV and work to control it.

### Blood Donors

The buying and selling of blood is a highly developed

industry in India. Private pathology laboratories collect and pay for blood from individual donors and sell this to hospitals and clinics. Despite the risks involved in the commercial blood collection system, India cannot afford to stop this practice because about half the blood used in large urban hospitals is obtained in this way. Commercial blood donors are a group particularly at risk of being infected with HIV. The virus can be transmitted through the use of unsterilized equipment in blood collection centres, and also by behaviours such as unprotected sex (both anal and vaginal) with multiple partners. Contaminated blood can then quickly spread the virus to blood recipients, to the sex partners of the infected person, to other donors (through the use of unsterilized needles), to blood products, and to the foetuses of pregnant women who receive transfusions.

The goals of the Gujarat AIDS Prevention Unit are as follows:

— To help ensure safe blood supply to the people.

— To protect commercial blood donors from HIV infection through unsterile equipment and procedures at the blood collection centres, and through other risk behaviours such as unprotected sexual intercourse.

— To protect the personnel working in blood collection centres from accidental infection with HIV in the course of their work.

To achieve these objectives the unit developed the following action plan:

— Educate commercial blood donors about safe blood-giving and how to practice safer sex.

— Test commercial blood donors for HIV infection, accompanied by pre- and post-test counselling.

— Provide commercial blood donors with alternative income-generating opportunities.

— Upgrade the existing guidelines for the prevention of infection and for handling body fluids in commercial blood collecting centres.

— Educate the staff at blood collection centres about the possibility of accidental transmission of HIV.

### BLOOD COLLECTION CENTRES

After setting up the HIV screening programme for commercial blood donors, the unit concentrated their efforts on the blood collection centres themselves. We began by surveying 75 registered pathology laboratories in the city of Ahmedabad. Most of these serve as blood collection centres which are in direct contact with the city's private hospitals and health clinics. The survey found that the level of HIV awareness among laboratory personnel was nil. Centres are usually staffed by one pathologist, two technicians and three unskilled personnel, who collect blood at a rate of one to ten units per day. Most of the laboratories did not follow the official infection control guidelines or the instructions for handling body fluids. The unit then began running crash training courses for technicians and unskilled personnel, and so far have trained 30 of each. These courses are designed to inform the participants about HIV/AIDS, and emphasize workplace precautions they should be taking to prevent accidental infection—either of themselves or of their clients.

The achievements of the Gujarat AIDS Prevention Unit are encouraging and significant, even if modest in the national context. The unit now have plans to help people who sell their blood for a living by providing them with vocational training and alternative income-generating activities. The unit also plan to establish, together with the commercial blood donors themselves, a co-operative blood banking system through which blood could be collected from people irrespective of their HIV status. This blood could then be screened and seropositive samples could be sold to research organisations involved in developing vaccines. The HIV-free blood would be sold to pharmaceutical laboratories. The project has helped to ensure a safe blood supply for the people of Ahmedabad, as well as helping to protect people involved in the blood collection industry from HIV infection. However, it is beyond the resources of a small NGO like ours to expand the project on a large scale.

## Selected Readings

A.M. Brandt, No Magic Bullet: *A Social History of Venereal Disease in the United States Since* 1880 (New York: Oxford University Press, 1987).

AIDS Information and Prevention (Policy paper, in English). (Amsterdam: Documentation Centre of the NCAB, 1986).

Bailey, M. 1991. "AIDS in India: The Current Situation." Processed.

Baines, D. (1992). Issues in cultural sensitivity: Examples from the Indian Peoples. In D. Becker (Ed.), *Health behaviour research in minority populations.* Washington, DC: National Institutes of Health.

Balachandran, S. 1987. *Managing change: An Indian Experience.* Bombay, India: Business Book Publishing House.

Bhatnagar, D. 1985. *State and Labour Welfare in India.* New Delhi, India: Deep and Deep Publications

Bhattacharya, R. D. 1992. "Commercial Blood Donors and AIDS Prevention—An Experience from Ahmedabad, India." Processed.

Bloom, D. E., and S. Glied. 1991. "Benefits and Costs of HIV Testing." *Science* 252.

Bloom, D. E., and A. Mahal. 1992. "The Economic Impact of HIV/AIDS in Asia: A Primer." Paper presented at the Second International Congress on AIDS in Asia and the Pacific, New Delhi, November 8-12.

Bloom, D. E., and G. Carliner. 1988. "The Economics Impact of AIDS in the United States." *Science* 239.

Bradley-Springer, L.A. (1994). Reproductive decision-making in the age of AIDS. *IMAGE: Journal of Nursing Scholarship*, 26.

Chatters, L.M. (1993). HIV/AIDS within the African-American communities Diversity and interdependence. A commentary on AIDS and the African-American Woman: The triple burden of race, class, and gender. *Health Education Quarterly,* 20.

Directorate General of Health Services. 1990. "Medium Term Plan for the Prevention and Control of AIDS in India." New Delhi, India: Ministry of Health and Family Welfare, in cooperation with the World Health Organisation.

Eastwood, A., and A. Maynard. 1988. Treating AIDS Patients: Is it Ethical to be Efficient" Paper presented at the First International Conference on the Global Impact of AIDS, London, March.

G.J.P van Griensven, "Epidemiology and prevention of HIV infection among homosexual men," Ph.D. Thesis (Amsterdam: University of Amsterdam, 1989).

Hassig, S.E., J. Perriens, E. Baende, M. Kahotwa, K Bishagara, N. Kinkela, and B. Kapita. 1990. "An Analysis of the Economic Impact of HIV Infection among Patients at Mama Yemo Hospital, Kinshasa, Zaire." *AIDS* 4.

Institute of Medicine, National Academy of Sciences, *Mobilizing Against AIDS* (Cambridge, Mass.: Harvard University Press, 1986), 26.

Kristol, I. 1992. "AIDS and False Innocence". The Wall Journal August 7-8.

Law Concerning the Prevention of Acquired Immuno-deficiency Syndrome, Ministry of Health and Welfare (March 6, 1987) 2.

Ministry of Health. 1991. *National AIDS Programme in Indonesia:* An Update.. Jakarta, Indonesia.

Nataraj, S. 1990. "Indian Prostitutes Highlights AIDS Dilemmas. *Development Forum* (UNDP) XVIII (6): 1, 16

Piette, J., Fleishman, J.A., Mor, V., & Thompson, B. (1992). The structure and process of AIDS case management. *Health and Social Work*, 17.

Roemer, M. I. 1991. *National Health Systems of the World*. New York: Oxford University Press.

*The Jakarta Post*. 1992. Suspected AIDS Carrier to be sent to Switzerland." January 9.

WHO (World Health Organisation). 1992. AIDS: *Global Situation*. New Delhi, India: Southeast Asia Regional Office.

Yoshiaki Ishida, "Objection to Legalisation of AIDS Countermeasures," *Asahi Shinbun* (February 9, 1987).

# Index